A Teen's Guide to Witchcraft

WHERE TO PARK YOUR BROOMSTICK

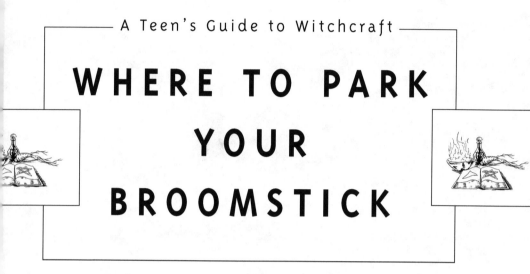

Lauren Manoy

•

With Illustrations by Yan Apostolides

A Fireside Book

Published by Simon & Schuster

New York   London   Toronto   Sydney   Singapore

This publication contains the opinions and ideas of its author and is designed to provide useful information in regard to the subject matter covered. It is sold with the understanding that the author and publisher are not engaged in the rendering of health, medical, psychological, or any other professional advice or services. The author and publisher specifically disclaim any liability, loss or risk, personal or otherwise, which is incurred as a consequence, directly or indirectly, of the use and application of any of the contents of this book.

FIRESIDE
Rockefeller Center
1230 Avenue of the Americas
New York, NY 10020

FIRESIDE and colophon are registered trademarks
of Simon & Schuster, Inc.

For information regarding special discounts for bulk purchases,
please contact Simon & Schuster Special Sales:
1-800-456-6798 or business@simonandschuster.com

Designed by Lisa Stokes

Manufactured in the United States of America

10   9   8   7   6   5   4   3   2   1

Library of Congress Cataloging-in-Publication Data

Manoy, Lauren.
    Where to park your broomstick : a teen's guide to witchcraft /
Lauren Manoy ; with illustrations by Yan Apostolides.
        p. cm.
    Summary: A guide to witchcraft and the working of Magick, explaining how to get in
touch with your own sacredness and create and cast various spells.
    Includes bibliographical references and index.
    1. Witchcraft—Juvenile literature. [1. Witchcraft.]   I. Apostolides, Yan, ill.   II. Title.
BF1566 .M278 2002
133.4'3—dc21   2002070470

ISBN 978-0-684-85500-4

This Book Is Dedicated To:
Faith, with all of my Heart;
Tempest Smith and her Mother,
With Hope for a Kinder World;
Rose and Joseph;
Anahepsut;
And to my Mother, my Heroine.

ACKNOWLEDGMENTS

My most heartfelt appreciation goes to Allyson Edelhertz, whose immense creativity, professionalism, and patience let me cross off one thing on my List of Stuff to Do Before I Die. When I learn all the languages in the world, I'll be able to express what this book meant to me. I couldn't have done this without your help. Many thanks to the wonderful team at Simon & Schuster who made this book possible. Eternal gratitude and Love to all who contributed directly and indirectly to this project: Gavin Bone, Janet Farrar, Stewart Farrar, Selena Fox, Gypsy and Richard, Isaac Bonewits, Julie, Sheila, Tara, Margot Adler, Z Budapest, Scott Cunningham, Starhawk, The Witches' Voice, Circle Sanctuary, the myriad beautiful Pagan writers who brought these paths to light, and the web mistresses and masters who keep the info flowing. To the teens who helped shape this book and lent me their eloquent insights: May you all have health, love, and happiness. To the Witches of Broome, for their incalculable assistance, support, and friendship. A thousand thanks to those who have stood at my side during my darkest days and who fill this life with joy and laughter: Faith and Yan, Catherine and Brian, the Apostolides family, Chrissy, Jerry, Karen, and Ronnie. To J. Hessling, E. Hehrli, K. McGovern. To ARC for their support. To MW, PS, the Fierce Nipples, Pan, Paul, and Rowan (you know who you are)!

CONTENTS

MERRY MEET!

PART I

You're probably in the midst of some kind of social crisis. You probably have a paper due for school tomorrow (which you haven't started yet), and your teachers are so mind-numbingly boring that you can barely manage to keep your eyes open in class. Your parents think you dress funny; and you have acne, are just getting over acne, or are extremely concerned about developing acne. Your hair is the wrong color, and you are *sure* that your nose is exactly the wrong shape for your face. If any of this sounds familiar, then you're probably an American teenager.

Maybe your friends think you're nuts for recycling everything, caring about the environment, or believing in ESP. Are you looking for answers to your heart's deepest questions? Do you desire a set of instructions for achieving supernatural abilities and amazing powers? I hope not. You will not find any definitive answers to life's deep meaning in this (or any) book, and you certainly will not find any hype about sorcery here, either. What you will find is a road map to your intrinsic remarkableness, a starting point for the discovery of your own perfectly natural powers and abilities. What you will find here is an introduction to Eclectic Wicca, a spiritual path that is being rediscovered and is finding a warm reception from people of all ages and in all walks of life.

My first encounter with Wicca came through a book called *What Witches Do,* by Stewart Farrar. I picked it up expecting to find fairy tales or some other kind of fiction. What I found instead was a journalist's investigation of modern people in our modern society who practiced something called Wicca and called themselves Witches. I couldn't believe it. I read the entire book in a matter of hours, completely amazed that there was a group of people who claimed to practice Witchcraft. Were they kidding? Were they delusional? Were they ex-hippies who had smoked way too much pot in 1969 and had totally lost touch with reality? But no, they were doctors and lawyers, mothers and fathers—everyday people who were also Witches. I sat in my room that night and pondered. It took me all of five minutes to decide that I would find out everything I could about Wicca and find someone who would teach me to practice real-life Witchcraft.

Wicca is a way of constant celebration. It is a vehicle for the achievement of grand acts of individual evolution, and it is a healthy, life-affirming, respectful philosophy that recognizes the Earth as a living Mother, the God as Her consort and lover, and all living creatures as their children. Male and female alike are revered; our connection to one another and to every other living being is treated as fact.

Oh, and you get to cast spells, too. No, really. I'm serious.

All right, so if your parents read that last part and call for an exorcism, remain calm! I highly discourage sitting down at the dinner table one night and excitedly exclaiming, "I'm a Witch! Please pass the pan-fried tofu." Please, learn from my mistake. My poor mother nearly passed out when I first introduced her to Wicca. I believe her exact words were "A Whu? What are you talking about? You're talking crazy." She went about six different shades of white and called a therapist. I am twenty-four now, and my mother still thinks I'm a little crazy, but she has become very accepting of my beliefs—especially when she wants a Tarot card reading.

Try to understand that the word *Witch* can really freak people out on a fundamental level. It brings to mind crazy, cackling old hags with oozing warts and funky houses made of gingerbread where small children are lured and then stuck in an oven. Assure your parents that you are not interested in eating children. Explain that you are a relatively sane human being who is not joining a cult that will force you to wear tie-dyed sheets and shave your head! Luckily, we're not burned at the stake anymore, so you folks don't have to worry about *that*. Perhaps this is not your first exposure to Wicca, and maybe you have already opened the lines of communication with your parental units. Good for you! For those of you reading this in your closets: hey, the closet is not a terrible place. We'll talk more about revealing your Wiccan-ness to friends and family later, but for now try to include your parents in your thoughts and ideas; we hope they'll respect you enough to grant you the right to have opinions that differ from theirs.

I don't mean to imply that one must give up one's particular upbringing to practice Wicca. There are no laws that state that a Wiccan cannot simultaneously practice another religion; in fact, Wicca itself combines many different ideologies. We do not answer to any particular authority or leader—except the Gods and our own consciences. While we're on the subject of what Wicca is not, let's get something clear: It is NOT Satanism! It IS NOT Satanism! Wicca is not a cult—we do not answer to some charismatic leader with a handlebar mustache who tells us to sacrifice cats to the devil! (Did I mention that WICCA IS NOT SATANISM!? All right, then.) Wiccans are not immoral, drug-crazed sex-pervert wackos who want to steal you away from your friends and family. Wicca will not teach you to control other people by casting spells on them. "As you harm none, may you do what you will" is a saying that most Wiccans are very familiar with. You and the Earth are included in that statement. The Threefold Law is also a common belief: Whatever you do will come back to you, three times more powerfully than your original action. This works for good deeds as well as not-so-good deeds. Lastly, Wicca is not a fashion statement. It is a way of life for those who choose to practice it.

The origin of the word *Wicca* is a matter of some debate. Some people believe it comes from a Welsh word meaning "to bend," while others think it is from the same root as the word meaning "wise one." While it's an interesting idea to debate, both meanings can be applied to the description of modern Wicca, in that Wiccans do strive for wisdom and employ various techniques of working with Nature's energies to shape (or bend) their own destinies and master their own lives. Many aspects of Wiccan rituals are similar to methods used by psychiatrists, like visualization, to create the positive mental attitudes necessary for personal growth. Other elements of Wiccan ritual draw on pre-Christian religions (Celtic and Greek traditions, for example) and other Pagan heritages like the herb lore of midwives and the navigation of the soul practiced by shamans and medicine women. In general, Wicca is a combination of philosophies and rituals that respect the turning of the Earth's seasons and acknowledge the link between human beings and the rest of the world.

Sometimes in our adolescent years, we humans tend to forget our bond with Nature, and it is easy to get caught up in the pressures of school, the need to be successful, and the demands of society to be "normal" (whatever that means). We are told to grow up and conform to some prefabricated concept of a normal person, to shove aside our imagination and quit playing. We are bombarded—by the media, our peers, and our own minds— with confusing and critical images of what we should be.

Despite all the turmoil, despite the seeming impotence of youth, this is a time of great power. Your body is young. Your mind is open to life's infinite possibilities. You contain vast energy and an honest voice. So, what does all that have to do with Wicca? By training yourself in the Wiccan way and by dedicating yourself to the lighthearted and imaginative practice of Witchcraft, you can reclaim your intuitive skills and experience the divinity inherent in each day of your life. You can take control of your own existence. You have the opportunity to create the future.

Your daughter or son has told you of her or his interest in Wiccan or Pagan beliefs.

First of all, don't panic.

Take a deep breath.

Heed an ancient piece of parental wisdom: Do not speak until you can improve upon the silence.

This, more than many other moments before it, is the time to listen.

You have a choice: Focus on your own feelings of upset (which can range from being mildly miffed to having deep feelings of anger, shame, or rejection) or listen to what your teenager is telling you is important to her or him.

If you choose to listen, try to hear the big picture. More likely than not, your teenager is trying to tell you about an Earth-based religion that centers around respect for all living things, an intense preoccupation with the natural textures of the world, a desire to find the quiet spiritual place within him- or herself (in the face of a pop-teen culture dominated by cheap fashions, bad bands, violent movies, and computer games).

Your child is trying to tell you about her or his soul.

You could, of course, focus on the minutiae: the differences between the religious beliefs and practices with which you have personally grown up and cherished and this new world of witchy stuff.

My own personal belief is that about 18 percent of the practitioners of every religion have developed into genuinely spiritual people. And those

18-percenters of each religion have more in common with one another than they do with the 82 percent of rigid literalists in their own religion.

Know that your child is likely not asking you to agree with him or her and to change your own beliefs. Your child is asking, whether consciously or not, to be respected as an autonomous, thinking, feeling being. He or she is asking to meet you on the Field of Ideas and be heard. Without interruption or debate.

However, should your child wish to debate you, I would urge you not to take the bait. (They are, after all, teenagers.) I would urge you, instead, to share what you have found beautiful or meaningful about your own religious traditions.

Better yet, let them see you live your beliefs and be joyous in your practices.

If you do need to talk about how upset you are with your child's break from your own traditions, by all means do so. But do it with a trusted adult. (I'm biased toward mental health professionals.) It may turn out that you're bothered by more in your life than your child's new beliefs.

Once the surprise has worn off, and you have reconnected with your loving heart, it may be possible for you and your child to see each other with clear eyes. And you may just be lucky enough to realize that your child has grown into a soulful being who resembles you more than you ever knew.

WHEN TO WORRY

Your child's involvement with Wicca or Paganism does not, by itself, warrant a trip to a mental health professional. However, one or more of the following warning signs would warrant some professional help:

· Experiencing a significant and prolonged drop in school grades, accompanied by a noncaring attitude
· Cutting, self-mutilating (no, not just a nose ring), or practicing other self-injurious behaviors
· Spending most of his or her time with much older "believers" whom he or she doesn't ever want you to meet

· Behaving with cruelty to animals
· Exhibiting significant substance abuse
· Suddenly dropping all previous friendships and/or hobbies
· Losing ability even to consider the future, colleges, possible career choices, etc.
· Listening primarily to "death metal" or overtly Satanic music (the messages of which are deeply antithetical to Wiccan beliefs)

Jerry Sander, A.C.S.W.
Warwick, New York

This is an *introduction* to Wicca and Paganism. There's plenty of information in here to get you started on your own path, with resources for you to explore on your own. The more you seek, the more creative you'll be in your own practice. The beauty of Wicca is that it creates a place for you, the individual, to encounter the infinite, divine energy of the Universe *for yourself.* Finding what makes *you* feel connected to Nature, divinity, and your own power is what Wicca is all about. If I didn't encourage you to do that in your own way, I'd be stealing something fabulous from you.

Speaking of direct experience, you'll notice that I included a bunch of spells, rituals, and recipes for you to play with. You can absolutely use the spells and rituals as they appear, and I encourage you to do that if you've never cast a spell or experienced a Wiccan ritual yourself. The best way to gain direct experience of divine, magickal energy is to do some rituals and see how the experience makes you feel. I included the formulas in this book to illustrate, by example, the concepts behind Witchcraft's techniques and methods. If you look carefully through the stuff I wrote, you'll start to see patterns running through the exercises and examples. Those patterns are the basic structures of Wiccan ritual and Witchcraft's methods. If you take a few moments to really absorb what each ritual or spell entails and examine the movements, props, and ingredients, you'll be able to strip the rituals down to their essential elements and utilize your *own* words, ideas, and techniques. That's the whole game.

Try the spells and rituals the way they're written here first, if you're unsure of how to get started, then tweak, wangle, and invent your own from there. You can change the props and ingredients according to your need, change the sequence of the ritual to fit your concept, and you can *always* use your own words. You can also work within your limitations (like if no incense or candles are allowed in the house), and I've given you alternatives for those items throughout the book. The Appendices include a Table of Correspondences that will help you substitute materials that you might not have on hand.

You'll also notice that the recipes included here are for everything from pimple-banishing concoctions to psychic-awareness incense blends. I've tried them all myself, and I included all sorts of substitutions, in case you can't find one item or another. Check the Appendices for quick fixes and for ideas to create your own recipes. I've noted the parts of each recipe that make up the base for that concoction. Stick to those proportions to ensure that you get the right concentration or consistency. Other than that, experiment and try everything!

And lastly, you'll notice that the first three chapters are a bunch of history, which you may find boring. Tough tomatoes! If you're serious about making Wicca or Paganism your way of life, you'll want to know where Wicca and modern Paganism come from. Plus, you'll need to tell your parents and friends something intelligent about your belief system, and you'll want to be able to converse intelligently with the adult Witches you'll come across. Besides, your magick will be greatly improved by a better understanding of where it originates. So pick a night when you've got nothing better to do and charge through it. Potentially unfamiliar words appear in *italics* first and then in regular text, explained immediately afterward or in the Glossary.

Let's go. . . .

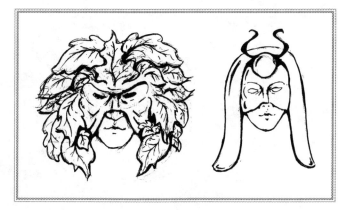

PART II

CHAPTER ONE
ANCIENT ROOTS

What practical information does the scribbling of ancient hands have for us moderns? Some people may scoff at the "childish" rituals, the "simplistic" view of nature, and insist that these people made up myths and superstitions to explain a seemingly incomprehensible world. "Science," they will say, "has far surpassed the cave dwellers. We know so much more now! It's stupid to bang rocks together and think it'll bring rain."

Primitive folks probably did develop their practices to help them understand what life was about and how they were supposed to interact within it, to ease their fears by explaining the seemingly inexplicable. I'm not suggesting that we live in caves, grunt, and let our backs get hairy. However, the common symbols used by Paleolithic man that have been found all over the globe makes me wonder: Did ancient man have a clue to the workings of the Universe that modern civilizations have forgotten?

These ancient cultures (I'm talking Upper Paleolithic, better known as the New Stone Age, about 30,000–10,000 B.C.E.) left behind many sculptures and paintings. Anthropologists can make reasonable inferences from these artifacts about their functions. They hypothesize about what Paleolithic humans thought and felt. Their interpretations are purely speculative, and there is a great debate raging as to whether or not these works of art and implements had religious implications for the tribes that crafted them.

The relationship between modern Witches and Paleolithic Paganism is this: Witches work for the deep connection with all of Nature that ancient humans must have known; we use those parts of our mind that are primal and that speak to us through the rich heritage of symbols that have been mankind's since the moment we crawled from the primordial sea.

PALEOLITHIC PLAYGROUND

Lightning, rain, the Sun, the Moon, the stars . . . The natural world was filled with miracles and mystery. Paleolithic man (I'll call him Paleo for short) could see, hear, feel, and taste these phenomena, but he couldn't possibly conceive of their significance or function. He probably saw lakes and trees and lightning as actual, living beings, a view of the world called *animism*. This was the beginning of humankind's religious impulse. Animism is a common thread that still runs through many modern Witchcraft cultures.

When I say religious impulse, I mean the need to express the connection between ourselves and the rest of the Universe, not an organized system of religion. Prehistoric humans didn't need religious systems. Paleo didn't see a distinct line between his own life and self and the world around him. His constant state of being was likely awe for the miracles of life, death, and renewal he saw occurring daily. Nature's force was around him constantly—sometimes bringing good, and other times bringing destruction. It's only a short walk from awe to worship, and Paleo almost certainly worshiped each and every manifestation of nature's sheer power as a manifestation of divine forces, a.k.a. *pantheism*. That premise is the logical beginning of Witchcraft: That the planet we live on and the other creatures that live here with us are alive, holy, conscious, intimately connected, and an expression of Divine presence.[1]

A common theme among Paleolithic cave paintings shows the primary job of men: the hunt. The prominent imagery of these paintings depicts the main food animals of the prehistoric tribes, often placing different species alongside one another. Since it's unlikely that bison and horses actually grazed side by side, it appears that these images represented Paleo's intended prey. Sometimes, the animal likeness stands alone, with no reference to the outer landscape or any other related scenes. The lack of reference and the skillfully detailed images, obviously drawn with care and high regard, implies that they were etched in gratitude to the animal's spirit, to show respect for the life that sustained the people. In this way, Paleo seems to have understood the web of life as continuous and interrelated.[2]

While actual human figures are rare in the earlier paintings, elements of the human form were sometimes drawn mingled with the animal that was hunted. Notably, the figures often include horns, which points to the culture's reverence of hunted, horned animals. This is a precursor to the Witch's Horned God, who appears throughout history in the ancient cultures. (He'll keep popping up as we go on—you'll see!) It's reasonable to infer that Paleo thought his art directly influenced the actual outcome of his hunt: if he drew the scene perfectly, or with a special type of mineral, or with the guidance of the tribal holy person, then the spirit of that bison was already caught. This was humankind's first act of *sympathetic magick,* a basic method of Witchcraft.

Well-rounded female figures carved from stone and bone have been found from France to Russia to the Czech Republic, and have been dated

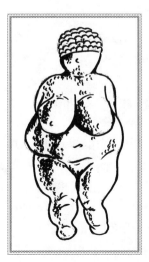

between 35,000–10,000 B.C.E. They express supreme femininity, the profusely fertile female body, and the obvious roles of womanhood: to protect and encourage fertility, to watch over childbirth, and to nurture the tribe. Whether the Venuses indicate a portrayal of guardian spirits encased in the sculpture is a matter of debate, but their function as an expression of woman's enormous power to regenerate is very clear.

This time in evolution was also marked by ceremonial burial of the tribe's dead, often with tools or other implements for daily life, which points to a belief in some kind of afterlife. Careful burial

> "The idea of the earth as a mother and of burial as a re-entry into the womb for rebirth appears to have recommended itself to at least some of the communities of mankind at an extremely early date. The earliest unmistakable evidence of ritual and therewith of mythological thought yet found have been the grave burials of *Homo neanderthalensis,* a remote predecessor of our own species, whose period is perhaps to be dated as early as 200,000–75,000 B.C."
>
> —JOSEPH CAMPBELL[3]

also implies love, the most spiritual of human impulses. Bodies were often painted with colored minerals and buried in a sleeping position, indicating that Paleo equated death with sleep. This brings us to Paleo's perception of his death as it related to Nature's cycles. Maybe Paleo saw his death as returning to the Earth to rest and be reborn, in the same way that plants died and came back to life as the seasons turned. The concept of Earth as a womb for life is one of modern Paganism's most basic ideas, and many Pagans also believe in some kind of afterlife or reincarnation.

As far as we can tell from incomplete anthropological findings, these similarities exist in ancient cultures around the world. Nobody knows about the exact rituals, and there's no one left to ask! While there are stylistic differences, the concepts were the same: if the tribe was respectful of the life around them, if they performed rituals to ensure their survival and the safety of the new generation, they would thrive. They would live, die, and live again.

Here's the challenge to the anthropologist and any person who lives in modern, Western culture: To acknowledge the possibility that it might actually have worked!

These ancient human civilizations discovered the magick of nature for us. They might not have had scented candles or guided meditation CDs, but they knew how to live with the natural world. That's what Witchcraft is all about. The symbols and knowledge still live deeply ingrained in our own minds, buried within the collective unconscious of the entire human race. As stinky and hairy as our Paleolithic ancestors must have been, they're still relatives! Paleolithic, Neolithic, and Mesolithic tribes mark the beginning of our species evolving into more recognizable people. Their marks are left for us to ponder, and perhaps we can arrive at some little bit of wisdom from their profound connection to the Earth and life around them.

THE BIRTH OF CEREMONIAL MAGICK: NEOLITHIC MIDDLE EAST

Nature worship is one thing. Ceremonial magick is a whole other animal.

As evolution continued, the Paleolithic age was left behind and replaced by the Neolithic, around 8,000 to 4,000 B.C.E. The nomads settled into villages. Permanent homes stood alongside fields of cultivated crops. Temples stood as separate houses of worship. This is important. As man built a house of worship, he relocated his spiritual impulse to a special residence. He moved his reverence for nature into its own home and created the gods to live in it. He also created Priests and Priestesses to commune with these gods, to dedicate all their time and energy to understanding the gods' symbols and omens. After all, Neolithic man was far too busy growing crops, building roads, learning arithmetic, and making war on his neighbors' fertile land to talk with the deities all the time! Ceremonial magick was born along with a system of written language and the newly established structure called society.

This new religious system portrayed the Divine with many faces and many names. Neolithic religion still expressed nature's forces, but now they were personalized as gods and goddesses. This system was much more complex—appropriate, since society had become more sophisticated.

Society's new address was the Middle East, specifically Mesopotamia, Babylonia, Sumeria, and Egypt—the area known as the Fertile Crescent and its outlying regions. Sumeria was located in the Arabian Desert. The Arabian Desert was—and still is—a rough neighborhood, but the Egyptians' land was abundant, giving them enough free time to invent philosophy. Both cultures were *polytheistic,* and both believed that they could use magick to work with the Universe's abundant energy to get what they wanted. Modern Wicca includes both of these ideas. We can still see a blending of animal and human forms in the remnant religious art, and the representations of humans mingled with horned beasts of the hunt now became deities.

Another culture that was important to ceremonial magick's development was Chaldea, a land between Sumeria and Egypt. This is reportedly the birth place of *Cabala* (a.k.a. Qaballa, Kabbala, and a few other spellings), the mystic tradition of the Hebrews. Cabala is still very much alive and well today, a tradition passed down for centuries through the rabbis with very few apparent changes. Many Wiccans incorporate Cabala in their magickal practice, and some of the more esoteric Tarot decks also incorporate Cabalistic symbolism. Chapter 3 has a little more info about these cultures' philosophies.

ASSIMILATION

You've got to understand that the development of written language was a huge breakthrough. Now people could record their daily experiences, review them over long periods of time, and start making connections. This knowledge brought incredible power, both spiritual and scientific. Many cultures still believe that to know, and especially to write, something's true name is to have the power of its spirit. On the scientific tip, people could finally organize their experiences and observations. Think about the implications! Humans now could chronicle which plants healed particular illnesses and trade knowledge, recording their myths and legends for the next generation.

Speaking of trading ideas, commerce played a huge part in cultural assimilation. People from neighboring cultures exchanged their papyrus journals along with spices and precious metals. Constant war also played a huge role in Middle Eastern religion. A conquering tribe would often impose their deities on the vanquished culture's existing religion. The conquered territory's gods often became the conquering nation's devils, the old gods' temples were either destroyed or rededicated to the new deities, and the victors often outlawed any mention of the old religion. This was as much a way to destroy a culture's pride and spirit as it was an expression of one country's superiority over another. There's no better way to control a country than to oppress the countrymen's heritage. This conquering/melding of cultures accounts for the similarities between different pantheons: the Sumerian Great Mother Goddess, Ishtar, corresponds to the Babylonian Inanna; Inanna became the Egyptian Isis, and so on. And here's a thought to really blow your mind: Scholars have found a distinct similarity between the languages and mythologies of such diverse cultures as India, the Slavic world, Greece, and Germany.[4] This common language thread has been dubbed Indo-European, and it establishes a strange cultural diffusion that ties us into a much larger global family than you might expect.

So what happened next? More wars, Pharaohs, slave trades, the furtherance of science, and a whole bunch of other humanity. Let's skip ahead to the ancient Greeks, Romans, and Celts.

THE WESTERN WORLD

The Greeks did Witches some great favors. Pythagoras, a philosopher and mathematician, asserted that numbers occurred in nature and were not made up by human beings: hence the birth of Numerology, which is practiced by many Witches. Empedocles asserted that the world is made entirely of the Four Elements—Earth, Air, Water, and Fire—and he attributed specific characteristics to each. These are used almost universally within the current practice of Witchcraft.

The ancient Greeks were polytheistic, with a huge family of gods and goddesses to express all the facets of human experience. In fact, they are credited with creating the first truly *anthropomorphic* gods. That is, their gods looked like humans, acted like humans, and often lived among us. They were, however, all powerful and deathless, and usually more beautiful than ordinary humans (being a god has its perks!). They likely borrowed some of their gods from their Egyptian contemporaries. This is most apparent through the Persephone myth, which relates strongly to the Egyptian Isis legend and, by connection, the Sumerian Ishtar and Babylonian Inanna. The Greeks also split the original concept of goddess—that of Mother and Destroyer as one Great Goddess—into several different goddesses. The Horned God was called Pan in Greek mythology. He was still the god of wild beasts, and he also represented music, frolic, and sexuality. While these don't have much to do with hunting, they certainly relate to the world of nature.

The Roman gods come directly from the Greeks, probably a result of the Romans conquering Greece and taking many Greek slaves as teachers. They have the same group of deities and similar mythology with Roman-ized names. The word *pagan* comes from the Latin word *paganus*, meaning "country dweller," or peasant. The peasants practiced fertility rites to en-sure the health of crops and children, and they differed from the sophisti-cated, urban religion of Rome. While the Romans built temples to their gods, they also kept personal altars in their homes for the god or goddess who was the specific patron for the family.

THE BRITISH ISLES

The countries most often associated with modern Pagan and Witch-craft traditions are found in the British Isles: England, Scotland, Ireland, and Wales. It's interesting to note that, while England does show Paleolithic remains, to date, Ireland has absolutely no Paleolithic record. However, there are Mesolithic sites.

The horned god appears in Ireland under the Roman-Celtic name of Cernunnos, also called Herne. And, again, he is the god of nature and wild beasts.

Classical times had much more than that going on, but I want to jump ahead to medieval Europe, a strange point in history. This is the beginning of widespread Christian influence, and the Church dominated Europe al-most completely. The Old Religion of the Great Goddess and Horned God was condemned as devil worship. Remember what happens when one tribe conquers another? Well, the Christian devil had Cernunnos's horns and tail, although the concept of the Horned God as an embodiment of evil is not to be found anywhere in Pagan mythology, either ancient or modern.

The question is this: Did the European peasants, pagans, and heathens continue to worship the old gods and celebrate the old festivals? Even fur-ther, did they continue to do so with conscious knowledge of their roots?

It's entirely plausible that midwives and country folk still observed the old rites in secret, but the existence of a semi-organized Pagan religion past the fourteenth century is extremely doubtful. The Church was now very powerful and vigorously oppressed any religion that it saw as a rival. How-ever, midwives still practiced their herbal art, and the making of charms was still evident. If celebrations were observed, they were either carried out in the utmost fear and secrecy, or they were marginally allowed and diluted through the Church's fusion of old celebrations with the new, Christian mythology. Read Chapter 15 to discover the ancient roots of Christmas, Easter, and Halloween.

Margaret Murray, an anthropologist and Egyptologist who wrote about the witch craze in Europe, insisted that Pagan religion had survived by going deeply underground and was still practiced by modern Witches, Priestesses of the Old Religion. I must state here that her views are extremely controversial among academics and Pagans alike. The most solid part of her thesis can be summed up in one simple statement: Immediate conversion of an entire populace from a well-established religion to a radically new one is pretty ridiculous.[5] She also traces the worship of Horned Gods of Nature through all the cultures we've discussed here, insisting that worship was continued.

If you want a good understanding of the history of Wicca and Witchcraft, you must pick up these two books: *The Triumph of the Moon: A History of Modern Pagan Witchcraft* by Ronald Hutton, and *Witchcraft: A Concise History* (an e-book, available at Amazon.com) by Isaac Bonewits. Anything by Janet and Stewart Farrar is also highly recommended.

What's obvious is this: Relics called Sheela Na Gigs have been found all over Ireland, France, Scotland, Wales, and England (although the greatest concentration is found in Ireland), dated approximately 1200–1400 C.E. They are images of women crouching to expose their regenerative members in a blatant display of female power—the power of birth and, by association, of death and rebirth. The odd part is that they are often found on churches! Not exactly Sunday school material! Carbon dating reveals that these figures are much older than the churches on which they are found, indicating that they were brought from other areas and grafted onto the new establishment—much like the Pagan deities themselves.

BACK TO THE HERE AND NOW

Modern man is so incredibly far removed from the necessity of a good hunt. We have penicillin and other little magical pills. We have the Weather Channel. We don't need to look to the Moon and stars for guidance about when the rivers will flood, or whether our actions are in accord with nature and the gods. However, just because we're less attuned to the Earth's natural energies doesn't mean that those energies are less real than they were when our ancestors saw them as proof of Nature's divine, animated presence.

CHAPTER TWO

MODERN WICCA

Guess what? *Wicca* is a relatively new word; it's used incorrectly; and it isn't the only kind of Witchcraft out there. And guess what else? The words *Witch, Wicca, Pagan,* and *Neo-Pagan* aren't interchangeable at all. Confusing? Don't stress. It goes something like this:

"Wicca" was coined by Gerald Gardner (see below); he might have conjured it up from the Anglo-Saxon word *wician,* which apparently meant "to practice Witchcraft," or he might have gotten it from the Scots-English word *(wica),* which meant "wise." [1] Other similar words come from the root *wic-,* which might be related to the words *willow* and *wicker,* which brings us to the concept of "bending" that I mentioned earlier. Wicca refers specifically to a male practitioner; *wicce* refers to the female practitioner. Gardner originally called his new religion *Wica,* with one "c," and Wiccan is actually plural (more than one wicca or wicce). Today, Wicca can refer to the religion itself or a practitioner of Wicca. Some people call themselves Wicca, others Wiccan, and still others use Witch instead.

Witches are sometimes Wiccan and sometimes not. Some folks practice Witchcraft but don't like to be called Wiccan because they don't consider Witchcraft

to be a religion. Many Wiccans *do* call themselves Witches, but other Wiccans don't and don't practice magick or spell casting. They may, however, consider themselves *Pagan,* which is a blanket term for people who are interested in reviving the old ways and who (1) aren't Judeo-Christian or Muslim and (2) practice an Earth-based spirituality that is often, but not always, polytheistic. This brings us to *Neo-Pagans,* who don't necessarily claim to be reviving any age-old tradition, but who do fit the definition of Pagan.

To sum up: Witches aren't always Wiccan, and Wiccans aren't always Witches; both can be either Pagan or Neo-Pagan, depending on their tradition. Yikes! All these words to divide us . . .

The brilliance of Eclectic Wicca is that it allows complete and total freedom of expression and evolves constantly. Besides, most Pagans are rabid individualists, so to lump everyone together and say "all Wiccans think this" or "all Pagans do that" will get me in big fat trouble.

Strictly speaking, most Wiccans are *duotheistic:* they see the Divine as both male and female, called the Goddess and the God, the Lord and the Lady, and other such. Many Wiccans feel that "all goddesses are One Goddess and all gods are One God"; for example, Athena and Aphrodite are really just particular faces of the One Goddess. Wiccans who view each individual god or goddess as being totally separate personalities are *polytheistic.*

WHAT DO WICCANS DO?

One thing to keep in mind when you're reading is this: While Wicca is a religion, Witchcraft, first and foremost, is a magickal *craft* (which is why a person can practice one and not the other). While Wicca often focuses on semiformal ritual and religious worship, pure Witchcraft focuses on creating, whether that means making candles for spell or healing work or creating incenses, charms, amulets, and the rest. Straight-up Witchcraft tends to be less formal, in general.

When reading, keep in mind that practices differ from coven to coven, and they also vary from individual to individual. This is just an introduction to a huge variety of info, so be sure to check out the Appendices for website resources and suggested reading to get a more complete picture!

MODERN WICCA

Witchcraft was not necessarily a religion in history, but Wicca and its accompanying Witchcraft tradition *is!* Complicate the matter further by realizing that Wicca is not an organized religion; that is, there are no holy men or wholesale prophets or bibles to follow, thank goodness. Again, the whole point is to interpret the myths, revive the gods, and personalize the experience of Divinity. On a related note, please don't let anyone tell you you're not Wiccan or a Witch because you don't practice their specific tradition. It just isn't true, and those people should go join a cult if they want to get snobbish.

In order to qualify as a religion, there are certain basics that need to be present. In her book *Wicca Covens*, Judy Harrow outlines these basics as she found them from Dr. Leonard Swidler, a professor of interreligious dialogue at Temple University in Philadelphia. These basics are credo, cultus, code, and community, and they go something like this:

Credo is a religion's belief system. It's a collection of myths and symbols that talk about how the religion views Deity. Wicca's credo varies with each tradition, and so does any other religion that has different sects or traditions, like Christianity with its Catholics, Baptists, and the rest. It's safe to say that Wicca looks at Deity as *immanent* (that is, present in all things at all times), *transcendent* (that is, a part of Divinity beyond human understanding), and *polarized* into male and female forces. The myths vary from group to group, depending on what cultures each draws from.

Cultus sounds alarmingly like cult, but don't freak out! Cultus is the form of ritual worship that a religion uses. All religions have cultus. In Wicca, for example, casting a Circle is a movable temple and also the most formal way to worship the Gods. Circle-casting styles vary from group to group. See the Witch's Circle section for the particulars on that.

Code is the ethic by which a religious group lives. The Wiccan Rede, in one form or another, is Wicca's code.

The Wiccan *Rede* (an old Anglo-Saxon word for "advice") says: "An it harm none, do as thou wilt." (If it harms none, do as you will.)

Essentially, this is the Golden Rule that all major religions follow—"Do unto others as you would have others do unto you"—but it has a bit of a twist. The first part, "an it harm none," seems straightforward enough. As long as your actions aren't harmful to other people, the Earth, *or yourself*, you are completely free to "do what you will." It seems simple, but it isn't. With great freedom comes great responsibility. You've got to think through all of the possible outcomes for any action you put in motion. That means taking time to consider deeply each and every other person, life-form, or institution that may possibly be affected by a word, deed, or—most especially—spell that you put out there. The main goal is that the highest good of all involved be respected. That's an enormous obligation! The U.S. Army chaplain's handbook refers to Wicca as a "high-choice" ethical system. Thanks, U.S.A.! We've always thought so. . . .

Community is the group that forms with any religion. Wiccans don't have churches, mosques, or synagogues; they have covens. The coven is a place for them to worship together, share one another's joy and trouble, and work on their personal and collective spirits. Some Wiccans prefer to practice Solitaire, and that's perfectly good, too. Solitaires still *have* a community in the larger Pagan family, even if they choose not to come hang out all the time.

As with any other religion, there are several interpretations, also known as sects or traditions ("trads" in mod-speak shorthand) within the general heading of Wiccan. Wiccans may use different names for God/dess, and there are many variations in ritual.

What makes a tradition? Good question. The Witches' Voice, one of the absolute best resources on the Web, considers a group to have started a tradition if three or more covens practice it for more than one year. Hey, why not? The whole philosophy of Eclectic Paganism is about individual freedom to communicate with the Gods without slavishly following any set rules about ritual or worship.

TRADITIONAL AND HEREDITARY WITCHCRAFT

Traditionalist Witches claim to practice Witchcraft that survived through the ancient, classical, and medieval cultures I described earlier! Specifically, their traditions emphasize pantheism and animism, and they often have little to do with formal ceremonies. They don't claim to have direct knowledge from our ancient ancestors, but they claim they are reviv-ing—not reconstructing, like Wiccans—the Old Ways as passed down through oral tradition. Another important distinction is that Traditional Witches may not view what they do as a religion. They employ herbal heal-ing, communion with the Spirit world, and other magickal work, but they don't acknowledge the Wiccan Rede or work in Wiccan ritual format for the most part. Traditionalists view cursing as acceptable if their family is in danger; they also may not believe in the Threefold Law or karma of the Wiccans. However, they do believe in fate.

It's entirely possible that there are Family Tradition or Hereditary Witches out there and that their practices have been handed down through family folklore, but keep in mind a few things when someone claims to be Hereditary: First, these folks are probably very few and very far between. Second, their tradition would have been passed down orally, since it would've meant punishment by death to find written material about Witchcraft, and also because very few people could read and write in the Middle Ages. This means that their tradition is *still evolving* and probably isn't exactly the same as it was five hundred years ago.

Traditional Witches don't cast Circles the way Wiccans do. They feel that, since all space is already sacred, it's not necessary to create a deliber-ate sacred space. There are some Traditionalist Witches whose Craft seems very similar to Gardner's outline, which is reasonable since Gardner basi-cally knitted together a whole bunch of other philosophies, and it's entirely possible that those Traditionalists were influenced by some or all of the same sources. However, there are other Traditionalists whose rituals and tools vary greatly from Gardner's methods. Those folks are probably prac-ticing Witchcraft from other cultures. Ronald Hutton points out in *Tri-umph of the Moon* that several of the Traditionalist groups were influenced by a lesser-known "cunning man" named Robert Cochrane, who practiced around the same time that Gardner was creating Wica but who wasn't as well published.

GARDENERIAN WICA

"Ye shall not be a Witch alone. . . ."

Considered the origin of modern Wicca, Gardnerian Wiccans trace their lineage to initiates of Gerald Gardner. Gerald Gardner, an Englishman who lived from 1884 to 1964, brought to light what he *claimed* was traditional British Witchcraft.

Gardner was a member of a secret society called Ordo Templi Orientis, whose most famous member was the magician and wild man Aleister Crowley. Crowley was also a member of the Golden Dawn (an *occult* society), which he left due to a mad ego and disagreements regarding methods: Crowley was a sex, drugs, and demons kind of Ceremonial Magician. Both of these groups practiced ceremonial magick based on the rituals of secret societies like the Freemasons and Rosicrucians, mixed with some Greek and Egyptian methods and Eastern philosophy (like karma and reincarnation, which they got from the Theosophical Society, another occult mystery club). Gardner took the occult practices of all these groups, synthesized them with whatever other knowledge he had about Traditional English Witchcraft, and created Wica. You heard me. He made it up. Well, he made up the rituals, basically grafting Pagan deities onto Masonic rituals. Witchcraft itself existed long before Gardner did!

The Witchcraft Laws were finally repealed in England in 1951, and Gardner published his first nonfiction book on what English Witchcraft was about in 1952. He asserted that the original Pagan religion, with Witches as its Priests and Priestesses, was alive and well, although scattered, fragmented, and secretive.

Gardner was central in creating modern Wicca, but he had quite a bit of help. Parts of Gardner's rituals were taken directly from the Freemasons and were heavily influenced by Aleister Crowley. The rituals were rewritten, reworked, and made poetic by a prominent Witch named Doreen Valiente.

Although Wicca is a relatively new religion, it is based on ancient ideas and timeless practices. The idea of Divinity being male and female alike is ancient. Leaving offerings to the gods is ancient. Living with Nature's cycles is ancient. Burning incense, dancing, and chanting until your mind is transported to another level of reality is ancient. Creating charms, amulets, and potions for health is ancient, as is using herbs and foods to heal or to harm. These parts of ancient religion are part of Wicca. What about the rest? It may be newer than you thought, *but it's just as valid as anything else*. Why? Because it works; it still talks to the ancient gods, and the ancient gods still listen.

Gardnerian tradition states that belonging to a coven is necessary to be Wiccan. Secrecy is very important, and Gardner's literature stresses it (remember, he wrote his stuff almost immediately after the Witchcraft Laws were taken off the books! If nothing else, he was brave!). There are 162 rules to follow, in all. Each coven has its own High Priest and High Priestess, along with a Maiden (who is the High Priestess's second in command and will take over whatever duties she can't take care of). Anyone who finds a Gardnerian Coven—which is a bit hard to do, since many are still quite secretive and exclusive—goes through several levels of training, moving from student to Priest/ess. The Witch has to have each degree for at least a year and a day before he or she can advance.

First Degree initiates may be referred to as "Outer Court" or "Outer Circle," and they're not allowed to take part in all the coven's rituals. Second Degree makes the Initiate a Priest or Priestess, and Third Degree creates a High Priest/ess who can then start his or her own coven.

In this tradition,

As Isaac Bonewits points out in *Witchcraft: A Concise History*, myths regarding Witches were made up by the Christian church during the Witch Craze (1450–1650, approx.). When Murray wrote her works, which were influenced by a selective interpretation of the trial transcripts, people who had some diluted Hereditary Witchcraft practices or who came from Freemasonry, Spiritualism, Theosophy, or another socially acceptable form of occultism essentially said, "Hey, I do some of this! We should try to revive our true roots!" Then some folks got together and decided to use Murray's language, calling themselves "covens"—secretly—and celebrating the "sabbats" and all the rest. Instead of doing their folk magick and practicing the little superstitions, they became the Witches that Murray had described. It's history from there![2]

"only a Witch can make a Witch." That is, Gardnerians feel that only those initiated by another Gardnerian are actually Wiccan. I think it's more appropriate to say that only a Gardnerian can make a Gardnerian, but the Gods make us Witches.

Speaking of Gods, Gardnerians usually call on Cernunnos (the Roman-Celtic Horned God of the woods) and Aradia (Roman Goddess of Witches, the daughter of Diana, the Moon Goddess). Other deities may be called, but these are the most common.

One of the key elements of Gardnerian Wicca is the Book of Shadows, a book of rituals and spells that's passed down from the High Priest and Priestess to each initiated Witch. Gardnerian tradition originally asserted that each ritual was to be followed exactly as it was written, with no additions or subtractions. Gardnerian rituals are often performed in the nude. Nope, that *isn't* a myth!

In fact, many Witches like to do ritual naked. Nudity was originally mandatory in Gardnerian covens, since Gardner claims that the energy Witches created in ritual is let out through the skin, and that clothing restricted it. To be perfectly fair, he states in *Witchcraft Today* that this may be mind over matter. I've never found ritual to be less effective with clothes on. I've done it in the buff, too—either among good friends with whom I felt completely comfortable or by myself. You certainly *do not* have to be naked at a ritual if you're not comfortable with that, but if you aren't comfortable being naked all by yourself, then you'd probably better find out why and get over it. Ritual nudity (sometimes called "going skyclad") also means ultimate naturalness, social equality, and humble worship of the Gods. We weren't born with designer clothes on! Plus, an enormous part of Gardnerian covens is "Perfect Love and Perfect Trust." Don't get naked without them!

According to my interview with Bonewits, Gardner's original intention was to create a method of Tantra (sex magick) for England, including the idea of a coven as a group marriage. Are you shocked? So was England. I don't personally advocate all Gardner's ideas and methods, but I also don't think they're wrong or evil. They're not for everyone. Neither is football.

You can find examples of Gardnerian rituals in several books (see the Appendices), and we'll talk more about details of ritual in Chapter 10.

ALEXANDRIAN WICCA

Alex Sanders, who lived from 1926 to 1988, was another British Witch, initiated into a Gardnerian coven along with his wife, Maxine. He essentially ran off with the *Book of Shadows,* changed a few elements, and started his own tradition. It isn't named for him; *Alexandrian* refers to Alexandria, a city in Egypt. Appropriately, his rituals had a much heavier Egyptian influence than Gardner's, and he also incorporated Cabalistic symbolism into the rites. According to Janet Farrar and Gavin Bone, two well-known Wiccan writers and initiated Alexandrians, Alexandrian ritual also drew a lot from the ancient *grimoires* (recipe books for spells and ceremonial magick from the Middle Ages). Sanders was also responsible for creating a more serious form of training. The ritual tools are essentially the same as Gardnerian, plus or minus* depending on the individuals.

I had the pleasure of interviewing Janet Farrar and Gavin Bone, and I asked them about their experiences in the Alexandrian tradition—although they don't align themselves with this or any other particular group anymore and prefer to be called "Progressive" (loosely equivalent to Eclectic) if a label is necessary. Among other words of wisdom, they had this to say about modern Wicca and teens:

> Right from the beginning Wicca has defined itself as a Priesthood, and therefore a tradition of service to the Gods, however you perceive them. It is a vocation, not a religion, although it would be true to say that Paganism is the base religion for it all. Like all Priesthoods, it is a mystery tradition, a tradition of self-discovery and connection with Spirit, defined within Wicca as the God and Goddess. As a Priesthood we do not believe it is for everyone, just

---

* a tool here or there

as not everyone can be a doctor or an airline pilot. Nobody would accuse them of being elitist professions, just professions where a certain type of person is required. So understand that we do not feel we are being elitist, just practical. We also strongly believe that you cannot have a Priesthood where there is no life experience among the members, so therefore this cannot be open to teens. This may seem harsh, but you have to ask yourself the question: Could you really take counseling from a teenage rabbi or Roman Catholic priest seriously? The answer must be no! After saying this, I do believe that the tenets of paganism should be open to everyone, especially if they are searching for a true spiritual path, and not just interested in "casting a few spells."

This should be open to young people, but must be done in a responsible way. When approached by teenagers, we recommend that they study *all* religions before embarking on a path of studying paganism. They may find that they're better suited to Buddhism, and we feel we have no right to dictate someone's spiritual path to them. This is the failing of many of the mainstream religions and something we do not want to repeat.

Now, don't take this the wrong way; they also said that Solitary practice is a totally valid Wiccan experience. Their opinion is a pretty common one within the traditional standpoint. Quite frankly, if you come across a Gardnerian or Alexandrian coven that mixes teens with adults, I'd caution you to be wary. The thing is, these traditions often incorporate techniques that just aren't appropriate for teenagers under eighteen, especially ones who are totally new to the Craft.

SOLITARY WICCA

Scott Cunningham made Solitary practice accessible and legitimate, whereas the preceding trads originally emphasized coven work. He still used the Gardnerian methods, but he adapted them for Solitary use. He also brought other cultures into his literature. This is the most prevalent form of Wicca today, as many American practitioners are either in the broom closet, can't find a coven they gel with, or are young like you!

This is an excellent place to start your journey, and I wholeheartedly recommend Cunningham's work to anyone. It's very down to Earth; it emphasizes personal interpretation while providing a good foundation in the traditional myths and methods; it concentrates on the creative, Craft aspect just as much as the magickal part of Wicca. Cunningham is totally unpretentious, and his books are all user friendly.

DIANIC

This women-only variation on the Gardnerian theme focuses primarily on the Goddess aspect, sometimes completely leaving out the God. Dianic worship often focuses on the Lunar Goddesses and Triple Goddess in Her aspects of Maid, Mother, Crone. This type of coven tends to have more free-form rituals, using the spontaneous energy that is created so easily when women are alone among women. It's just a lot more comfortable for some female Witches without the sexual tension and competition that unfortunately occurs within many mixed-gender covens. Sometimes Dianic covens exclude men, and some—but not all—Dianic Witches are lesbian separatists. Z Budapest, an exile from Hungary, is one of the most prominent Dianic Witches, and her books rock.

FAERIE

Also called Faery, Fairy and—originally—Feri, this is a shamanic system started by a fellow named Victor Anderson, added to by Gwydion Pendderwen. Anderson's background was a crazy mixture of Voudoun and Hawaiian shamanism, while Pendderwen brought in the Celtic lore.

As you might have guessed, this tradition calls on the mystical energy of the Faeries, a.k.a. the Fey, the Little People, the Shining Ones. Faeries make an appearance in lots of mythologies, including German, Italian, British, Irish, and Scandinavian. They are variously portrayed as benevolent Nature spirits, powerful magick workers, evil sprites, mischievous pranksters, or a combination of all the above, depending on to whom you're talking. The main focus of Faerie rituals is ecstasy, connecting with Nature energy, trance, and an experience of "divine madness" (my phrasing): that place shamans, poets, artists, and madmen go to draw their Divine inspiration— Faerieland!

Faeries are not all like Tinkerbell. This tradition is proud of embracing life's darker aspects. They encourage a "Warrior" mind-set, and they refuse to bow down or submit to any weakness. They don't subscribe to the Wiccan Rede or Threefold Law. The tools are varied.

RECLAIMING

Started in 1980 in the Bay Area of California, this radical group of Witches mixes magick and politics within a structure that could happily be called anarchistic! There are no High Priests or High Priestesses here; the emphasis is on equality. They tend to lean more toward shamanism than ceremonial magick. They use the ecstasy of dance and chanting to raise energy, and their focus is often on political, social, and ecological reform and healing. They don't subscribe to a central Book of Shadows, and anyone can write, lead, or participate in any ritual. Initiation is not considered necessary to call yourself a Reclaiming Witch. They don't work with any particular pantheon. Reclaiming definitely has a feminist edge to it, and they call on the Goddess more often than the God. Still, they are inclusive and not as militantly feminist as some Dianic Witches.

Reclaiming is a legally registered, incorporated, nonprofit religious organization. Training in magic, self-empowerment, and politics goes on at Witch Camps.

The notion of Reclaiming seems to mean: Reclaiming your power, your connection to the Earth, and your responsibility of ensuring liberty and justice for all. This is a great path for Pagan teens with a strong political voice, and one Reclaiming group allows teens to participate in their Witch Camps. See the Appendices for details.

Starhawk, Reclaiming's catalyst and a prominent writer/activist, was also deeply influenced by Faerie before beginning her own tradition. Several parts of Fearie magick were incorporated into Reclaiming, and her books are suggested by members of both systems.

AMERICAN ECLECTIC

Wicca itself is totally eclectic to begin with. I've already described how Gardner incorporated bits and pieces from all over the occult world and brought them together. The thing is, some people hang on to the notion that Wicca is the Old Religion and won't incorporate other Deities or methods into their practice, preferring to stick to the Gardnerian/British model.

In our glorious melting pot, we have access to so many other cultures and traditions, and many other religions have great wisdom to offer! Why restrict yourself to one small part? In fact, many other religions use rituals and techniques that are very compatible with Gardnerian-style Witchcraft; it's interesting to note the similarities, and it's equally fascinating to explore the differences.

One example of an Eclectic Wicca tradition is Circle Amaurot, based in upstate New York. They've been crafting their tradition for several years, utilizing Wicca's basic ritual framework and incorporating Celtic, Hindu, and Syrian pantheons. They also keep an open mind to lots of other cultures, including the Native American, Egyptian, and Gypsy heritages. Deep understanding of the cultures they work with is key to Circle Amaurot's philosophy, and they feel that the harmonious blending of diverse kinds of wisdom makes for a very rich spiritual experience. In fact, when asked why they felt the need to break away from the British model, they insisted that they weren't. Instead, they view their tradition as a modern interpretation of Wicca that unifies the common elements within a wide range of religious systems.

Santeria, Stregheria, Native American Shamanism, Voudoun, Buddhism, Taoism . . . all these religious philosophies fit with Wiccan beliefs, and the Eclectic uses them all. Read on to find out a little bit more about these other cultures that help make American Eclectic Wicca what it is. . . .

CHAPTER THREE

THE MANY FACES OF THE GODDESS AND GOD

The following is an unbelievably basic, supershort look at some other cultures. All of the following are either religious traditions that incorporate Witchcraft, religious philosophies that are useful to Witchcraft, systems that deeply influence modern Wicca, or other Neo-Pagan paths about which you may want to learn. I always say that a well-rounded Witch is a happy Witch. The more avenues and cultures you explore, the more knowledge and experimentation you seek, the better your magickal practice will be. Embracing our differences, celebrating each other's knowledge, and generally giving up the notion of "one right Path" frees your mind and soul like nothing else!

EGYPTIAN

There are some surviving papyri that tell us quite a bit about Egypt's magick. They absolutely used talismans, amulets, and spell craft that included sacred herbs and magick words. Ancient Egyptian magick was also very concerned with making the soul perfect to ensure its survival with the gods in the afterlife. All these aspects of magick are alive and well in modern Wicca, and the Hermetic Order of the Golden Dawn (a huge part of Gardner's inspiration) drew on this system very heavily.

There are a couple of problems when talking about Egyptian magick in the modern age, though. First of all, the vowels that are inserted into the popular names for their gods are assumed. Their deities' names were written without any vowel sounds, so we stuck some in there for good measure.

This presents a problem, because from what we can tell from the surviving evidence about Egyptian magickal systems, *Perfect pronunciation of words, spells, and the gods' names was considered absolutely imperative to the magick's effectiveness!* Without the vowels, we've got a conflict!

Beyond that snafu, we can tell a bit about their ritual structure that's pretty helpful. As I said, they placed a lot of emphasis on exact pronunciation. We can apply that concept to our own Gods, being careful to speak very clearly and using, to the best of our ability, the original language of the Deities we're calling. Also, Egyptian rites consisted of two parts. The first part was a l-o-n-g invocation to the Gods or a detailed set of commands aimed at the person or situation the magician wanted to control. This is great stuff! A major part of Wiccan spell craft is building emotion to a peak and aiming that emotion toward your goal. Impassioned verbal commands can certainly help that. The second part of the Egyptian rites used physical motions, to invoke the Gods or move energy toward the goal. Hello! Wiccans do that, too!

While we can't reproduce these rites down to the last detail, we can certainly learn from the Egyptians. They were eerily lovely, stunningly civilized, disciplined magicians who knew without any doubt their Gods were alive and listening. . . .

RESOURCES FOR FURTHER STUDY

Any books by E. A. Wallis Budge
Osirisweb.com
Idolhands.com

CABALA* (A.K.A. KABALA, QABBALA)

An incredibly ancient magickal tradition, Cabala comes to us through the Hebrews and is thousands of years old. The main idea of Cabalism is that the universal divine force has different levels and forms of manifesta-

* Jewish mysticism

tion. Each of these forms has a place on the Tree of Life, a diagram of the universal forces that's expressed by three pillars, one to represent the feminine forces, one to represent the masculine forces, and the center pillar that stands between the two representing ultimate harmony. Each of the pillars has spheres, called *sephiroth,* placed at certain points on it, ten in all. Each *sephira* represents a specific manifestation of God. The *sephiroth* are connected to one another by twenty-two paths, and each of those twenty-two paths is represented by the twenty-two letters in the Hebrew alphabet. Each of the Hebrew letters also represents a concept of divine creation. Ten *sephiroth* plus twenty-two letters equals the Cabala's thirty-two Paths of Wisdom on the Tree of Life, which is an expression of the connections between God and Man. Each *sephira* also has a whole host of corresponding counterparts in the world, including a specific color, body part, sound, stone, animal, symbol, herb, flower, and archangel.

The idea of letters and numbers being sacred expressions of the divine force that we can decipher to learn more about the interconnectedness of the world is absolutely compatible with Wicca. Many Witches incorporate this aspect of Cabala into their practice, along with the generally known Cabalistic correspondences. Some Witches also call on angels and archangels in their work, and others use the Cabalistic Tree of Life as a model to base their magick on.

This magickal tradition is not one that you can learn from books, though there are many that can get you acquainted with Cabala. You need to study it with an initiated rabbi to get an inkling of its philosophy, and many initiatives won't teach you Cabala unless you're over thirty-five, married, and have a family. That's not a matter of exclusion. Cabala is such an involved and absorbing tradition of magick that you need to have very firm roots to keep you grounded.

RESOURCES FOR FURTHER STUDY

Dion Fortune's *The Mystical Qabalah,* 2nd edition (York Beach, Maine: Red Wheel/Weisa, 2000).
Golden-Dawn.org

VOUDOO (A.K.A. VOODOO AND VOUDOON)

YORUBA AND DAHOMEY

It's an almost impossible task to talk about African religion, since Africa is actually composed of many different countries, tribes, and cultures. Voudoo is a religion that started when African people from Dahomey, Nigeria, Senegal, and Guinea, were sold into slavery and brought to Saint-Domingue (Haiti) in the seventeenth century. They were baptized and converted to Catholicism by the French landowners in Haiti, but they retained as much of their traditional practice as they could by combining their gods with the Catholic saints, much like Santeria (see below). The word *Voudou* means "a god, spirit, or sacred object" [1] in the language used by the people from Dahomey and Togo.

Voudoo's worship focuses on spirits and gods, called *loa*, which are variously described as spirits, angels, or "winds." That is, they're archetypal energy forms that express every possible facet of natural forces—human experience, fate and divine power, and the constant presence of dead ancestors. There's no way to catalog every *loa*; there are thousands of *loa*, varying by region and by the personal interpretation of the *mambo* (priestess, also called *maman-loa*, "mother of the gods") and the *hungan* (priest, also called *papa-loa*, "father of the gods"). Behind Voudoo's intricate religious system is *Mawu*, the supreme god of Voudoo.

The ultimate goal of Voudoo ritual is to be possessed by the *loa*, which is considered a great honor. By achieving ecstasy through drumming, dancing, and chanting, the *vodû-si* (companion of the Voudou) connect with universal energies and divinity—like Witches!

Voudoo rituals also resemble Wiccan rituals to some degree. The *loa* are invoked by drum, dance, and drawing their particular *vèvè* (symbolic drawings that represent the *loa*'s power). The *vodû-si* chant and sing, and the *mambo* or *hungan* pours libations for the *loa* in front of the *poteau-mitan*, the middle post of the *humfo* (temple room) or at the four cardinal directions. Leaving offerings for *le morte* (our dead ancestors) is also key to Voudou's spirituality.

Voudoo is still alive and well today, especially in New Orleans, where the Creole population has found a happy home.

RESOURCES FOR FURTHER STUDY

Mamiwata.com
Voodooshop.com

SANTERIA (A.K.A. THE WAY OF THE SAINTS, *LA REGLA LUCUMÍ*, AND THE *ORISHA* TRADITION)

In Nigeria, West Africa, there is a city called Ile Ife where the Yoruba live. They are ancient; their language is believed to be several thousand years old, and their culture is rich with art. They worship Oloddumare, the supreme creative force, their god. Oloddumare made the *orishas,* separate beings that protect and care for humans and represent all of Oloddumare's different natural forces. To the Yoruba, everything in the world is made of *ashé* (divine energy), and Oloddumare and the *orishas* can give us their *ashé.* When you need help from the *orishas,* you have to leave them *ebbó* (sacrifice or offerings) so they will give you their *ashé.* You must also remember to honor and "feed" your dead ancestors, the *eggun,* so they will continue to watch over you and aid the *orishas.*

The Yoruba were brought into Cuba as slaves in the seventeenth century. The Spanish ruled Cuba at the time, and it was a Roman Catholic territory. The Yoruba were strictly prohibited from practicing their native religion, but they found a way to preserve Oloddumare and the *orishas.* They gave each of the Catholic saints the same powers that their *orishas* had! So, even though Santeria has African (Yoruban) roots, it is also distinctly Hispanic.

In America, the men and women who are initiated into Santeria are called *santero* and *santera*—priest and priestess. Initiation has several degrees. Before being initiated, you must find out who your special *orisha* is by casting cowrie shells, the Santeria divination tool. You can call on other *orishas* when you need their particular powers, but your *orisha* will protect and keep you the rest of your life. A santero/santera will take the name of his/her *orisha* and be given a *libreta,* a special book of spells, advice, and traditions that the santera's *padrino* (godfather) hands her at her *asiento* (third-degree initiation, approximately). During the *asiento,* it's considered a blessing if the initiate becomes possessed by his or her *orisha,* which is referred to as being mounted or ridden. This is similar to the Wiccan rite called Drawing down the Moon. Santeria's rituals produce altered states of consciousness through drums, chanting, and dancing—the same way Wiccans do.

An interesting part of Santeria is the fact that *they don't call this Witchcraft!* This is just their religion, their personal connection to the divine, and it's seen as perfectly natural. Love that! Also, Santeria has definitely affected American Eclectic Wicca. We're realizing how rich African spirituality is and how closely our ways are related.

The Yoruba ways affected other countries, as well. In Brazil, a variation on the Yoruban traditions is called *Candomblé,* and it's called *Macumba* in Trinidad. These systems are both similar to and different from Santeria, but I don't have the space to go into it, unfortunately. Do your own research and find out about it yourself! Santeria is very much alive, especially in Los Angeles, New York, and other areas with a lively Hispanic culture.

RESOURCES FOR FURTHER STUDY

Migene Gonzalez-Wippler's *Santeria: The Religion,* 2nd edition
(St. Paul, Minn.: Llewellyn Publications, 1994).
Church-of-the-Lukumi.org

BUDDHISM

There are several different sects of Buddhism. The most well known forms in the Western world are Mahanya Buddhism and Zen. Both have very practical advice for Witches. Buddhism is a philosophy more than anything else. It's extremely spiritual, but it doesn't have any elaborate rituals. The only ritual I've seen mentioned is that of leaving offerings for Buddha, usually in front of a small statue. The offerings are thanks for all the hard work the Buddha did while he was alive. The most important part of being

Buddhist is living your daily life in a way that exemplifies the Eightfold Path, a set of moral guides that are very compatible with the Wiccan Rede: right understanding; right speech; right action; right livelihood; right endeavor; right mindfulness; and right concentration.

The main concepts here are disciplining your mind (*Samadhi*), and controlling your speech and actions (*Sila*) to keep destructive emotions from polluting your soul and the world. Keeping your body healthy is also stressed, and developing a deep understanding of your own mind and body are key to Buddhist practice. Complete tolerance of other people and other ways of life are also major parts of Buddhist philosophy. All these ideas are very much at home with Wiccans. Remember, some of the occult teachings that influenced Gardner, especially Theosophy, were strongly influenced by Eastern mysticism.

While other forms of Buddhism can be quite intellectual and academic, Zen puts an emphasis on peaceful meditation, especially *zazen,* which means "sitting." The goal of *zazen* is to reach nirvana, a spiritual level of existence that connects you with the Divine and is described as quiet ecstasy. Witches use lots of different meditation techniques, and sitting meditation is certainly one of them. A major part of many Witches' rites is designed to bring ecstasy, as well. It's that whole "connection to the Gods through joy" thing. While our rites often go for the wild ecstasy of dancing and howling with a bonfire, the calm ecstasy of Zen Buddhism is a great alternative technique.

The goal of Buddhism is to continually perfect your soul, balance your karma, and become a Buddha yourself.

RESOURCES FOR FURTHER STUDY

Buddhist Study Association
  16 Stanford Avenue
  West Orange, New Jersey 07052
Buddhanet.net
Tricycle.com

HINDUISM

Also from India, Hinduism is a very formal religion of many gods and goddesses, in sharp contrast to Buddhism's simplicity. Worship of the gods (*puja*) takes place after the Hindu has bathed and purified himself or herself. Hindus leave flowers to their gods, even at the simplest ritual; this is done in a very stylized, formal way, while the Hindu chants a prayer. Their goal is to unite their soul (*Jiva-atman*) with Brahman, Absolute Truth and Soul of the World, roughly!

Yoga is part of Hindu philosophy. Its movements are devised to create the ecstatic union of Jiva-atman with Brahman—to unite the human soul with Divinity through ecstasy. Sounding familiar at all? The cool thing about Yoga is that it helps your physical body, too. It's not just spiritual and intangible. Yoga also helps to open the *chakras,* specific points on your body that hold, release, and generate energy (*prana* or *shakti*). Hinduism also uses *mantras,* chants that are repeated during meditation, *mudras* (ritual gestures), and *mandalas,* geometric illustrations used to concentrate your mind. Hindus recognize all life as sacred and practice noninjury; that's why many are vegetarians. They believe in *devas,* spirits that guard animal and plant life, sort of like our faeries.

This is a very intellectual religion, and there are elements of occultism throughout Hinduism. The main ideas are found in many texts, the most famous of which is the *Bhagavad Gita,* but the Hindu holy books are collectively called the Vedas and Upanishads.

RESOURCES FOR FURTHER STUDY

Spiritweb.com
Hindunet.org
bhagavad-gita.org
Himalayanacademy.com

TAOISM

Sage old men with laughing eyes and youthful hearts, the gentle stream in your backyard, and screaming toddlers: this is *Tao*. Actually, this *isn't* Tao. Actually, Tao cannot be put into words, and any words you use to describe Tao are not Tao. . . .

This is the general feeling you'll get when you read the *Tao Te Ching*, by Lao-Tzu. This fourth-century book is considered the ultimate source book for an ancient Chinese philosophy. Its advice is practical today, and it's especially helpful for Witches.

Like I said before, any words I use to describe Tao are not Tao. It's not an intellectual concept. Tao is the all-inclusive energy that fills the world and makes it live. Tao is everything; Tao is nothing. Go with the flow. The world, humans, nature, everything flows with Tao, and there's no beginning or end to Tao. There aren't any gods or goddesses in strictly Taoist literature; Taoists say that gods and goddesses are just ideas we make up to put a name to the nameless.

One of the most important ideas in Taoism is *wu-wei,* or "no action." Taoists say that it's better to be weak, "limp," and still than to force your ideas onto Tao. Why would a Witch subscribe to this, with all our spells and potions? Usually, we don't. I think it's a good idea to stuff it into your bag of tricks, though. Sometimes, it's more important to stand back from the world's wild illusions and just let it stream around us.

Taoism also uses a classic divination tool, the *I Ching*. It's a bunch of yarrow stalks (you can also use sticks or coins) that you throw to form patterns. Then, you look in the *I Ching* book to see which pattern you threw. Each formation has a thought-provoking little riddle that goes with it, as well as a traditional interpretation for divination. *I Ching* works on the principle that, since Tao is everywhere in all things at all times, the yarrow stalks (or sticks, or coins) are part of Tao and can tell us how Tao is moving.

Speaking of thought, it has a less important place in Taoism than in many other philosophies. Instead of thinking their problems to death, Taoists teach us to look at nature for answers to dilemmas and be still in ourselves to let Tao move us where it will.

RESOURCES FOR FURTHER STUDY

TaoRestore.org

Lao Tzu's *Tao Te Ching*, reprint edition (New York: Viking Press, 1985).

ASATRÚ

Sometimes mistakenly called Odinism, this religion worships the old Norse gods, taking their cues from mythology and classical works of Norse literature, mainly two works entitled *The Poetic Edda* and *The Prose Edda*, the first whose author is unknown, and the second written by Snorri Sturluson. Asatrú means "loyalty to the *Aesir*." The Aesir are the sky gods of the Scandinavian Pagans, complemented by the *Vanir*, or the Earth/underworld gods, who control agriculture, death, and other Earthy things.

People who practice Asatrú are called Asatrúar or Asatrúarfolks, and their groups are called *kindred*, which says a lot about their value of family, a main component in Asatrú. Asatrúar usually have a Scandinavian heritage; that is, their families are descended from Norse, Germanic, Icelandic, or Scandinavian folks. There is a sense of ethnic pride in the Asatrúar, and they don't use any mythologies, methods, or gods other than the Germanic ones.

The Nine Noble Virtues are their moral code: courage, truth, honor, loyalty, hospitality, industriousness, perseverance, self-discipline, and self-reliance. Some Asatrúarfolks feel that magick is a part of their tradition, while others don't. They use the Germanic runes.

Their religious leaders are called *gothi* and *gythia* (priest and priestess, approximately), and they are responsible for running the *blóts* (sounds like "bloat"), where the gods are honored with offerings of food and drink, as well as through giving thanks and praise with the *sumbel*. The *sumbel* is a ritual that is often described as a toast, in which the Asatrúarfolks pass a drinking horn filled with ale, beer, or mead around an informal circle. Each Asatrúar will take a sip and tell a story, recite a poem, and offer toasts to the gods. After each Asatrúar drinks a small bit to become connected to one another and to the gods, the rest is poured onto the ground as a libation and honor.

They don't follow the same holidays as Wiccans, but Yule is essentially similar to Wicca's Yule and considered the most important holiday.

RESOURCES FOR FURTHER STUDY

> *The Poetic Edda,* e-text trans. Henry Adams Bellows, 1936.
> Snorri Sturluson's *The Prose Edda,* trans. Jean Young (Berkeley: University of California Press, 2002).
>   (Both can be found at Sacred-Texts.com)
> Irminsul.org
> Asatrú Folk Assembly: Runestone.org

STREGHERIA (A.K.A. *LA VECCHIA RELIGIONE*)

Nestled in the sensual Mediterranean Sea is passionate Italy, the home of the *Strega*—the Italian Witch. Raven Grimassi is the modern reviver of what he claims to be *La Vecchia Religione,* the Old Religion of the pre-Christian Etruscans. He says that the Pagan ways of Italy were never destroyed completely and that *Stregheria* is a continuation rather than a reconstruction of an authentic Witchcraft tradition. He cites classical writers such as Ovid and Horace, who wrote about Witches "calling down the Moon" as early as 30 B.C.E. There is also evidence that some Italian women were hand-copying *The Key of Solomon* in the seventeenth century. It's totally obvious that Italians were pretty darned Pagan for a good part of their history, so I'll go out on a limb here and grant that Witchcraft's survival through the ages—at least in some diluted form—is possible in this region's rural areas.

In 1890, folklorist Charles Leland produced a very controversial work entitled *Aradia, Gospel of the Witches.* This book was supposed to have been written in part by a woman who claimed to be a hereditary Strega, Maddelena. The thing with *Aradia* is that it's very anti-Christian in tone; however, it would make sense that a Strega who held on to her beliefs would feel quite put out over being threatened with imprisonment or death for them as a result of supreme Christian influence. Raven Grimassi, Strega's foremost writer, asserts that Leland's work is full of false info. Some scholars think that Maddelena was full of malarkey, lying to protect the true rites, or nonexistent.

An interesting aspect of Stregheria is its main *avatar,* or prophet, a woman who named herself Aradia after the Italian goddess. Legend has it that she lived in the fourteenth century (1313 is the mythological attribution). She was also called *La Bella Pellegrina,* the beautiful pilgrim, and she traveled around teaching Witchcraft to her disciples. I love this! It's not often that we see a female prophet, and much less often when she's a proudly self-declared Witch!

Stregheria's tools are very similar to Wicca's. There are two additions to Wicca's working tools: one is the *nanta bag,* which serves as a constant reminder or talisman of the Witch's power. Wicca uses that type of magick as well, but the *nanta* is a constant tool. In addition to the common Wiccan altar tools, the Strega uses a Spirit Bowl, usually of cast iron. A small amount of Strega Liquore (which is actually available at your local liquor store, believe it or not! It's this weird bright-green color, and on the label is a picture of women dancing with Pan in a forest . . . interesting!) is poured into the spirit bowl and lit. The blue flame that results represents Divinity's presence.

Stregheria also celebrates the Wheel of the Year, but their holy days are called *Treguendas* instead of sabbats. The mythology attributed to the holidays is also a little different from Wicca's.

The Strega calls on Diana as his or her supreme goddess, and Aradia, the Goddess of Witches, Diana's daughter. They use the old Etruscan gods, as opposed to the Roman gods that we're familiar with, although that varies within the tradition. The similarities between this system and Wicca are striking. Then again, remember that Gardner was impressed by Leland's book, as well. It's reasonable that the two would look a lot alike!

RESOURCES FOR FURTHER STUDY

Any of Raven Grimassi's books on Stregheria
Stregheria.com
Fabrisia.com

DRUIDISM

In ancient Ireland and Gaul, the Druids were the priest caste and intellectuals of the community. Contrary to popular belief, the megaliths (like Stonehenge) aren't attributed to Druids; they were created before the Druids got organized. The Druids lived in Ireland and Gaul (France) around 600 B.C.E. Classical texts by authors like Pliny, Cicero, and Julius Caesar mention the Druid's awesome powers to enchant, to frighten away soldiers, to control the weather, and to tell the future.

The word *Druid* is associated with the Gaelic word for oak, which also has the connotation of strength, solidity, and order. Oak and mistletoe were both sacred to the Druids. Where the Witches of ancient times were lone midwives, herbalists and spell casters for the general population, the Druids were an organized priesthood that worked for the people in general and the aristocracy in particular. In fact, one reference to Druids says that a king must have a Druid in his close circle of advisers.

There's a movement going on right now to revitalize and reconstruct the Druid priesthood. One of the most prominent men in this reconstruction is Isaac Bonewits, founder of *Ár nDraíocht Féin* (ADF)—Our Own Druidism. He was totally honest in his intentions and methods; he didn't claim to be practicing Druidry as it was thousands of years ago. Though Bonewits has stepped down from his position of Arch Druid, ADF is still going strong. ADF is about finding the classical references to ancient Druids, putting together as many of the pieces as possible, and creating whatever works along similar lines.

The cool thing about ADF is that they have a definite teaching curriculum. The first level includes classical literature, archaeological scholarship, meditation techniques, ritual-tools crafting, and service to the community in which you live. The *coolest* part is that they accept teen applicants—with parental permission, mind you! This is a really fabulous resource for any Pagan teen. While Druidism is a Celtic path, ADF doesn't restrict their practice to those cultures.

There are some distinct differences between Druid worship and traditional Wicca. Neo-Pagan Druids are truly polytheistic. They don't go for the "all gods are one" view. Neo-Pagan Druids worship each god/dess as an individual, and they're not limited to the Celtic pantheon. According to Bonewits, ADF is geared toward public worship of the old gods in medium to large groups, where Wicca is more of a private, small-group situation. There are different degrees of initiation into ADF; clergy is expected to have mastered very specific skills, whereas Wicca says that each Wiccan is a Priest/ess after his or her first or second initiation, depending on the tradition. Druidism is inclusive and open. It isn't a "secret mystery school," as Mr. Bonewits put it to me. It's an attempt to build public Pagan "churches" (for lack of a better analogy), and they're dedicated to scholarly research. Since many Wiccans prefer to keep to themselves, it can be sort of difficult to gain entrance to a coven, but ADF accepts everyone who's genuinely dedicated.

RESOURCES FOR FURTHER STUDY

Neopagan.net
ADF.org

SHAMANISM

NATIVE AMERICAN, SIBERIAN, AFRICAN

The image of the Native American medicine man, complete with impressive headdress and mysterious tools made of earth and bone, lives in American popular culture. The more accurate word for him is *shaman,* and shamans come from all over the world. In fact, if anyone can claim descent from Paleolithic Paganism, it is the cultures who have a shaman as part of their spiritual practice. The indigenous people of Siberia, the Americas, Africa, Australia, and others still put their faith in the shaman, the gifted healer who visits and talks with the Spirit world to cure illness. He enters the Spirit world at will by using altered states of consciousness (are you beginning to see a trend here?), and he sees every object as part of the Divine, with its own unique soul. Remember our discussion about animism and pantheism? The way of the shaman is both animistic and pantheistic.

The shaman's function is to maintain the health and balance of the entire tribe or community, along with treating individuals. Something I found interesting in my research was the common experience among shamans of being "called." Many didn't want to be shamans, and many resisted. They were plagued with horrible visions and happenings until they relented and took up their path in earnest. Many Witches whom I've spoken with describe a similar experience: the harder they fought against their natural psychic abilities, the longer they tried to fit into the current Christian mold and forget their early connection to other gods, the more intense their discomfort became, until they finally found out that they weren't alone!

RESOURCES FOR FURTHER STUDY

Animalspirit.com

Shamanism.org

Michael Harner's *The Way of the Shaman* (San Francisco: HarperCollins, 1990).

Shirley Nicholson's *Shamanism* (Wheaton, Ill.: Theosophical Publishing, 1987).

THE WITCH'S PATHS

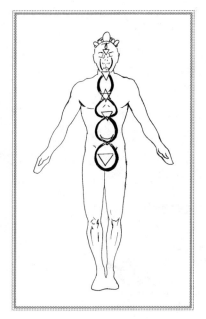

PART III

CHAPTER FOUR

INITIATION TO THE SPIRAL

So, you made it through the history, and here you are. (Or maybe you just flipped through all the preliminaries, and here you are even sooner. I understand the temptation, but it will bite you in the behind later!) Ever onward.

This chapter is a beginning, an introduction to the elements of Wiccan spirituality and its many symbols.

The exercises in this chapter are structured in a specific way for a reason. I don't want to imply that Witchcraft is a rigid practice. It isn't. However, when you're just starting out, it's helpful to understand why a certain element is useful, how you can use it, and what to do with it! Once you learn the basic "rules," you can break them in an intelligent manner, so jump in, tear it up, and have a good time.

You should do the following exercises for one full Lunar cycle. As the Moon progresses through Her natural course, so will you. You'll start to know yourself intimately and to see the connections among all of your layers; you will know that your internal life is in circuit with the wild life of the natural world. You'll begin to feel the presence of Divinity in your everyday world. Once you're attuned to these energies, you will be able to work with them to draw what you need into your life.

In order to practice Wicca, you need to accomplish two things: primarily, you have to listen carefully to your inner Self, and then you have to become sensitive to the natural world. This chapter is mapped out so you begin by exploring your Self, move to exploring the Elements, and finally begin to work with the Deities. The goal during this month is to stimulate

"At the core of Pagan spirituality is communing with the Divine through Nature. This underlies key Pagan spiritual practices. These include attuning to and celebrating the cycles of Moon, Sun, and seasons, and work with the sacred Elements—Earth, Air, Fire, Water, and Spirit. The Divine in Nature at the core of Paganism is also reflected in a variety of Pagan sacred symbols. These include the Circle (representing the interconnecting Spirit that is indwelling in all), the Spiral (the ever-turning wheel of life through and beyond time), and the Pentagram (the balance of the five Elements of Nature). Other major Pagan symbols include the Tree (growth, renewal, being centered between the realms of Land and Sky), Sun Wheel (Solstices, Equinoxes, and in many traditions, also the midpoints between sometimes called the Cross Quarters or Celtic Fire Festivals), and Triple Moon (cycles of the Moon, with waxing and waning crescents and full Moon disc between— the Goddess as Maiden/waxing, Mother/ full, and Crone/waning)."

—SELENA FOX, CIRCLE SANCTUARY

and connect with all of your senses and incorporate parts of life and your mind that you aren't used to using.

If this chapter seems a little serious, it's because you'll need *some* little bit of discipline to get the energy moving. While Devotion requires discipline, it should also be fun. You should never feel that ritual or magick is a drag or requires slavish blind faith. You may feel somber during some rituals, and that's fine. Seriousness is a sign of deep thought, and deep thought is a necessary part of Witchcraft. However, throwing energy balls around with your best friend late at night or making little spheres of white light and blowing them like bubbles through the air is fun. Don't think that laughter and playfulness makes your magick less powerful. Quite the contrary, in fact! Wicca is joyous, and the power of Witchcraft depends on the celebration of Life.

If you don't do it already, I highly recommend keeping a daily notebook where you can write down all of your thoughts, dreams, and feelings as you start your journey. The purpose of keeping a notebook is not to write stunningly beautiful poetry or doctorate-level theses on the meaning of life but to keep track of your thoughts in such a way that you can go back later and ponder them. Even if your daily entry is a one-liner ("Um, school rots and I had a dream about toads last night"), it's still a way to keep up with your mind. Sometimes we aren't aware of the patterns in our thoughts and in our lives until we write them down. In order to work magick, you have to be com-

> "It is a very hard thing to break free of the idea that the Gods are not with us, that we have to walk into a building and let a Priest talk to God for us. We are fully capable of talking to the Gods ourselves, and we are also a part of the Gods."
>
> —WYLD WYTCH, AGE 19

pletely honest with yourself and confront with bravery destructive patterns, bad habits, or internal conflicts. This is a major key to practicing Wicca: we try to refine ourselves as best we can and to realize that we are unique and wonderful, no matter what our personal quirks are. Be willing to encounter those parts of yourself that are frightening or unattractive. It is only through self-examination that we can learn anything useful and grow into fabulous creatures.

For your Month of Devotions and Elemental exercises, you will need the following:

- Three candles, preferably two different-colored candles plus a plain white one. If you aren't allowed to light candles in your room, don't worry. You'll still be able to do your Devotions.

- A mug or cup that can hold hot liquids. One made from a natural material like glass or pottery is best. Use this mug and only this mug for your Devotions, and be sure to wash it thoroughly after each use.

- Two bowls. One bowl will serve as a place to leave offerings, whether those offerings are food, objects, or words on paper. The other bowl will act as a kind of mini-cauldron, where you can mix ingredients or place articles to be blessed. Be sure to use each bowl for the same purpose every time. This will help to keep your intention constantly focused on each act that you perform.

· Salt. Sea salt is preferable, Kosher salt is great, but table (iodized) salt is perfectly fine.

· Tea. Plain old black tea is perfect, preferably decaffeinated (you don't need the caffeine jitters). If you like green tea, that has superior health benefits.

· A compass, or at least the knowledge of which wall in your room corresponds to which cardinal direction: North, East, South, and West.

You may wish to include:

· Incense. It definitely sets a mood. If you can't burn incense, potpourri is a good substitute.

· Images of Goddesses or Gods. Wiccans do not worship images as being holy in themselves, but representations are a nice, solid reminder of the beauty of Divinity.

· Crystals or stones that you may have already.

· Unlined paper and variously colored inks, paints, markers, or even crayons—hey, they're cheap and you'll get plenty of hues with which to work.

Begin your Month of Devotions by cleaning your bedroom to literally clean out your space: put everything where it belongs, put a dent in the inevitable pile of laundry, and hide the rest of your dirty clothes in a closet or under the bed—anyplace out of sight—and dust the surfaces. Really put your back into it, and wash every inch of your room. Vacuum the rug or floor. As you do this, know that any bacteria and other little germies are being sucked up and washed away.

Choose a surface like your dresser or nightstand to set your candles, mug, and bowls on, if you can. Arrange them any way that looks groovy. This is your Devotional altar. I usually set the candles on two sides of my altar and place all the other objects between them. I also use a square altar most of the time. I like the solidity of the square and its relation to the four directions, four seasons, and the four physical Elements. I can then create a circle of objects within the square's four sides. If your parents freak about your keeping a Witch's altar in your room, don't fret. You can simply use the items for Devotions and then put them away when you're done.

SYMBOLISM AND THE SUBCONSCIOUS WORLD

Some of the articles Witches use during ritual are powerful in themselves, such as salt, water, a bonfire, or herbs. These items obviously have the power to replenish, burn, or heal without having a Witch tweak them. Other objects, like wands and ritual robes, are *symbols* more than anything. By using the same materials over and over again, and by using them only for rituals, those items become charged with your personal energy. It's like wearing your lucky hat to pass a test. The hat isn't really lucky by itself, but the energy you put into it makes it a symbol of good luck. Whenever you pull it on, you know you'll ace the test. Our subconscious mind—the part of our mind that rules the dream state and intuition—speaks in the language of symbols.

The trick is to lull your conscious, rational, intellectual mind into a peaceful state so it will stop worrying you with the stuff you forgot to do today, the stress you'll have tomorrow, etc. Repeating a single word or a phrase over and over again, called chanting, is a simple way to do this. Another way is to stare at geometric patterns, those *mandalas* from Indian culture, to occupy your conscious mind and free your subconscious to interpret your symbols. Staring at a candle flame has a similarly mesmerizing effect, and so does the repetition of sounds, like rhythmic drumming. Meditating with these tools lets you shift your awareness from the physical world and open your mind to the symbolic world.

BE THREE TIMES MORE

Many Wiccans feel that the Self is actually composed of several "bodies," or layers. To make it convenient, I'll break them down into the physical body, the emotional body, and the astral body. The physical body is, of course, our wonderful conglomeration of organs, limbs, and skin. It houses and facilitates the intellect. This is obvious, but the connection between this vehicle and the rest of us is too often ignored. Our emotional body is the swirling medley of feelings and impressions that fluctuates from moment to moment. This part of ourselves is distinct from our physical selves but is completely entwined with it. The last layer is our astral body, and it contains the essence of our selves—our Soul or Spirit. The astral body can move from lifetime to lifetime. Sometimes it moves around in this lifetime, too; this is called astral projection. If you've ever had a very vivid dream of flying, then you've probably experienced astral projection without even knowing it.

It's not difficult to become aware your different aspects. All it takes is a willingness to do so and a minor effort to look really closely at yourself, to willingly encounter the depth and breadth of your entire life. If a piece of your being is ignored, it'll get your attention in visible ways.

"The line I love most in the Charge of the Goddess is 'If you cannot find what you seek within, do not bother looking for it without. . . . ' One can't begin to understand something so vast without starting with one's own sense of balance and effect in the world. I am both Destroyer and Creator. When I do not have balance, the Goddess gives me the opportunity to see that and change it, not wallow in self-pity."

—ATHENA, AGE 17

All these layers are knitted together; one won't function properly independent of any other. If one part of the Self is out of balance, the whole Self is out of whack and generally miserable. When you maintain a balance between all of your aspects, you'll begin to feel your awareness unfold, and you'll start seeing connections between you and the big crazy world.

QUESTION YOUR MORAL STANDARDS

You can also use your notebook to write down the questions that you will have as you read this book and any other literature to start a dialog with yourself. It's important to question yourself and others, and if you write it out, you'll be able to keep your thoughts sharp and clear. A strong, lucid mind is integral to practicing Wicca; if your thoughts are muddled, your magick won't be as fabulous as it could be, and you won't reap all the benefits of spirituality in general.

USE MORE OF YOUR GRAY MATTER

Speaking of strong minds, there are three basic kinds of psychic ability that Witches use. The most well known psychic gift is *clairvoyance,* which comes from a French word meaning "to see clearly." Some people see future events in their dreams, while others receive visual flashes when awake that predict future events. The ability to see spirits of the dead or other spirit beings also falls under this category. Some Witches really do use a crystal ball (usually either clear quartz or obsidian, which is black molten lava that has cooled very quickly). This is called *scrying,* and we'll talk more about it in Chapter 11.

Less well known is *clairaudience,* or hearing thoughts or voices from the Spirit world (from a French word meaning "clear hearing"). Don't think that all people who hear little voices in their heads are schizophrenic or delusional! It is often a very subtle impression, such as the voice we all hear in the back of our minds that whispers about the rightness or falseness of a situation. Some clairaudients also hear the voices of ghosts or spirit beings. They can receive guidance or information about circumstances from these beings or warnings about danger.

Clairsentience is another form of psychic ability, again from a French root, meaning "to perceive clearly." It is the ability to accurately intuit situations, sometimes through physical sensation (i.e., feeling nauseated by negative energies in a particular area) and other times just by deeply sensing the truth of a situation. Clairsentience is often overlooked as the psychic

"Questioning motives and beliefs is something very important to both Judaism and Paganism, and it is one of the reasons I feel very comfortable with both religions. There are some things about Judaism I disagree with, though. I was at a Teen Chavurah [youth group thing] meeting a while ago, and we were discussing what happens after death. I asked a hypothetical question: 'What if there's this Pagan who follows all the Jewish ethical code things and is very, very socially active, but has no intention of ever becoming Jewish . . . and there's this Jewish person who thinks s/he's holy but doesn't do anything above the minimal amount of *mitzvahs* [Jewish word for "good deed," except it isn't optional]? Who gets preference in Heaven?' The rabbi said she didn't know. That disturbed me."

—MARJORIE, AGE 13

ability that it truly is because almost every person has had the empathetic experience of sensing good or bad "vibes."

You may have already had some experiences with one or more of the above; if you haven't, please don't worry! These aren't gifts that are given to some people and not to others; they are skills that all human beings have. With time and practice, we can all develop and use these facets of our minds.

The world is filled with life that we cannot see, hear, or feel with our regular senses. We can't see atoms with our naked eyes, but we acknowledge their existence. When you look through a microscope, all matter is revealed to be infinitesimal particles and vast stretches of space—a very different reality than the one you "see" every day. Learn how to be still and quiet within yourself, and you'll begin to perceive the subtle energies clearly.

KINETIC FRICTION, METAPHYSICAL STYLE (AN ENERGY-BUILDING EXERCISE)

One of the first laws of physics states that energy is neither created nor destroyed. Energy is present at all times in all things. You can move the energy present in your own body. You can move it through your body, around your body, and out of it. You can also take in the energy present in another object. Remember that everything is connected, so every object's energy is connected to you and your energy. Focus your Will to consciously interact with your own energy and that of everything around you.

After you pinpoint the area of your body that's most receptive to subtle energies, you can strengthen your own energy surrounding that particular spot. Start by rubbing your palms together in a circular motion; do this until you feel your skin get warm. You may notice a tingling, anything from a very slight "pins and needles" sensation to a pronounced sense of prickling on your skin. You have just harnessed the energy of kinetic friction—the energy generated by two objects touching (your hands) and moving in opposite directions. Place your dominant hand over the sensitive spot. Visualize the heat from your palms as bright, white light. Imagine this light as a filter or as an impenetrable barrier, depending on how much protection you need. The most important part of this exercise is to *know* that your energy barrier will insulate your sensitive area from danger. Simply placing your hand over the spot will create a barrier, too, but when you boost your energy this way, it stays there to protect your points of entry after your hand is removed.

> "You, the reader, are looking for (or perhaps have already found) a religion that coincides with what you deep down really believe, what you feel is right. Any religion can give you many answers about theology. But only spirituality (that inner knowing, or rather seeking) can truly guide you to your questions' answers. One aspect of Wicca that I truly admire is that it focuses on the individual, not the adherents as a whole. It is about you and your relationship with the Divine."
>
> —ATHENA, AGE 17

THE WEB OF LIFE

I recommend that you cut back on meat during this month, for two reasons. First, because animal protein is hard to digest. If your body has to spend a lot of its energy digesting what's in your stomach, then it won't have the energy necessary for meditation, spell casting, or anything else.

If your parents are big meat eaters and dinner often centers around it, you can just abstain and eat the side dishes, or you can offer some help in the kitchen. Make something you want to eat alongside your parents while they cook. It's a great chance to do the bonding thing, and it's also an opportunity to introduce them to some of your beliefs!

Second, it's helpful to become sensitive to the fact that meat is the flesh of another animal, and that animal gave up its Life for you to nourish yourself. Don't misunderstand me. I don't think it's wrong to eat meat, and I'm not telling anyone to become a vegetarian. I *do* think it's important to be conscious of what you eat, however. Whatever you put into your body becomes part of you! It's important to view human beings as connected to Life, not as superior to all creatures. Our place on the food chain is exalted, but being part of a larger whole means respecting each part, not trampling blindly on it. This month is an experiment, and as part of the experiment, I suggest that you shift your awareness of meat away from the neat little packages it comes in at the supermarket and truly understand what it means to eat another animal. If you do cut back on meat, make sure you get plenty of protein from other sources. Nuts, tofu, and a combination of rice with beans can provide protein. If your body craves meat specifically, however, then eat it. Your body knows exactly what it needs, and you should listen to it carefully.

Once you accomplish harmony within yourself, you can start to feel synchronized with the rest of the natural world. Being locked away in a climate-controlled classroom or house all day and all night is not natural! It's great to know oneself and get groovy with the All in meditation, but if you're shut off in a four-walled box for most of your life, you're missing the point. To work with the energy of Witchcraft, you really have to understand and feel that energy. It's the energy of Nature, of rocks and plants and good, raw earth. This was the hardest part for me. I was never a big hiker or granola-crunching Nature buff. I could always see the beauty in Nature, but Nature always seemed like something outside of me, not connected to me in any real way. I had to make a conscious effort to understand the simple joy of dirt and Sun, and it took me some time to understand that these were part of me.

THE FIVE ELEMENTS

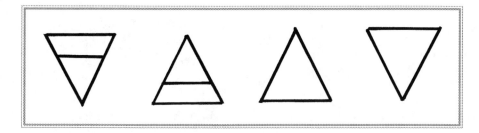

The energies of our world come from the Five Elements: Earth, Air, Fire, Water and Spirit (also called *Akasha,* a Sanskrit word). Everything comes from these basic Elements. To work with them you have to introduce yourself to them. The following exercises are open to interpretation, and anything you add to them will strenthen your connection to the Elements. Heart-felt improvisation is a great way to bond with elemental energy.

DEVOTION TO EARTH

KITCHEN WITCHING

North is the direction associated with Earth. Earth's colors are all the shades of brown and green. Healing the body with Earth's bounty is one of the most powerful kinds of magick that a Witch can work. Cooking is definitely working with Earth energy, because our food comes directly from the soil. Of course, working with herbs is one way of practicing Witchcraft, but in addition to herbal medicine, ordinary foods have tremendous healing powers. Garlic and cinnamon are both antibacterial and antibiotic, for example, and citrus fruits contain vitamin C, which boosts the immune system. (Witchcraft has roots planted firmly in science.) Your body relates directly to Earth. It is made of Earth. It has the wisdom of all Earth's years encoded within each solitary cell. Your body will tell you exactly what it needs by craving particular foods. Similarly, if you feel repelled by a certain food or group of foods, then avoid them. Try baking cookies or a loaf of bread if the thought of making an entire meal is overwhelming. As you measure out ingredients and mix them together, think about how you are creating a healthy body. As you eat, feel the food's energy circulating through you and sustaining each individual cell.

Cooking an occasional meal also offers a chance to open the lines of communication with your family. Besides the fact that you're performing a really nice service for your folks, you can start to introduce them to the simpler elements of Wiccan philosophy in a relaxed way.

EARTH AS A LIVING CREATURE

Pick up a handful of soil. Feel its texture, enjoy its scent, and notice the different shades of brown it encompasses. Know that you have picked up thousands of microorganisms, and that the Earth is alive. Try rubbing it between your palms and speaking a few words of love to your Mother.

Lay your body directly on the ground one day. The Earth will contour itself to the imprint of your body; it will comfort and welcome you. If you can, sleep outside one night. It may be the best sleep you'll ever have.

> "What can burning candles do? Salt? Holy water? Symbols? Dance, laughter, song, petitions, drums, words . . . ? Alone, they can do nothing. Oh, they have energies of their own, but like the many humans who bumble through life without realizing what energies they spread by seemingly simple and even unremarkable actions and words, they are like leaves scattered in the wind, randomly dancing to their own tune with no direction or purpose. So what is magick? What is ritual? Raking up the leaves, I suppose."
>
> —ATHENA, AGE 17

DEVOTION TO AIR

BREATH OF YOUR BODY

Air is essential to sustain Life. It permeates nearly everything and lives within us as breath. Air is the Element of intellect, and it is traditionally associated with the East. It is both gentle and immensely powerful at the same time, and its colors are light yellow and pale blue.

You can attune immediately to the Element of Air simply by breathing in deeply. Breathe normally, and feel the Air travel through your nose and into your lungs, expanding your chest. Feel the warm rush of Air as it passes out again; be aware of your breath. When you feel comfortable, breathe in rhythm: inhale to the count of three, hold your breath for a count of three, exhale for a count of three, hold for a count of three, and repeat. Make an effort to consciously expand your chest and abdomen as you inhale. Contract your abdomen and your chest as you exhale. Continue this for as long as you like.

> All the herbs I use for the food and tea recipes are edible, but you might be allergic to something and not know it! Please use caution when trying new herbs and spices! Either use a substitution you're familiar with, or taste a very, very small bit of the new ingredient the first time you use it. Then, pay attention to your reaction, if any. If you experience anything weird, like nausea, hives, rash, or headache, don't eat that herb again. If you don't notice anything unusual, try another small bit. Repeat this process for three days, increasing the amount a little each time. Be sure not to eat anything else that's new while you're testing an herb—that way, if you have a reaction, you'll be sure it was from the new herb you tried!

WIND AND STORMS

Air is an active Element. The next time there's a good storm outside that's really kicking up the wind, go outside and stand in it. Find which direction the wind is coming from, stand with your back to it, and then jump as high as you can. You will feel the wind cradle you and lift you, playing with you. Yell into it, and feel your words being carried away from you. Dance in it, mimicking the rhythm and movement of trees swaying.

DEVOTION TO FIRE

SOUL FIRE IN THE INFINITE CONTINUUM

Fire is vigorous, aggressive, animated. Fire is the Element of passion, sex, creation, and destruction. Fire purifies and releases. Its colors are red, orange, yellow, white, and blue. It's associated with the direction South.

This first Fire exercise requires a lit candle, so if you can't light one in your room, then find a spot outside. It isn't necessary to use candles in your work on a regular basis, but it's important to acquaint yourself with Fire's reality at least once. Then you can call upon a mental image of Fire with certainty.

Place your white candle somewhere stable and light it. Have a seat and loosen up. Roll your head from side to side, stretch your arms and legs, and then sit in whatever position feels most comfortable. Try not to slump. Hold your receptive palm above the flame closely enough that you can feel its heat. The energy produced by the candle's Fire does not end at the flame; it extends forever.

Continue to hold your receptive palm at a comfortable distance from the flame. Close your eyes. Feel the heat of Fire warming your palm and arm. Move the sensation of heat through your arm to your chest and then to your sternum. Move the heat down into your abdomen and let it blossom there, below your navel. This is where Fire resides in your body. Feel heat course through you, radiating from your abdomen, flowing up and down your spine, rushing toward your limbs, all the way to the tips of your fingers and toes.

DANCING CANDLE FLAME

After you have done that meditation a few times, try this: Pull Fire energy in through your receptive hand and run it through your body, the way you did in the first exercise. Concentrate your will, extend your energy, and try to push the flame as you slowly move your dominant hand over and around it.

Open your eyes and gaze at the flame for a moment. Close your eyes and see the flame's image on the back of your eyelids. You can invoke Fire at any time without a candle, using this mental image, and stir your inner flame with your visualization.

DEVOTION TO WATER

RESTORATIVE BATH

Water is associated with the direction West. Water is the Element of the subconscious mind, of psychic abilities and dreams. It purifies and nurtures Life. It is the Universal Solvent. Water is directly related to the Moon, since the Moon regulates the tides. Its colors are deep blue, silver, and white.

We enjoy Water's healing and rejuvenating power every day. Water will eventually dissolve most substances, given the time—stress, angst, and general mental funk included. Water replenishes you and nourishes your body and emotions.

To make a rejuvenating herbal bath, gather fresh or dried herbs and put them in a clean jar or large bowl (see the recipes in Chapter 12, or choose some herbs from the list in the Appendices). Pour two or three cups of boiling water over the herbs and allow them to steep for three to five minutes, just like making a cup of herbal tea, called an infusion. Strain the herbs out or you'll have little plant bits left in the tub; your parents probably won't appreciate the mess. Run a very warm bath, and pour the infusion into the tub. Then, steep yourself! Alternatively, you may want to use sea salt in your bath. It cleanses and draws out impurities, and it reminds us of the womb and the ocean from which Life comes.

SIMPLEST PSYCHIC AWARENESS POTION

To rev up your psychic abilities, try this: Pour Water into your mini-cauldron/bowl. Rainwater is nice for this. Hold the bowl between your hands and concentrate on whichever ability you want to develop. Put the bowl down, and rub your palms together to channel kinetic energy. When you feel that you have built enough energy, place the index finger of your dominant hand into the bowl of Water, stirring it with a clockwise motion. Drink it, and feel energy flowing through you. You can also make a big batch of this and place it in a window where the full Moon can shine on it, empowering your water with its rays!

DEVOTIONAL CLEANSING

Now you're ready to cleanse your room—this is slightly different from cleaning. While you were *cleaning,* you got rid of the physical mess and disorder. *Cleansing* gets rid of the psychic debris that accumulates in any room. The movements you will make when cleansing your space are deliberate. Move counterclockwise, starting in the East, moving to the South, then the West, to the North, and finishing in the East. You will use the Elements in a particular order: Air first, then Fire, then Water, then Earth. By moving this way and using the Elements in this sequence, you are banishing negativity from your space. If you proceed in the exact opposite manner by moving clockwise and employing the Elements starting with Earth, moving to Air, then Fire and lastly Water, you can invoke an energy (like protection) or charge your space (with creativity, for example). Clockwise motions are considered positive or invoking, because moving clockwise reflects the Sun's motion through the sky. Counterclockwise motion is considered negative or banishing because it is a reversal of the Sun's natural pattern. We'll talk more in depth about the techniques of ritual in Chapter 10, but this exercise is a good start.

CLEANSING RITUAL

Fill one bowl with water from the faucet (if you have spring water, that's great, but tap water will do—unless you live near a nuclear power plant that leaks crazy chemicals.

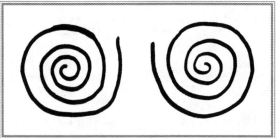

Move clockwise, called deosil, *to charge up with energy, and move counterclockwise, called* widdershins, *to banish energy!*

You don't want to cleanse your room with radioactive tap water! I wish I were kidding). Set the bowl of water near a window and watch as the Sun casts light into it. Pour salt into the other bowl and leave it next to the first. Open your window, even if it's freezing outside. Starting in the East corner of your room (break out the handy compass!), feel the wind whisking all negative thoughts and feelings out of your personal space. Know that the fresh Air is replacing any negativity with clean, sparkling joy. Let the Sun's Fire into the room, watch its bright light burn away darkness and restore a brilliant glow to everything in your room. Carry the bowl with Water as you walk the perimeter counterclockwise (moving from East to South to West to North), dipping your fingers in it and lightly flicking Water droplets at each corner and on the floor. Then take the bowl of salt and walk slowly around the perimeter of the room, sprinkling a few grains at each wall and in the corners. Don't forget the doorway and the windowsill, and draw a faint line of salt directly along your threshold and window. These are the points of entry to your domain, and salt will protect your area by grounding negative energy before it enters. If you can light incense, do that now, as you move back to the East. Carry the incense around your room.

LUNAR RHYTHM

Now that your room is cleansed and your tools are gathered, try connecting with Spirit. If you like, you can start at the dark Moon and work along to the full Moon. This is a symbolic gesture, starting your journey in darkness, allowing your consciousness to grow as the Moon swells, and then ridding yourself of all fear and negativity as She becomes smaller in the sky. It has a definite rhythm to it and, if you keep this thought in mind as you proceed, your intention is strengthened by your focus. This is my suggestion, but you can start any time when you feel inspired. Keep this in mind: As the Moon

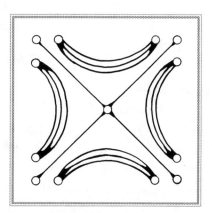

Ceremonial Seal of the Moon

"Each Moon phase gives off a specific energy. The new Moon is associated with new starts and planning for growth, as well as inner reflection, divination, and binding or banishing. The waxing Moon's vibration is that of growth and increase. The full Moon is a time for any magick; it's in all its glory, emanating surges of power. The waning Moon signifies a time to release, banish, or decrease."

—GWINEVERE, AGE 16

moves from invisible to full, so do you grow; when the Moon hangs ripe, so are your aspirations; as She wanes from large to small, so do your obstacles. First, you must ascertain what phase the Moon is in, of course! Step outside each night of this month and peek at Her, even if you can manage to do so for only a minute or two. Many standard calendars tell where the Moon is in Her cycle, as well.

Do something special when the Moon is full. Make a cup of tea and meditate outside under Her light and do a painting of moonlight or write a poem. Witches often celebrate the full Moon to worship the Goddess at rituals called Esbats. The full Moon creates very special energy that you can work with. Experience it for yourself!

Ladies: When you get your period during your Devotional Month, pay very close attention to what makes you joyous, angry, or sad, and any instinctive feelings or premonitions. During this time, your powers of intuition are greatly enhanced. Treat yourself luxuriously during your period. It's a sacred privilege— despite the cramps!

DEVOTIONS TO SPIRIT

You have to ask yourself: "Why am I here? Why did I seek out this religion?" If your answer is "Just curious," that's perfectly fine! If you were raised with a particular religion, then think a little bit about what you do and don't like about that tradition. Examining your beliefs is very useful in finding out about yourself.

The most important exercise you can practice is whatever activity makes you feel truly alive, whether it's painting, singing, writing, riding horses, running, gardening—whatever brings you joy. Notice how you feel when you are doing what you do best, and look more deeply into the reasons why you love this activity so much. Is it the play of colors on paper? Is it the wind in your hair as you run or ride over dirt? Is it the intellectual stimulation? Knowing the reasons will help you to understand your strengths and weaknesses. You can help to build those parts of yourself that are less developed by calling on a particular Element or Deity and taking that energy into yourself.

INTELLECT IS A VEHICLE ON THE DIVINE PATH

Find out as much as you can about every form of spirituality that intrigues you. Something can be gained from every concept that every person has ever postulated, and every religion has Divinity coded into it somewhere. Moreover, your research will help you to understand your own ideas more fully. For example, if you find something about another culture fascinating or if it feels right to you, then you just discovered something about how you view life. On the other hand, if you're repelled by a certain philosophy, then you know what you think is wrong or useless. It's a process of elimination as much as a course of discovery.

GODDESS, GOD, SOUL OF THE WORLD

The Devotions that appear here are to help you attune with the Goddess or God or both, depending on your inclination. Some women find it important to work specifically with the Goddess first, since She is so often forgotten in our culture. Some men are most comfortable working with the God at first for the very same reason. Any way you choose to find Deity

Symbol for Magickal Energy

is the right way. If you work with only one force, at least acknowledge the other for the sake of balance.

Simply concede the possibility of this universal energy and realize that it is both feminine and masculine, dark and light. Think about the world's energy as male and female, and realize that opposing forces actually make each other perfect and balanced. This is part of how Witchcraft works. Relate it to physics: for every action, there is an equal and opposite reaction. Whatever function you perform on one side of an algebraic equation must be performed on the other side to solve (balance) the equation. It's this concept of balance, opposites united, and action causing reaction on which Witchcraft is largely based. Tell that one to your math teacher!

If you decide to name these forces, find out whatever you can about Their culture and particular affinities. For example, if you choose to connect with Aphrodite (Greek Goddess of Love and Beauty), then you might choose symbols that are related to Her, like the seashell. You might leave foods that are traditional to the Greek culture as offerings to Her, like honey, olives, or lemons. Do you see where I'm going with this? Use symbolism to communicate with your subconscious, and Deity will do the same.

Designate one colored candle to represent the Goddess and feminine energy and the other to represent the God and masculine energy (remember the candles we talked about on page 68). Choose whatever colors speak to you for now—we'll get into color symbolism later. If you can't work with candles, that's all right! Instead, find a smooth and round stone outside to represent the Goddess and an interesting piece of wood to represent the God. You can also create a yin and yang image, either on paper or with clay, and hang that on your wall. Or, you can designate a pretty glass to represent the Goddess and a pointed crystal or rock to represent the God.

DIVINE ABUNDANCE

MORNING INVOCATION

When you wake up in the morning, set aside five minutes to make a cup of tea. I chose tea for this aspect of Devotions because the plant comes from

Earth, is infused into Water, heated on Fire, and produces vapor (Air); it also has health-giving properties. If you don't like tea, use hot chocolate; chocolate is sacred and creates a chemical in your brain that simulates the feeling of being in Love (and it's yummy, too)! Use your Devotional mug. As the water boils, clear your thoughts and just breathe. As the tea steeps (or the cocoa dissolves), hold the mug in both of your hands. Feel the heat of the liquid. Watch the steam

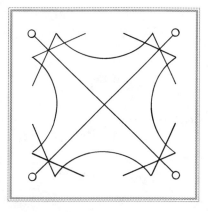

Ceremonial Seal of the Sun

curl up, and breathe in the vapors. As you hold your drink, give silent thanks to Goddess and God for Water, for the Earth that grew your tea (or chocolate), and for your senses to appreciate it.

With each sip, feel the warmth of Divine abundance slide through your mouth and into the pit of your stomach. As you swallow, promise yourself that you will give thanks often and receive generosity with grace. The warmth and comfort of their blessings will remain with you, remembered by your body as a warm glow in your belly, and available for you to call on whenever you need to. Just think back on your Morning Devotion, and your body will be triggered by your mind to reproduce that gentle radiance. You can also use coffee, if you are a coffee drinker—I am—but I feel that the higher caffeine content in java is too much of a jolt for Morning Devotions. Coffee also has an acidic quality that can make the stomach uncomfortable. Pains in the belly are not a pleasant way to remember the Gods! If you must have a cup of coffee first thing in the morning, do your Devotion after that.

GREET THE SUN

When you have finished your morning drink, stretch your body out a little bit. Try bending over to touch your toes and then slowly rolling your body upright again spreading your arms out and splaying your fingers wide for a moment; then bring your arms slowly in and cross them over your chest, resting each hand on the opposite shoulder. This is the God position, and it is a great way to greet the Sun and the morning.

DAILY INVOCATION

If you're using candles, light both colored candles for a few minutes in the morning. Know that the flames represent the eternal Light and power of the Goddess and the God. Say "good morning" to Them. Ask them to protect you through the day. Ask them to help you develop your clear sight, clear hearing, and clear perception. If you wish, light some incense and blow the smoke into the air, envisioning your prayers being lifted with it. If you cannot light candles and incense, just hold those same thoughts in your mind while breathing in deeply; as you exhale, your breath will carry your intentions to the Gods. Make sure to put the candles and incense out when you're finished. Setting your house on fire is decidedly un-Divine!

LIVE DELIBERATELY

As you move through your day, make an effort at different times to be completely aware of your body. Feel each muscle's action as it moves when you walk. Chew and swallow deliberately and slowly, relishing each gesture of tongue and teeth, each sensation and flavor. Give quiet thanks to your body for all of the joy it brings you. Make an effort to think good thoughts at yourself, because your body takes in every thought to each of its cells. If you take the time to program your body with messages of love and acceptance, it will continue to be good to you!

Pause before you speak, and choose your words with conscious intent. This is very important. Thoughts are

Morning Sun Tea: Get a glass jar and put several tea bags in it, depending on the size of the jar and how strong you like your tea. Fill the jar with water and put it in a sunny place to steep for several hours. Remove the tea bags before drinking, and keep the jar in your refrigerator. You can also add herbs that relate to the Sun—generally, any herb that makes you feel warm or increases your circulation, like ginger or cinnamon!

things, and words express thoughts. Words can never be taken back. If you speak words of love and kindness, then you have generated love and kindness. If you respond to someone in anger, then you have created anger. It will rever-

> Evening Moon Tea: Do this by the cupful, not in quantity. Brew your tea as usual, with boiling water and black or green tea. Leave it to steep in a window where you can see the Moon. Now add herbs that relate to the Moon. Some good choices for Moon Tea spices are nutmeg (increases psychic awareness), chamomile (encourages sleep), or jasmine (has an affinity with the Moon, as it's a night bloomer).

berate forever as sound wave after sound wave, long after your angry words are spoken. Be sure your words are truthful and that they represent your thoughts clearly. If a situation calls for tactfulness, by all means be tactful—there is very little point in telling your mother that her beef stew sucks and her hair is frizzy, even if it's true! Instead, find a way to get your point across without hurting other people's feelings in the name of brutal honesty.

Listen very carefully when someone else talks to you, and look him or her in the eye. (Don't get creepy and stare them down, but maintain eye contact.) When you are truly listening to another person, you won't be thinking of what you want to say. Instead, allow yourself to take in each syllable that she's speaking to you, and your mind will be open to all of the subtle messages she's sending. You're respecting that person's Spirit when you give it your undivided attention.

NIGHTTIME INVOCATION

In the evening, after dinner and before bed, make another cup of tea or hot chocolate. Pour it into your mug and hold it in both hands as before. This time as you feel the heat of the water, feel the warm glow of peace and quiet that sleep brings. Thank the Goddess and God for each moment of the day. Be comforted by their presence.

EMBRACE THE MOON

If you can, take your tea and step outside for a moment. Find the Moon. Again, after you drink, stretch your limbs. Reach down to the ground, roll your body up, and spread your arms out as wide as you can as you turn toward the Moon. As you stand with your arms and legs spread, you are taking the Goddess position. Feel Her energy streaming toward you, entering your body at your breastbone in the center of your chest, and flowing to the tips of your fingers and feet.

DREAM A VISION

Before you go to sleep at night, light your Goddess and God candles (if you can) and pray in whatever way you like. Ask the Goddess or God with whom you are working to send you a dream. They often appear to us in the dream state in many different forms; keep track of your dreams in your notebook. If you see animals in your dreams, they may be messengers from the Gods. If you dream of an event, make a note of it and see if a similar event occurs in the next few days. If you dream of a person, keep an eye out for that person and be sure to talk with him or her, if possible. These symbols in dreams are often clues with which the Gods provide us to further us on the Path.

Celebrate these Devotions as consistently as possible for the entire month, and you will surely feel their impact. When you get to the point of allowing your imagination and spontaneity to guide your practice, your Life will become filled with creative opportunities. Each moment will become an act of magick, and you will cast a forceful spell each time you laugh out loud, simply because you are filled with joy.

CHAPTER FIVE

REFLECTION
AND MEDITATION

There are lots of ways to meditate, and there are several reasons to do it. First of all, meditation is like a mental coffee break. It relaxes your body and clears your mind, getting rid of everyday stress and mental clutter. When you take a few minutes to bond with Eternity, your English midterm is put in perspective—which will help you do even better on it, by the way! Meditation is also mental discipline. It's a way for you to get a grip on your thoughts and emotions, so *you* control *them* and not the other way around.

Controlling your mind and will are totally essential to magick. We use techniques very similar to the Eastern styles, but there are also less formal ways to relax your mind and get in touch with your subtle self. Meditation can be as simple or as complex as you want it to be. As crazy as it may sound, washing dishes and vacuuming are two of my favorite ways to meditate.

BUDDHA MONK MASTER, TAKE 1

Really stretch yourself out. Tense and release each major muscle group, starting with your feet, working up to your legs, then your trunk, your arms and hands, your neck and head. Breathe deliberately for a few seconds, making sure to expand your chest and belly while you inhale, and compress them completely when breathing out. When you find a comfortable breathing pattern, close your eyes and listen to your breath.

You can try a couple methods for getting into the meditation mind-set. Count your breath, listen to it, and keep your mind focused on that. Whenever your mind strays from your breath (And it will, believe me! You'll start hearing bits of songs in your head; you'll start thinking about your day. You'll realize that you're hungry, your nose itches, your feet feel weird. . . .), gently bring your concentration back to the sound of your breath going in and out, counting "one, one, one . . . two, two, two."

BUDDHA MONK MASTER, TAKE 2

One technique I found in a wonderful Buddhist source book[1] suggests using an object on which to concentrate. Visual aids can help your mind stay focused. Anything you find interesting will work, and geometric patterns seem to work especially well. Grab a poster, picture—whatever—and tape it to a wall. Set yourself up in front of it, close enough that you can see all the details, but far enough away that you can see the whole image. You can also use a statue, a candle (the first meditation I was taught), whatever you like.

Try it with a big circle. Draw a blue circle on a white sheet of paper. Use a compass or a template to make it as perfect as possible. Tape it up on a wall and sit in front of it. Let your mind focus completely on the circle, and say, "Circle, circle, circle." Then, close your eyes and picture the circle as perfectly as you can. If you see a shadowy image of it (it should be an orange afterimage, if you used a blue circle), keep your eyes closed and look

at the image. Try making the circle appear and disappear on the back of your eyelids. If you don't see an image when you close your eyes, open your eyes again and continue looking at the circle intently, closing your eyes occasionally until the image appears. This technique helps cleanse your mind of negativity; if your mind is filled with a pure image, there's no room for anger, jealousy, or hatred.

GUIDED MEDITATION

This type of meditation uses audio guidance to take you into a light trance. The goal is to get you into your subconscious, and you're often instructed to find an object, person, or other symbol that you mentally "bring back" into your waking consciousness. If you do this on a regular basis, the theory is that you create a sacred place in your mind where you can go when you need to recharge your mental battery or wrestle with your issues. I've never had much luck with this technique. I had a psychiatrist try to hypnotize me once (very similar to guided meditation), and he said I'm not "suggestible." You may or may not be suggestible (open to someone guiding you through a series of mental images), but it's worth a try. Lots of people have good experiences with guided meditation.

Have a friend read the meditation out loud to you, or tape yourself reading it and play it back. Make sure you read it slowly, clearly, and in a soothing voice. Start by counting backward from sixty. While you listen to the voice counting, tense and release each of your muscles, starting with your feet and ending with your face. Lie down, close your eyes, and imagine the following scene as vividly as you can. . . .

THE HOUSE OF THE MIND

You are lying down in a field of grass. It is warm but not too warm, and a slight breeze is passing over your body. It was a lovely day, and now the sun is almost setting. You can hear crickets singing in the distance, and all you want to do is lie in the grass, relax, feel the ground cradling you. Your eyes are closed against the sun, and you can feel its red warmth and see its orange rays through your eyelids, bright yellow. You can feel the grass underneath your back, and you can smell the fresh, green scent of it. The sun is shining on you like a blessing and warming your eyes, your head, your face, your neck, your chest, your arms, your stomach, your legs, your feet . . . you could lie like this forever. . . . (Pause about ten seconds before moving on.)

As pleasant as this is, you want to get up. You sit up slowly and open your eyes. The sky is dusky blue, deepening to violet. The field is quiet, and you move slowly through it, noticing the gentle slope of the ground. You are on top of a small hill, and you can see a large house a short distance from the bottom of the hill. It is white, with light-blue shutters, and a light-blue door. You can see lights on in the windows as you walk toward it. As you get closer, you see a small, black rectangle on the door. As you walk closer, you can see that the rectangle is a sign. When you stand in front of the door, you read the sign's silver letters: "This is the House of Your Mind. You are Welcome!"

The door has a silver knob on it, and you reach out, turn it, and open the door. You are standing in a small foyer. There are white tiles on the floor. The walls are white. There is an archway in front of you, and you can see a beautiful dining room beyond it, with a long wooden table and many chairs. You look to your left and see a hallway. You look to your right and see another hallway. You go to the right. You feel cool, white tile under your feet, and the walls are bright white. It is a long hallway, and you pass many doors along the way, but you keep going because you want to go into the room at the end of the hall, the very end of the hall.

When you get there, the door is open. The room is empty except for a small table. You walk closer to the table, and you see that there is an object on it. You move closer and pick it up with both hands. What is it? Look at it very closely. You will take it with you.

You turn toward the door and notice a light switch next to the door. You turn the lights off. You walk out of the room and close the door behind you. You walk back down the long hallway with the white walls, and at the end of the hall you see a light switch. You turn off the lights at the end of the hall, and you walk to the foyer. You turn toward the door, and you see a light switch there. Again, you turn off the lights. You open the door and step outside.

It is dark outside, and you can see the Moon and stars. You look at the Moon. It's very round, it's full, and it's very bright. Your eyes are filled with the bright light. Your eyes are filled with light. Your eyes are open! Welcome back!

What was the object you saw on the table? Remember it as completely as you can. Don't worry if you didn't get a really strong picture. Just use your imagination, and think of the first thing that popped into your mind when you were looking at the object in the room. Go back and do this as often as you like, changing it a little each time. You might want to go left next time and see what's down there. . . .

MOVING MEDITATION

Crazy as it might sound, playing basketball, running, or swimming—any sport, really—can be a meditation. Playing a sport is mindfulness; if you've ever played competitively, you know exactly what happens when you get out of the zone: you move badly, you fumble the easiest plays, and you lose the game. Same deal with life in general.

Keep your mind focused on your body's movements, and don't let your thoughts stray. Doing something that's rhythmic, like swimming, running, walking, bouncing a ball, etc., will make this really easy. Just concentrate on the sound you're making, and make sure to bounce, run, swim, etc., in a definite rhythm.

IT'S A SHORT WALK TO ENLIGHTENMENT

Put on comfortable clothes and shoes, and head outside. Before you get going, stretch a little: bend to touch your toes, straighten up and stretch out your arms, roll your head from side to side, whatever loosens you up and gets you ready to move. Pick a stopping point. Make it a few minutes away, maybe a five- or six-minute walk. Start your rhythmic breathing, and walk. Time your pace so it creates a rhythm with your breath. As you walk, concentrate only on your breath and step. If you lose your rhythm, stop. Take a moment, calm your breath, concentrate, and get moving again. It helps to look down at the road when you do this—fewer distractions!

THE SOUND OF ONE MIND MEDITATING

When you hear different types of music, you probably have very different and obvious reactions. Classical music makes me feel either really relaxed or exuberant, depending on the piece; techno makes me want to dance or trance; punk makes me want to paint my house and overthrow the government (not recommended for meditation!). Find whatever music makes you feel relaxed and focused. Close your door, find a comfy spot, and press play.

You can use the music to practice mindfulness, listening to every nuance. You can close your eyes and see what pictures the music conjures. You can just enjoy the relaxing pleasure of hearing something that speaks to you.

AN INSTRUMENT OF THE DIVINE

If you play an instrument, you can use that as a tool to focus your thoughts. I played violin for a few years, and it was definitely a meditation. My posture had to be perfect to get the best sound, and I had to concentrate very carefully, watching each finger's movement, maintaining my hand's positions, and reading music at the same time. This is mindfulness.

Play an ascending scale or arpeggio repeatedly. Scales are usually simple, and if you've been playing for even a month or so, you probably have at least one down cold. If you play it over and over, without a break between repetitions, you'll probably find that it becomes weird to you—the same way saying "purple" over and over makes the word lose its meaning. You have to concentrate to play an instrument well, even just a scale. Ascending scales have the added benefit of uplifting your spirits.

If you don't play an instrument (or even if you do), sing a scale. Singing is a great way to connect with your breath, and it acts like a wee yummy massage for your organs. Singing scales will also get you ready for chanting later on; your diaphragm—the muscle underneath your lungs—will be in good shape and ready to chant up some magick.

If you're really, *really* self-conscious and insist that you truly can't sing, then just try ripping on one note. You can hit one note, can't you? Come on, get over it! You'd better pump up your self-confidence and get rid of any shyness if you want to work Witchcraft.

TAROT TO TICKLE YOUR INTELLECT

Tarot cards are excellent meditation tools, among their other uses. If you don't have a deck, definitely grab one next time you have about $20 lying around. If you can't afford a deck, don't despair; we'll make one in Chapter 11.

The goal of Tarot meditation is to start your mind working, making connections within your subconscious. It's mental aerobics!

There are a few ways you can use Tarot to meditate. The most basic way is to pick a card you really like, tape it up on a wall, and sit across from it. Examine it really closely, and then step back. Close your eyes and picture the card in your mind. Try to remember as many details as possible. Write down each object you remember, and then check how close you came. Lather, rinse, repeat.

WRITE WHAT YOU LIVE

I'm relentless in insisting that you write, write, write. It's such an outstanding skill to have. It's self-expression, it's therapy, and it's power. It's also a considerable meditation technique.

You can write about what happened during your day, including all the littlest details, and that's practicing mindfulness. Start with waking up; how did you feel? Go through each moment of your day. What did you have for lunch? What classes did you have? With whom did you talk? By being conscious of each moment and action, you'll be able to see a full picture of your life. Also, keep a notebook close to your bed at night. As soon as you wake up, jot down any dreams you can remember. Make this as detailed as possible. When you have a chance later on, go through your notes and pick out each detail: colors, descriptions of people, places, and things. Write down your intuitions about what each detail means.

AROMATHERAPY

Using your sense of smell to stimulate your mind and concentrate is a helpful tool. Ever notice how certain scents make you respond emotionally? Baking cookies or homemade soup makes me feel comfortable and re-laxed because I associate those scents with being happily at home. Aro-matherapy works on the same principle, and certain smells are better than others for meditation.

Lavender is the first one I think of for meditation. It's very soothing and will help you relax your body and mind for intense meditation. If you can burn incense, try using a commercial one. If you can't, gather some laven-der flowers or dried lavender. Put the flowers in a pot with just enough water to cover them. Turn the stove on with a very low heat, and simmer the lavender while you meditate. This method works with pretty much any plant substance, even pine needles and orange rinds! Check out the recipes in Chapter 12 for more ideas.

GROWING A WITCH'S GARDEN

A Simple Witch's Garden

> Sage
> Rosemary
> Roses (there are several miniature varieties that grow best in a pot on a
>   windowsill)
> Chamomile
> Mint
> Lavender

Taking care of another living creature pulls your focus away from your-self and your raging brain. You have to concentrate on giving your energy to that other creature, and you have to pay close attention to figure out what it needs and wants—if you want it to live, that is. Growing a Witch's garden is a way to meditate daily with lots of perks.

Having plants in your home makes you healthier! They clean the air for you, and they release pure oxygen. Plants are alive. Their energy will boost your own and make your house cheerful. Don't worry if you've got a black thumb; I do, too, actually. I've found that you really have to pay attention to plants—not just watering them—but also pruning them back, feeding them, dusting them, and generally letting them know that you care.

The herbs listed above are all pretty hardy. To determine the plants' specific needs, check the back of the seed packet or read the little stick tucked into the soil of plants that you buy at a nursery. They should do fine in a windowsill, but keep them in separate pots. Each one will have its own watering and sun requirements. Definitely put them outside during the warm weather, if you can. They like that. You can keep these all year, but you'll notice their flavor isn't quite as strong during winter and fall. That's all right. You'll use them for spell craft later on, so taste isn't the ultimate concern.

Grab a copy of *The Old Farmer's Almanac* when you can (available at most major bookstores). You may be surprised to learn that farmers often plant and sow along with the phases of the Moon!

CHAPTER SIX

CREATING SACRED SPACE

Witches don't usually worship in specific buildings like churches, although some covens and groups *have* established permanent places to gather and have rituals, and this seems to be a growing trend. We usually get together at each other's houses or at special places outdoors. It's part of the whole Wiccan concept that every place is sacred, including every square inch of our bodies and the Earth, but most of us keep places in our homes that are just for worship and magick. Even if we're lucky enough to have a special meeting place for a coven or community, it's really important to set aside our own private space. Most Witches still practice Solitaire even when they have a coven.

Keeping an altar of your own is a powerful way to remind yourself of your connection with the Gods and Nature every day. Plus, altars are totally a work of art in progress; you can add stuff to your altar as you need it: to remind yourself of a problem you're trying to solve; to boost your psychic energy; to reflect the changing seasons; or just to build a lovely piece of sculpture!

PORTABLE CIRCLE

If you absolutely *can't* keep one single tiny Witchcraft doohickey around, fret not, young Pagan! You can make a portable Circle that's there when you need it, but tucked away from the general public.

You will need the following:

· A large square of light, solid-colored piece of cloth or canvas.[1] The size will depend on how large you want your Circle to be. If you want to go with the traditional nine feet, then make your square about ten and a half feet on all sides . . . large enough to fit the Circle and any decorations.

· Fabric paint or markers

· A length of string

· 5 thumbtacks or weights

Spread the cloth or canvas on a floor. Use one that has carpet, because you're going to tack the corners down. If you have hardwood floors, use weights instead of tacks.

Find the cloth's center by lightly drawing two diagonal pencil lines between the two sets of diagonal corners. Use a tape measure so they're perfectly straight. You'll end up with an *X* marked on the cloth.

Stick a thumbtack (or place a weight) in the middle of the *X*. That's the center. Now, attach your string to the tack (or weight). The string's length will be half the Circle's total diameter. A traditional Circle is nine feet across, but you may not have that much space. Do make it big enough to sit comfortably inside.

Now, tie your brush or marker to the string's other end. Fabric paint markers would be the best, since they're easy to control and permanent. Pull the string tight, and walk around your fabric, drawing a circle very slowly and lightly. If you go too fast, you'll bunch the fabric, so take your time.

Get as wild with it as you want. You may want to decorate with the astrological symbols, or you may use symbols for the Elements in each corner. Or, you can make several smaller Circles inside the main one and do both! If you want to keep it simple, maybe you could stamp a flowery vine type pattern around the borders. Whatever works for you.

·　·　·

Now you've got a permanent, portable Circle! You can roll it up and stuff it in a closet or under your bed when you're not using it; when you want to, you can pull it out, plunk yourself in the center, and have all the benefits of an instant temple. Use it for meditation, to reinforce your Circle casting, or any time you need to concentrate your energy—like when you have a big test to study for.

SIMPLE ALTARS

If your parents or housemates are okay with your keeping an altar, grand! You really *should* be as respectful as possible on this one, because your altar's main job is to be a sort of psychic pit stop; thing is, some people aren't comfortable with that, and some are ultrasensitive to magickal energy—even if they aren't Witches. You don't want to be responsible for disturbing someone else's psychic health. "Harm none," remember? We hope you live with people who respect *your* need for expression, too.

"When it comes to setting up your sacred space in your room without tightening tensions in the household, try lighting candles to begin with, saying you like the aromatherapy. Carve out a shelf or dresser top and begin putting little collectibles on it. . . . Some artwork, porcelain figures, keepsakes, candles, feathers, rocks, etc. Eventually, you should be able to turn this into your own altar, although setting out your athame, chalice, wand, etc. full time might be a bit too drastic."

—ATHENA, AGE 17

Many Wiccans keep a formal altar with their working tools on it, set up according to their tradition's guidelines, and you can check out Chapter 9 for those details. My altar changes all the time, depending on what I'm working with at the moment, and I usually prefer to keep a formal altar along with a less structured one. You may not have all your tools—we'll work on that in Chapter 9—but you can still set up an altar.

Things to consider when you're setting up your altar:

· You have to relate to each object. If it doesn't have meaning for you, it won't do you any good!

· Have a theme in mind. Is your altar a place to meditate? Is it a place to do divination? Do you want to represent all the Elements (pretty traditional theme)? Make sure every item reflects that theme, and set them up in a symbolic way.

· Make sure it's nice to look at—unless you're doing some less-than-pleasant work, like banishing. More on that later!

· How witchy can you really be in your house? You may *want* to include a big old pentagram on your wall or black candles with runes carved on them, but will your parents freak out?

· What don't you mind other people seeing or touching? Some Witches don't want *anyone* to touch (or sometimes, even *see*) their ritual stuff; others don't mind at all. I think the middle road is a good choice here. You may not mind if your brother sees your scrying sphere, for example, but you may not want anyone else touching a charm.

THE GREAT OUTDOORS

If you have some space outside, set up an outdoor altar. If you're going to practice Witchcraft, you'd better be comfortable outside. That's where most of the power is, after all! Spells cast on the ground with natural tools work so much more easily, and forging that connection to Nature is totally key.

Besides, you can find all sorts of pretty things with which to make an altar right in the backyard. Go for a nice, long walk one day, and be sure to take a backpack or something to carry all the goodies you find along the way. Walk around and look for sticks and stones that appeal to you. Feathers are nice, too. My friend Chrissy always seems to find heart-shaped rocks when she goes hiking, so she takes them home and sets them up around her house. You may luck out and find some raw quartz or even pretty rose quartz. Don't stray too far from home, though; lugging a five-pound chunk of rock on your back gets old fast.

If you're lucky, you will find a thin, flat stone to use for your altar top. Put this on top of one, two, three, or even more stacked flat rocks, and you've got a fabulous stone altar. Set it up in a corner of your yard that's semiprivate. If you've got a natural circle of trees, you're one lucky Witch! Try to find at least one tree to sit near.

You can decorate with flowers (planting some around your spot would be awesome), statues, whatever says "temple" to you and fits your space and budget. A simple birdbath or feeder would be nice, too. Or you can plant flowers that butterflies like. There's at least one commercial butterfly mix on the market. If you can't find that, poke around a garden supply store and ask someone who works there which flowers will bring the butterflies over to your house.

NATURE WORSHIP

A pretty and inconspicuous altar that takes up only a wee corner of a room (best if it's your bedroom), set this one up for a little Nature worship indoors. This is good for urban Pagans who don't have a backyard, or for those of you who can't bust out the pentacle and leave your athame hanging around! The end result is a private little jungle you can call your own. All the stuff for this altar is really cheap, and you can find it all at a gardening center or even a local supermarket.

You will need:

· A couple healthy ivy plants (Ivies grow pretty well in semishade, so a bedroom with one decent window will work! Also, buy the plant itself; don't try to start ivy from seed.)

· Small pots to put them in

· A little potting soil. Don't just grab dirt from outside. It doesn't have the nutrients that potted plants need, and it won't drain well enough, either.

· Plant hooks

· An old table—check out garage sales, flea markets, or cheap stores. It doesn't have to be fancy at all, just sturdy.

· A chair or cushion. See above!

Pick a sunny corner in your bedroom. Ideally, it should catch at least six hours of sunlight each day, but you can help this out with a fluorescent light or two. Take the ivies out of their pots by turning them over and tapping gently on the bottom. They should pop right out.

Break the ivy apart into as many plants as you like by gently separating their roots; don't worry, separation won't hurt them! Repot them by filling the new containers about two-thirds up with the potting soil. Stick a plant in, and fill the rest of the way with the soil. Do the same till all are installed in a new pot. Give them a nice drink of water when you're done.

Now, figure out where you want to hang them. The idea is to almost create a separate room with hanging plants. Hang the ivies a few inches apart to fill the ceiling in your corner. Ivy grows really quickly, and you'll have a bunch of lovely trailing green stuff to bring the outdoors in! You can train the vines into patterns by wrapping them around clear thumbtacks, if you want to.

Put your table catercorner against the wall, so it backs up where the two walls join. Drape it with a little fabric if you want to—an old sheet that you've painted or dyed would be good. You could also paint the table and do a whole symbolic masterpiece on the top, if you want. Put items that are meaningful on it: statues, crystals, a pretty bowl with potpourri in it, photographs, and whatever else looks great and is special to you. Put your chair or cushion in front of it—the perfect spot for meditation, charging charms, making incense, reading Tarot cards. . . .

When you want to cast a spell or do a ritual, you can put your tools on the altar to charge with all those green vibes. Pull it out of the corner, and do your thing. When you're done, your corner just looks like a plant-lovers nook . . . very low profile! There's a *lot* of room to get creative with this, depending on how crazy you want to get. Think velvet draped along the walls, think murals, think huge chunks of rose quartz at the foot of your altar . . . think I'd better get a grip! I'm sure you get the point.

CHAPTER SEVEN

VISUALIZATION

Visualization is the ability to see an image from your mind very clearly. There are two types of visualization: *internal,* when you see something "in your mind's eye," like a daydream; and *external,* when you imagine an image so vividly that you can see it superimposed on the real world. The first is simpler than the second, and you'll need to work on internal visualization first—unless you're an artist, in which case you probably use visualization all the time. Visualization is important in spell craft; the more clearly you can *see* a goal or object, the more effective your spells will be.

Perhaps you'll find some of these exercises a little wacky. They're mental games. Lighten up. Revel. If you don't get the results you think you *should* get, pretend them. Enjoy your mind, and use fun and make-believe in your magick. These games are more effective than you may think.

I've included a few other exercises to get your mind moving.

MEMORY BOOSTER

Get several small objects from around the house. You could include pieces of fruit, jewelry, or silverware, whatever you have lying around. Start out with eight or nine; fewer will make the exercise too easy, but more will make it too hard to start off. Arrange your objects in a circle on a tray or plate. Look at your arrangement for a few minutes. Then cover them with a towel.

Draw a circle on a piece of paper and write each object's name in its right place on the circle. Check your accuracy. Rearrange the objects several times and repeat. When you get the order right a few times, include more and more objects!

VARIATION

Gather a bunch of similar objects, like several nail polish bottles, an assortment of coins, or a bunch of bottles. The point is that they're the same type of object; this makes placing them in the right spot later more difficult.

TRICK OF LIGHT

Look closely at the Moon, a candle flame, or a lamp. Squint your eyes a little bit. See the little rays coming off the main light source? They may appear like a stream of light or a glowing halo. If you wiggle your eyelids (Okay, do this one when nobody's watching! You'll look a bit goofy!), you can move the glow around, making it shorter and longer. Stretch the light as far as you can get it.

Now try holding an object in your hands and bringing the light down to it. Practice this technique. It's useful when you want to charge an object with light or bless a charm.

YOUR EYELIDS ARE A BLACKBOARD

What do you see when you close your eyes? Is it pitch-black in there, or can you see swirling colors and shadowy shapes? (I usually see the second.) If you don't see any light or movement when you close your eyes, you have a nice clean blackboard to draw shapes on.

Close your eyes and relax. Imagine that you're in a black room standing in front of a huge blackboard. Now picture a small speck of white light on the blackboard. This may take a few minutes, so just relax. When I first started doing this, I found that I could picture the speck of light, but it kept moving around on me! The first few times you try this just let it move around. If it draws anything, record that in your notebook. If you don't see any pictures, don't sweat it. Just concentrate on seeing the light and watching it move around.

After you've done this a few times, try to move the speck of light where you want it. Simple geometric shapes seem to work well. Try drawing a shape with it. Again, when I first started doing this, I could get the shape (triangles actually worked better for me than a circle—I kept getting caught up in trying to make it perfect), but then it would sort of slide away. That's all right, too. Just keep conjuring the image until you get bored. Next time you do it, see how long you can make it stick before it fades. You'll get better and better at it each time.

AURA YOU READY?

Auras happen! I have to tell you, I was always skeptical about people who said they saw auras—and you *should* be skeptical, you should *always* doubt until you feel something's been proven to you. Even then, believe but get skeptical the next day. I definitely acknowledged that people generate energy. That just seemed like a basic, scientifically provable fact, but . . . auras?

I saw an aura for the first time a few months ago. It was the weirdest thing because I wasn't trying to see one at all. It wasn't even on my mind. Actually, I've found since then that *not* thinking about seeing auras actually lets me see them more easily. Anyway, I was sitting with my friend Joyce in her living room, and we were just yapping away, when I suddenly saw a deep purple smudge of light about two or three inches off her shoulder. I didn't think anything of it, except that it didn't go away for several minutes. Then, when I was hanging out with another friend, John, a few hours later, I saw a dim grayish-white glow two or three inches over his head. I suddenly realized that I was seeing auras. I *had* made some powerful incense earlier in the day (see the recipe section), and I think it helped to stimulate my psychic flow a bit. . . . Since then, I've seen auras on and off: usually when I'm not looking.

When John and I were hanging out, I asked him to do me a favor and play a little. I asked him to stand in front of a white wall and send me a color. He did, and I saw a little puff of fog over his head: light blue.

Grab a friend and ask him or her to stand in front of a white wall. Look a bit to the side or above his or her head, and just relax your eyes. Let them go unfocused. You might see a solid color, several layers of color, or a dim, shimmering light. Once you can see something, have your friend concentrate on a specific color, and see if you can get that impression. Keep track of how many times you're right and wrong; if you're right over 50 percent of the time, consider it more than coincidence.

GARAGE SALE PSYCHOMETRY

Okay, so I really think garage sales are cool. Here's a fun psychic day trip:

Check out a garage sale at the house of someone you don't know. (Bring a parental unit or someone else with you.) Walk slowly through the place, and pick up a few objects that seem old, funky, or as if they had sentimental value. Hold it in your receptive hand (the one you don't write with). Look very closely at it. See what pops up in your mind. Did you feel happy when you picked it up, or did it make you sad? Did any pictures flash through your mind? Make up a history for your garage sale treasure. Then, find the person running it, and ask them about the thing you picked up. See if their story has any parallels with yours.

CHAPTER EIGHT

RAISING ENERGY

To practice Witchcraft, you need to feel your own energy and the energy of Nature, as you've read about in Chapter 4. Take it a step further and you'll realize that, since your own energy is connected with the energy present in every object at all times, you can raise up that luminous stuff and use it! The energy is already present; what you have to do is *amplify* it, conjure it out of an object or yourself, Will it to accumulate in a hefty quantity. This is sort of vague, I know, so I'll relate it to some experiences you have perhaps already had to give a clearer picture of the energy scene.

Remember a time when you were absolutely furious about something. I mean ripping mad, to the point that you were physically shaking or screaming at the top of your lungs. That's not necessarily the best type of energy to work with, but I'm sure you can relate, at least. What did it feel like in your body? Maybe tingling, maybe hot, maybe like your blood was buzzing? That's energy. What do you do with that feeling? Do you scream and yell and generally go ballistic until you feel better? That's an example of *releasing* energy. If you go for a run to get rid of the anger in a constructive way, that's an example of *channeling* energy—letting it run through you and transforming it into something else.

Now remember a really big party you've attended. There was a constant hum of voices and laughter, faces swimming around in a sea of people . . . depending on the party, you might have felt excitement when you walked into the room, or you might have felt horribly bored. A party—or any large group of people in one spot—always has its own vibe. So does the actual place they're at. That's energy, too. If you've ever been to a totally boring party and tried to liven it up a bit, that's a simple example of *shifting* energy. If you tried to get things moving by motivating people to be a little wild or to start laughing, that's *raising* energy: pulling out what's already there—laughter, fun, wildness—beneath the surface. If you get things going at a party by acting nuts, turning up the music, eating fire—whatever you do to get people stoked—and they respond by being more fun to hang out with, then you've raised the party's energy level from blah to groovy. Your physical actions call up energy; music definitely calls up energy; and this works for calling up Nature's own power.

Best to start with what you know best: your physical body. You did the kinetic friction thing in Chapter 4, right? If not, go do it! That's the simplest way to raise a little energy from your own body. It works well for charging charms, but you'll want to do it on a much larger scale to cast a spell. Dancing is one of the absolute best ways to raise energy, and it has a great side effect: ecstasy, an altered state of consciousness. It's also the best way to *start* raising and moving energy, because the results are immediate and you can easily feel what you're doing. Dance is a powerful combination of moving meditation, visualization, and energy raising. Don't be self-conscious about flopping around if you're not a great dancer. WHO CARES? The Gods aren't laughing at you, okay? Besides, the more you do it, the better you get at it, which is a definite bonus in both the real world and the magickal one. Before you even attempt spiritual, energy-raising dances, just bounce around your room to see how it makes you feel.

If you want to use music (you certainly don't have to, but it's a lot easier), pick something you're really familiar with and have it ready before you start: hit repeat on your CD player, or tape the same song a few times in a row. You won't be casting a spell here, so you don't need ritual tools or anything else, really. If you can dance around like a lunatic outside, that's the best way to go, but if your neighbors will freak out about it, just dance around your bedroom. Use whatever music makes you want to dance. I think (good) techno/electronica is great for raising energy, and I also love tribal drumming type stuff. Irish music, like The Chieftains, gets me going, too.

ENERGY IN MOTION

The motions here are very specific, so read through them a few times before you get going. This isn't the only way to raise and move energy with your body, but it works well. As I was writing this, I had Transglobal Underground blasting on the stereo (they rock), and I got up and went through my usual energy-raising routine to make sure I got it all down. I never realized it before, but I *always* use the same series of motions to do this. . . .

Stretch out a little bit (have you noticed that I advocate stretching?) to warm up your muscles. Breathe deeply a few times. Bare feet are best; feel your feet touching the ground/floor, and feel their connection to the Earth. Imagine the Earth has a pulse running through it, like a heartbeat, and imagine that it's in rhythm with your heartbeat. Feel the pounding under your feet and traveling up through your legs, up your spine, into your skull, through your chest, down your arms, until your whole body is throbbing with your heartbeat, the Earth's rhythm, the beat of the music (heavy bass and drums really help to make the sensation immediate and obvious), all of them mingling together in your head and body. Then, try to visualize the beat throbbing around you. You may imagine it as a mist, a pulsing web— however you picture energy. Thinking of it as a mist or an electrical pulse seems to work best for me, although I'm pretty comfortable working with an invisible substance as well.

Start moving slowly . . . you want to concentrate on each movement. Spread your feet apart; feel that pulse coming up through the ground; consciously *move* the feeling up through your legs and up your spine. Run it up and down your spine. Let it rest in your pelvis, and move your hips around; *feel* and *see* your energy coursing, imagine your blood as pure energy, pure light. Your personal energy should be moving now, since your body is moving . . . work it through your spine again, up your neck, down your arms.

Reach your hands down, touch the ground beneath you, and imagine your personal energy flowing out of your hands like light pouring from a huge spotlight. Now, *see* the Earth's energy flowing around you like a fine mist. If you can't quite see it (don't sweat it, you will!), just feel it and imagine. Cup your hands and literally pick up the energy radiating off the Earth.

Feel Earth's energy filling your hands. Picture your energy mingling with Earth's. You can even go for a scooping motion, as though you were picking up bunches of thin mist. Your movement will create a slight breeze. Picture yourself catching and throwing that breeze between your palms, still moving your hips and bending with your movements. Feel that energy running through you like an electrical current, or like a strong river flowing in your blood. See it swirling around your body.

Pull your arms up slowly, still imagining your hands filled with that mist-breeze-light. Position your arms so they're a little higher than your shoulders, slightly bent at the elbows, with your palms facing up. Turn yourself around in small circles, just big enough to get your body around, very slowly at first, your hands still full of the energy. Try a dancer's trick to keep yourself focused: pick an object in your line of sight (your dresser, a picture, etc.); each time you turn fully around, snap your head and return your focus to that object. Do this until you can really feel yourself humming with energy. Keep picturing the energy gathering around you, as if your body in motion pulls energy to you like a magnet, especially concentrating in your palms. Do it in rhythm with your music. It's not a frenzied kind of motion. It's very controlled (at this point, at least), and you should let the music dictate what your motion is like.

Now that you've got it in motion, you can start putting some real force into it. Let the energy continue to swirl around you in a larger bubble. See it moving from your body and hands outward to fill the whole room or space. This is your matrix, and it's real. It's pulsing around you, swirling, moving. You generated it, so it's connected to you, touching your body. Now you have to get as wild as you possibly can, dancing hard with your whole body, generating more and more energy with your motions and pulling it from the Earth.

Use gestures that imitate what you're doing: pulling energy from Nature and your own body and feeding your energy matrix. Keep moving your arms and hands in pulling/pushing motions, pulling energy from your body, the air, the Earth, and pushing it into your matrix.

Now what do you *do* with it?

First, you need to calm yourself down a little. You'll be sweaty and panting, and you should be able to feel the matrix you created. Your head

might feel swimmy and you'll probably feel a little dazed, a little drunk—
ecstasy! Well, a sort of beginner's version. Slow your body down until you
stop. Try kneeling on the ground and stretching your arms above your
head; pull the rest of your energy from your body into your hands and let it
seep out slowly to join your matrix. Keep your arms up, like a conductor
who's about to signal his orchestra.

You can do a couple of things at this point. You can take the energy
back into your body (nice, but it might shock you a bit), you can disperse it,
or you can send it somewhere. Since this was your first exercise, it's probably best just to ground it. You didn't really start with any intention, so or-
ganizing your thoughts and will at this point can be difficult.

Grounding is really easy and really important. With your arms raised,
push the energy into a small area (I like to use a sphere). It might take a few
minutes, but keep imagining the energy coming together, getting more
compact, creating a shape and hovering a few feet in front of you. See the
energy floating there, and then start to move it slowly downward. When
you have it slightly above the ground, move it into the Earth (if you're inside, just picture it going through the floor and then into Earth). See it go
in. Imagine the Earth absorbing it. Reinforce your visualization by bending at the waist (you should still be kneeling down), flattening your body
to the ground, and stretching your arms above your head to touch the
ground. You just gave back what you used, and it's nice to feed the Earth
like that.

CHANTING UP SOME GOOD VIBES

Somewhat less physical than dancing, chanting is also a good way to
raise energy. Your breath itself is powerfully magickal; it's part of your life
force, after all. Sound is magickal; it *is* energy, real, actual, physical energy
that bounces around.

There are a couple ways you can use chanting to raise energy.

The simplest chanting method is to repeat a single word or sound over
and over again, usually on one note. In Hinduism, these are called mantras,
and the most famous is Aum (OM). If you feel silly saying "OM," you can
rip on an open note, like "AHHH." This is good for focusing your mind

during meditation, and you can also use it to raise energy. Get used to chanting by doing it this way a few times:

Sit in a comfortable chair and close your eyes. Breathe deeply a few times, and then find your breath's rhythm. As you inhale, feel the air feeding your cells with its energy. As you exhale, imagine your breath as a dim white light, flowing out through your mouth. Start chanting your mantra very softly as you exhale, sounding one long note. Each time you exhale and sound your mantra, do it a little bit louder than the time before. Imagine the light of your breath getting brighter and brighter each time you exhale your mantra. Keep going until you've reached a loud, strong, resonant tone. When you reach your peak, visualize your breath-energy-light as a glowing shape in front of you. Then ground it, like we did before.

PART IV

CHAPTER NINE

RITUAL TOOLS

Witches use tools for two reasons. First, they're symbols of power. Like I explained in Chapter 4, if you use specific objects during ritual all the time, they help your mind get into the magickal mode. It's like putting pajamas on before you go to bed. When you slide into your comfy clothes, your mind makes the connection that it's time for bed. Similarly, when you cast your Circle or start a spell, you pick up your tools. Your mind gets the signal that it's time for magick.

Some tools are useful because they hold on to energy—especially crystals or metal things. And some materials—like plants, dirt, wood, and stones—have their own Nature vibe that works with and magnifies your own energy.

You don't have to spend a lot of money on an ornate wand or cauldron, unless you want to. I think it's much better to make your own tools, because the concentration and energy you put into making them will boost their potency and make them totally yours. I've included some suggestions for making your own tools. Any other supplies you might want should be available through arts and craft stores or in your backyard. Also, garage sales and yard sales are a good resource. You can pick up some pretty weird stuff; it's supercheap; and you can always paint, carve, or otherwise freak it out for your Witchcraft needs. And you won't feel too badly if it breaks or if you don't like the way it looks after you modify it. If you want to include a more exotic tool or ingredient into your practice, you'll find plenty of Pagan supply shops in the Appendices. I've made sure that all of those stores accept money orders (so you don't need a credit card), and all of them do mail order.

While you're reading, keep something in mind: tools are just that—things to use that help you get results. They're not powerful in themselves. Your mind and your constant use of them gives them power (for the most part, there are some exceptions to this, like herbs, fire, and water, for example . . . they *do* have their own life force). My point is, *you* are the only totally necessary and most powerful tool in Witchcraft. Tools are pretty and fun to collect, but don't get too caught up in them. You should train your mind to do most of your magick by itself.

I divided the tools up in two categories: "Working tools," which are the most basic, standard magickal tools that traditional Wiccans use during rituals; and "Craft tools," other random stuff you'll find useful in Witchcraft.

WORKING TOOLS

THE PENTACLE

The pentacle symbolizes Earth on an altar, and it is associated with the direction North. Its five points also resemble the human figure standing with feet apart and arms raised—the Goddess position. The pentacle can be used to capture unwanted energy, to invoke protection, and to materialize energy. It's usually made of clay, wood, or metal[1]—Earth materials. It's often used in spells involving money and health, since these are earthly matters. Many Wiccans and other Witches wear a pentacle, often on a necklace or ring, as a symbol of their religion.

Don't confuse this with the pentagram. It's basically the same symbol, but the word *pentagram* usually refers to the symbol that's drawn in the air during rituals, and it doesn't have a circle around the star.

❋ MAKE YOUR OWN ❋

There are a couple ways to make your own pentacle. The easiest and often the most effective is made of dirt. It's pretty cheap and easy to find.

All you need is a bowl or plate, some good old dirt, and your finger. Draw a pentacle with your finger in the dirt. It seems too simple, but it's a really good tool for two reasons: first, the pentacle represents Earth, right? So all the better that it's made from Earth! Second, if you're using a pentacle to nab offensive energy, dirt itself is great for that. You can also use salt instead of dirt, with the same results.

If you want a more permanent pentacle for your altar, paint a rock! If you're feeling more creative, try using some polyform clay. It's not natural, really, but it also doesn't require a kiln to harden. If you have access to a kiln (can I come over to play?), by all means use natural clay. Polyform is really cheap and easy to work with, and any half-decent art supply store will have it. Warm up your clay by kneading it with your hands. Get your energy moving, and concentrate on what you'll be using your pentacle for. Roll it out to about an inch thick (you can use a rolling pin or an empty bottle). Grab something circular, like a dessert plate (dinner plates may be too big, but if that's what you're going for, do it up!), and place it over the clay. Trim around the circle with a knife. Smooth the edges with your finger. You have a couple of options here. You can inscribe your pentacle with a pointed stick before you let the clay dry, or you can let your disk harden and paint it. I think the second choice is better, only because it'll be easier to get a really clean line and neater results. Draw your design lightly in pencil first, so you're sure you like what you've got before committing to it with paint.

THE ATHAME

The *athame* (dagger) is a double-edged knife, usually with a black handle on it (the *bolline*, another knife used in some traditions, is often white-handled with a crescent blade). It represents Air[2] on the altar, and the direction East. The athame is used to direct and control energy. In many traditions, you use the athame only during ritual, and it's used only for directing energy in a Circle, while the bolline is used to cut herbs and do other magickal preparation outside of Circle.

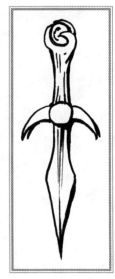

Never use your athame to harm any living creature, and never use it to threaten anyone. How much less spiritual could you possibly get? In fact, it's better if the blade is a little on the dull side so you don't have any accidents.

✳ MAKE YOUR OWN ✳

Unless you're a metalsmith, you'll have to buy your dagger or something similar. Raymond Buckland's book, *Buckland's Complete Book of Witchcraft,* details a method for making your own athame. I haven't tried it, but you're welcome to.

It's pretty easy to find one in antique shops or at garage sales. Don't haggle for it, don't steal it (duh!), and make sure you clean it and *cleanse* it really well. If you can't have one or can't find one, use a letter opener! Why not?

By the way, if you *do* go buy an actual dagger, I think using it all the time is better than keeping it in Circle. Use it to cut herbs, use it to inscribe candles, use it for everything that relates to your magick. It only gets better with use!

✳ THE WAND

The wand represents Fire on the altar, and it's associated with the direction South. Wands are used to invoke or generate energy, and they're usually made of wood. Wood has its own natural power, since it comes from trees, which are living creatures. Your wand will help you magnify energy, and you'll be able to use the energy of the tree it came from, too.

You can find sexy metal ones in Pagan supply shops, but I don't recommend them. See the first footnote on the whole metal-during-ritual controversy. Besides, wands are really easy to make yourself, and the time and effort you put into making one will add power to it.

❋ MAKE YOUR OWN ❋

The simplest wand is a stick from your backyard. First you have to find the perfect twig. If you want to use a specific kind of wood, look on the ground near whatever tree you want to use. I don't think it's a good idea to cut a living branch off a tree because it's totally unnecessary; there are plenty of twigs lying around out there, so why slice a living piece off a poor old tree? What did it ever do to you?

Pick a twig that's in good shape, no rot or anything funky on it, and definitely use one that's thin. You don't want to heft a log around during your rituals! The traditional length for a wand is the distance from your elbow to the top of your middle finger. It's appropriate that you'd measure according to your arm, because your wand acts like an extension of your hand and your own energy. If you can't find one that fits exactly, grab one that's a little longer and cut it down to size. You can use this as it is. It's perfectly effective. Or, since it's so easy to elaborate on, you can really go for it.

Start by smoothing your soon-to-be wand with sandpaper to give it a nice surface for embellishments. You can cut runes or other figures on your wand and go over them with ink, if you want. There are a couple of books that outline traditional markings for wands, but I think it's most important that you relate to the symbols you use. Some ideas for wand symbols are the infinity symbol, since the energy you're using is infinite; your astrological sign, since it represents part of your magickal nature; and the God symbol, since the wand is a totally masculine tool.

Figure out with what you want to adorn your wand. Keep in mind the idea that your wand will magnify your own power, and pick your materials accordingly. Quartz points are absolutely perfect for this because crystals—especially quartz—act as energy amplifiers. They're readily available, and they cost only a few pennies. Any stone or crystal you like is fine, but try to stick to pointy ones; they concentrate energy best.

You can glue these onto your wand with epoxy or wood glue, but first you have to hollow out the tip(s) a little to make room for the point. You'll need a sharp knife (*please*, please be careful! I can see the angry letters from your parents already. . . .). Just twist it around a little until you've got a small indentation in the wood. You can also wrap the part where the crystals stick in with embroidery floss, if you want to add some color symbolism to it.

Feathers are nice, too, especially if you decide that wands will represent Air for you. If that's the route you're going, then you can also just use a lit stick of incense for a temporary wand. The smoke that comes off the end is useful for training yourself to see energy you've invoked.

Do whatever you want with it, and make it totally yours!

THE CHALICE AND CAULDRON

The *chalice* and/or *cauldron* represent Water on the altar. The chalice is placed in the West corner of the altar, while the cauldron (if you use one) can either be underneath your altar, on the side, or somewhere else altogether. There's no set, standard material for either of these items, although I seem to see cast-iron cauldrons more than any other kind. I prefer glass or clay for my chalice, and I prefer copper or glass for my cauldron. These are powerful Goddess symbols; your life began in Water when you were swimming around in your mother's womb. Chalices and cauldrons represent a womb, and they're used to create potions, tonics, and other healing liquids. You can cook up fabulously enchanted soup, too . . . never underestimate the power of good soup! You'll also use these tools to bless Water for your rites.

❄ MAKE YOUR OWN ❄

Get a nice, simple wineglass (I happen to like glasses recommended for red wine because they have a larger bowl) or a goblet, either from your cupboards or—yet again—a garage sale. The simpler, the better, I think; if it's simple to begin with,

you can add your own design more easily. You can paint on glass with special paints (not very expensive and available at arts and crafts stores), and that's a good way to personalize your chalice.

You can paint the whole chalice with a multitude of colors in a pretty, swirling design. Go for blues, purples, light greens—Water colors. Or, you can paint symbols that relate to Water or to a Goddess. The Triple Moon symbol would be totally perfect, or you can go for a crescent, or an inverted triangle (a Goddess symbol). You may want to paint the Water signs from the Zodiac (Pisces, Cancer, and Scorpio) around the base. Use what speaks to you.

CRAFT TOOLS

The following list includes the items I think are totally necessary to have on hand at all times for Witchcraft. You don't have to run out and grab everything in one day. Start with one item in each group and get the rest when you can. You can almost always substitute, and I think it's good to learn how to be resourceful. For example, if you need to do a banishing ritual and you can't find frankincense, sage will work perfectly well. Get it at the grocery store!

Every spell, recipe, or project in this book can be made with the materials listed below. You may need the occasional stick or rock, but I think you can find those pretty easily. Check out the Appendices to determine how you can easily substitute any ingredients with whatever you have on hand.

HERBS AND FLOWERS

Sage
Cinnamon, sticks or powdered
Lavender (dried herb and/or essential oil)
Chamomile
Nutmeg, whole
Rosemary
Mint
Ginger, fresh or powdered
Rose petals and rosewater

Cloves

Whole black peppercorns (Sorry, already-ground pepper just won't do it!)

Vanilla beans and extract

ESSENTIAL OILS

Anise

Bergamot (can make your skin sensitive to sunlight; use sparingly)

Frankincense

Lavender

Patchouli

Peppermint

Sweet orange

Tea-tree (sometimes spelled "ti-tree")

KITCHEN STUFF

Honey

Salt (preferably sea salt)

Milk (whole milk or dried milk)

Oil (Preferably jojoba, extra virgin olive, sweet almond—although some people are allergic to sweet almond—and grapeseed. All are available at health food stores.)

Cocoa butter (also available at health food stores)

Tea (Decaffeinated is best because caffeine is highly addictive.)

Two bowls

A double boiler, or a pot that fits into another pot, or a bowl that fits into one of your pots (You won't be able to use the top pot or bowl for making food anymore, so ask your parents before you steal their kitchenware!)

OTHER SUPPLIES

Charcoal tabs (These are made especially to burn powdered incense on. Get them at Pagan supply shops, health food stores, New Age bookshops. . . .)

Beeswax (You can use this for making candles and lotions.)

Epsom salts (You can get this at drugstores, and it's supercheap—about $3 for three pounds!)

Candles (Every size, shape, and color you can get your hands on. Definitely stock up on white ones, though.)

Thread, in various colors

Sewing needles

Plain cotton or muslin, several yards

String or embroidery floss, various colors

Paper of various colors

An assortment of paints, inks, and pens

Assorted bottles and boxes (Check out thrift shops, garage sales, and reuse stuff from your kitchen.)

Oak tag, cardstock, or some other stiff paper

Seeds, especially alfalfa and wildflower

2 notebooks—one for your exercises and one for your Book of Shadows

An almanac and/or *ephemeris* (Use this to look up astrological correspondences, Moon phases, and other Zodiac goodies.)

WITCH'S WISH LIST

You don't absolutely *need* this stuff, but it's really nice to have on hand!

· Mortar and pestle (Perfect for crushing up herbs and resins. Or, use two rocks, an old bowl and the back of an old wooden spoon, anything that you can crush stuff with.)

· Athame (You can also use the first finger of your dominant hand [the one you write with]. Wear a ring on that finger to get the metal edge!)

· Censer (These are containers, often made of metal, in which to burn incense. They're pretty, but a bowl with some sand in it will do the trick, or a rock with an indentation.)

· Cauldron (You can certainly buy a fancy cauldron from a Pagan supply shop, but a spaghetti pot will do in a pinch. Copper pots are actually better than cast-iron cauldrons, in my opinion. Cast iron is a good conductor, but it's also reactive. If you put anything acidic into it, such as lemon juice or tomatoes, it'll rust. Plus, small bits of iron will leech into your mixture, which isn't harmful at all, but sometimes stuff tastes funny. Ditto for aluminum. Copper, on the other hand, is an excellent conductor and won't turn your stuff weird. Copper is also a sacred metal that looks lovely, and it needs to be polished occasionally; you get to charge your cauldron more often that way. On the downside, it's also pretty expensive. Try hunting down a copper pot at a garage sale, if this is the way you want to go.)

· Ritual robes (Sexy . . . mysterious . . . and totally unnecessary! You can pick some clothes from your existing wardrobe that work for ritual, like a pretty dress or a specific pair of pants, and decide to use them only for ritual. If you have them, white clothes are particularly handy because you can paint or embroider whatever symbols you want to them. Or, you can always go sky-clad! Naked, that is.)

· Broom (Some Witches use these to physically and psychically cleanse their ritual space. It's kind of a cool symbolic thing to have around, very witchy. You can also use a fan or feather for the same purpose.)

· Tarot deck (We'll make one in Chapter 11, but there are stunning decks out there, like Dali's. They're a bit pricey, but well worth it if you want to take on Tarot.)

CHAPTER TEN

CASTING A CIRCLE

The **image** of Witches and Magicians standing in a smoking Circle while crazy demons appear out of the shadows is forever entrenched in our minds and almost totally wrong. I guess some Magicians are interested in conjuring demons—although I don't really know *why*—but most Witches aren't. We often invite deities to come and join our rituals, but Circles are important for other reasons.

First of all, casting a Circle is a way to put yourself "in between the worlds." You're in a temple, you're in sacred space, and you're in that twilight state of mind where magick happens. Besides all that, drawing a psychic and physical Circle around yourself contains the energy you raise until you're ready to let it fly; it also keeps any static *out*. You don't want any little black cloud of energy beasties coming around while your mind is wide open and dancing around the dimensions. Circles are for concentrating and protection.

There are lots of ways to cast a Circle, and you should try all of them, adding and subtracting according to your taste. The main thing is to use all the Elements to declare your sacred space. The other important part is visualizing your Circle really clearly. Magick starts in your mind, always! Look through the following styles, try them all, and pick what you like best. As Carl Jung, noted psychiatrist and groovy guy, points out, the Circle and four directions as a symbol of Deity and as a temple has been around a long, long time in lots of different cultures. In *Psychology and Religion: West and East,* Jung states: "The wholeness ('perfection') of the celestial circle and the squareness of the earth, combining the four elements or psy-chic qualities, express completeness and union."

TRADITIONAL CIRCLES

Gardnerian Circle casting (and therefore Alexandrian, also—remem-ber, Sanders essentially made off with the Gardnerian goods and tweaked a few things) is serious business. It includes a whole host of tools, very strict adherence to Gardnerian liturgy, precise motions, and an instruction man-ual: the Gardnerian Book of Shadows, hand copied and passed down from Priestess to Initiate.

The Gardnerian Circle–casting model works because it demands in-tense concentration. However, it's *not* the end of the road for all Witches. It has some definite advantages, so you should check it out. Try *The Witches Way,* by Stewart and Janet Farrar; they have reprinted the most complete version of Gardner's Book of Shadows. When you create your own rituals (I hope you do!), you'll want to see what other people do that works for them.

What I don't like about Gardnerian Circle casting—and Gardnerian tradition in general—is that it has no place for the Solitaire, and I don't dig a lot of Gardner's symbolism. That's just me. It doesn't mean I think Gard-nerian Wiccans are wrong, I just don't relate. Remember, covens that prac-tice Gardnerian Wicca (and Alexandrian, while we're at it), aren't open to teens, and the Gardnerian method depends on working in a coven. The Cir-cle casting method reflects that, since the High Priest and High Priestess each have their own roles.

I recommend . . .

SEMI-GARDNERIAN WITH A HALF-TWIST

Definitely take the time to construct a Circle if you're doing anything more complicated than blessing a charm. When you're doing magick, you're opening your *mind*. You've got to make sure that you have those boundaries up to keep yourself balanced and your psyche protected, not necessarily from otherworldly beings, but from an overwhelming flow from your own subconscious. I'm not trying to freak you out here! I just want you to be able to stay on an even keel. Walking between the worlds is a fabulous way to live, but you're going to need some ordinary

> One word of advice: When you find what you like, do it the same way a few times. That's another key to Witchcraft and ritual. Once you establish your style, stick with it until you find something else that really calls you. That repetition strengthens your concentration after a while, and you'll slip into the other worlds more quickly. It becomes a mental trigger.

Earth time to decompress the old psyche every now and again. Casting and releasing semiformal Circles will help you keep your experiences from becoming overwhelming.

After a little monkeying, I've come up with a few ways to construct Circles without a whole lot of pomp and ceremony but with enough concentration to keep your boundaries firmly in place. Here are the major points, in order and based on the Gardnerian model. Plug in whatever symbols you like, but keep the basic structure intact until you feel strong enough to meddle effectively! I know this Circle-casting method includes things that you might not be able to use all the time, like incense and candles, if your parents don't like them. That's okay. You don't have to do it this way all the time, but if you can do this even once, it will make an impression in your mind that you can call up mentally any time you need to cast a Circle but can't do it formally.

CIRCLE CASTING 101

Here's an example of a generic formal Circle casting (not exactly black-tie, but more than jeans and a T-shirt!):

INTENTION

To cast your first official Circle!

TOOLS

Four white votive candles, one placed at each Quarter.

Two other candles, which will represent a Goddess and a God.

One more candle, to be used as the working candle. Light all the other candles from this one.

Bowl of salt.

Chalice filled with water.

Dish filled with dirt.

Charcoal tablets (not the kind you use in the barbecue!).

Frankincense and/or sage pounded in a mortar and pestle or whatever you're using to substitute for one. Put this in a dish.

ALTAR LAYOUT

BLESS THE WATER AND SALT

Place your hands above the salt, moving them clockwise over the bowl until you feel the salt is charged. Do the same thing with the Water. Take a pinch of salt with your fingers and drop it into the Water; stir it clockwise. Imagine that this Water represents the Water of the Ocean and the Womb. Traditional Wiccans would use the tip of their athame to put salt into the water and stir it. This symbolizes the Great Rite; it represents sexual union (think about it). It's also a statement: Male and female are equal opposites that unite to make each other complete.

CIRCLE CASTING

Draw your Circle with your athame or your finger. See it there!

"Earth, Air, Fire, Water. I call you. I am your daughter (son). Thank you for blessing this Circle."

(Light candle in the East)

"Element of Air, you are the Breath of Life. Thank you for lending your power to this rite."

(Light candle in the South)

"Element of Fire, you are the Divine spark. Thank you for lending your power to this rite."

(Light candle in the West)

"Element of Water, you are the Blood in my veins. Thank you for lending your power to this rite."

(Light candle in the North)

"Element of Earth, you are the Bones of my body. Thank you for lending your power to this rite."

Draw a pentacle in the dirt. Put this in the center of your altar. Light the charcoal, put it in the center of your pentacle, and put a generous amount of the frankincense/sage mixture on it. Put your hands over the smoke, and gently waft the smoke around your body, imagining it cleansing your mind and spirit. This is called smudging in Native American traditions. You'll probably get the sensation of cleansing just from the scent. Frankincense and sage smell astringent, like rubbing alcohol. Carry the pentacle with the incense clockwise around the Circle three times. Your Circle is now purified by Air. Put it back on the altar.

Hold the candles representing the God and Goddess about a foot away from your body, around your breastbone area. Imagine the flame burning away any negative feelings. Carry the candle clockwise around the Circle three times. Your Circle is now purified by Fire. Put them back on the altar.

Sprinkle yourself with the Water, with some on your forehead, hands, and feet. Carry your chalice clockwise around the Circle three times, sprinkling Water as you go. Your Circle is now purified by Water. Put your Chalice back on the altar.

Take the salt clockwise around the Circle three times and sprinkle it around. Imagine that the grains will keep out any negative influence from your Circle. Your Circle is now purified by Earth, and it's done!

Now, imagine your Circle as white light glowing brightly around you. Hold the image in your mind for as long as you can, and meditate on your breath for a few moments.

INVOKE A GODDESS AND GOD

Concentrate on whatever deities you picked for your ritual, and try to include some representation of them. For example, if you're calling on Athena and Apollo, you may have an owl statue and a picture of the Sun to represent them. You may also offer them traditional foods, like a bowl of olive oil with lemon and herbs in it. Try invoking them in Greek, too. Why not? If you're inviting someone to a party, it's nice to invite them in their own language! Carve your deities' names on the Goddess and God candles. Chant their names until you feel the energy is with you. Light their candles. The flames will represent their presence.

RAISE THE ENERGY

You have a couple of choices here: dancing, chanting, drumming . . . it's up to you! I think it's good to use a little of everything. Sound and motion are powerful energy raisers, and they work even better when used together. Get wild—in a controlled and focused way! For rituals that need something quieter, use concentrated breathing to raise energy. Look over the mantra exercise you learned in Chapter 8.

Whatever method(s) you go with, be sure to visualize that energy contained in your Circle, so you can . . .

SEND THE ENERGY OUT

Once you've got enough energy raised—you'll feel it, trust me—then you can send it toward your goal. How you do this will depend on what that goal is, of course! If your ritual was

> It's a good idea to work with deities from the same pantheon in any given ritual. Some Eclectic rituals call on deities from all over the place, but I think it's a little confusing. Besides, how do we know that those deities get along? In Santeria, certain *orishas* are never called to be at the same ceremony, because they have conflicting energy.

solely an act of religious worship, you wouldn't necessarily send it anywhere. But if you do a ritual to heal yourself, for instance, you may want to direct the energy into a potion or even a loaf of bread that you can eat later. If you're healing someone else (with that person's permission, of course), then you may direct the energy to that person by focusing on a picture of him or her. If you want to charge an amulet or bless a charm, you'd send the energy into that object.

> "Using a magick Circle is completely optional, although I recommend it because the Circle helps the practitioner focus, concentrate, and achieve the correct frame of mind. It is also a protective barrier [protects from negative/hostile energy] and aids in directing spells."
>
> —GWINEVERE, AGE 16

Many Witches use the image of a "cone of power," visualizing the energy as a huge cone above their Circle, flying toward their goal. It's a good one! I usually visualize several different ways, depending on my need. I like to visualize thick rays of specifically colored light (see the Table of Correspondences in the Appendices).

GROUND

You've done this before, in Chapter 8. It's not hard at all! Just fall to the ground and see the rest of your energy flowing into the Earth.

You'll also need to center yourself—to bring yourself back from that floaty, ecstatic state. After you ground, try sitting cross-legged and breathing deeply a few times. Some people recommend imagining that you're a tree with roots in the Earth. Sharing "cakes and ale" is a traditional way to end the Circle, and a light snack helps you ground and replenish your own energy. You don't have to eat cakes or drink ale, of course. Have whatever you like.

RELEASE THE CIRCLE

Release the Circle by walking around it counterclockwise (widdershins). Imagine the Circle flowing back into your athame or finger. As you walk, stop by each Quarter and release that Element, remembering to say thank you, and state that the Circle is open but never broken. You've pulled it up, but it's always there in your mind when you need it.

CHAPTER ELEVEN

DIVINATION

Most people define divination as "looking into the future." I think that's an inaccurate way to express it. Divination is looking into the "now," and seeing what possibilities await you if you continue on exactly the same pathway in the cosmos. Is that too hippie? I hate it when I sound like a hippie. Anyway—the way divination works for me is by using a tool (like Tarot cards or a scrying ball) to open my subconscious mind to give me a clue about the way the Universe is expressing itself at one specific moment in time so I can have an idea about where, when, and how I can move to make sure my actions are in agreement with the flow of things.

Lots of Witches use divination before they cast a spell. First of all, this will give them an indication of whether the spell will work and what side effects it might have. Second, it helps us decide if this is the right time to work that particular energy. If I want to cast a spell to call a lover and I do a reading that doesn't have any cards that relate to a love relationship, I probably won't do the spell at that time. My reading might give me some clues about what I need to work on before I can have the relationship I want. For example, if I did the reading and got a few cards that related to balance and health, I might think about getting my emotions under control and balancing my energy a little better before I try to call a cutie.

There are *hundreds* of divination methods, and I don't have the space to go into all of them here. I picked a few that I particularly like and that are relatively easy for a beginner. Try them all.

RUNES

Runes are magickal alphabets that have been used in several cultures, especially Germanic/Norse and Celtic civilizations. You'll see one of the most common alphabets, Futhark, below. This is divided into early and later Futhark.

For divination, the runes are drawn on stones or pieces of wood and then cast, or thrown. Put them in a bag, shake them up, and concentrate on

1. *Fehu: (cattle) wealth, success*
2. *Uruz: (auroch) strength, defense*
3. *Thurisaz: (thorn) power, Thor's hammer*
4. *Ansuz: (male deity) magickal force, inspiration*
5. *Raidho: (travel) journeys, cosmic motion*
6. *Kenaz: (torch) creative energy, change*
7. *Gebo: (gift) interplay of energy*
8. *Wunjo: (joy) comfort, favorable fortune*
9. *Hagalaz: (hail) protection, control over a situation*
10. *Naudhiz: (need) inner strength, resolve*
11. *Isa: (ice) binding, control*
12. *Jera: (year) abundance, living with the seasons*
13. *Eihwas: (yew tree) enduring crisis, magick*
14. *Pertho: (dice) luck, chance*
15. *Elhaz: (elk) God energy, protection*
16. *Sowilo: (sun) movement, cosmic guidance*
17. *Tiwaz: (Tyr) victory, justice*
18. *Björk: (birch, goddess) Mother Earth, cycle of birth and death*
19. *Ehwas: (horse) fertility, marriage*
20. *Mannaz: (human being) male and female united with the divine*
21. *Laguz: (water, leek) virtue, growth*
22. *Ingwaz: (Ing) beginning manifestation, incubation*
23. *Dagaz: (Dag, day) spiritual awakening, hope*
24. *Othala: (property) home, prosperity*

your question. When you feel that your energy has been passed into the stones, pull one, two, or several, to get your answer. You can also use a spread and give each rune a position that has a meaning. For example, if you want to find out about why your boyfriend is acting weird, you could do a past, present, future spread. Shake the runes and pick one, putting it down on a table. That's the "past." Then choose another and lay it to the right of the first; that's the "present." Pick one more, and lay it to the right of the "present." This one represents the "future." Then you would refer to whatever book you're using for interpretation, or use the list above, and read each interpretation according to its place.

Another way to cast runes for divination is to draw a circle on a piece of paper or trace one on the ground. Then, shake, concentrate, and throw all the runes out. Read only the ones that fall into the circle.

❄ MAKE YOUR OWN RUNES ❄

It's so incredibly easy to make your own runes. Just gather a bunch of stones that are about the same size and shape—river stones work best because they're smooth and round—and paint the symbols on them. Pick different colors for each rune, if that will help you remember the interpretations. You can also engrave on the stones, if you have a dremmel.

Make yourself a pouch to store them in, too. Keeping them in a pouch helps keep them psychically "clean." Get two squares of muslin or cotton, and fold the tops over so there's about a half-inch overlapping. Sew each one that way. You'll be left with a little hole in the middle of the lip. Then, sew the two pieces together, wrong sides out, and leave the top open. Turn them right side out, and you're almost done. Thread a single piece of cord through the two top lips. Draw the fabric closed with the cord and knot it to keep your runes together. Lots of Witches don't let anyone else touch their runes, so the runes'll be infused only with the Witch's energy. If you want to do a reading for someone else, just have them concentrate on their question while you shake and throw them. The runes, not your friend!

SCRYING

Scrying uses a reflective surface, like a mirror or crystal ball, to see images that tell you about possible future events. When I say "images," I don't necessarily mean whole pictures. If you're a very visual person, you may very well see clear images. I'm sort of an abstract person, so I often get abstract images, like geometric patterns, color flashes, or flashes of images that don't always make a lot of sense until I write them down and think about them for a while.

There are a variety of objects that are good for scrying. I've had good luck with an obsidian sphere, a dark window at night, and candle flames (when you use a fire or candle flame, it's called *pyromancy*). Other good scrying tools are a bowl of water with ink or olive oil dripped into it, a mirror that you use only for scrying, and clear quartz or even glass spheres.

To get yourself ready, try burning some Vision or Power incense (you'll find some recipes in Chapter 12), or some straight-up dragon's blood resin and/or frankincense on a charcoal. If you want to cast a Circle, that helps, too. Remember to grab your notebook because you'll want to write down your impressions. Let the smoke fill the room. If you can't burn incense, try making a cup of tea with chamomile, cinnamon, and ⅛ teaspoon of freshly ground nutmeg. In fact, make the tea even if you *can* burn incense. Just relax, and do a little deep breathing.

If you're using water with which to scry, put it in a bowl and stir it clockwise. Recite a little incantation over it, such as: "Visions now appear to me, only true ones will I see." Repeat this until you feel your consciousness shift.

Pour a few drops of oil or ink into the water while it's still moving. Breathe on the water to make it ripple. Now sit back, relax, and gaze. Here's the tricky part: You have to let your focus get dim and look with your third eye. Okay let me back up a minute and explain.

Stare at your bowl. Feel where your energy is? It's in your eyeballs, right? Well, take that feeling and move it to a spot between your eyebrows and slightly higher while you continue to gaze at the water. If you concentrate on that spot, you'll feel a slight opening sensation and your vision will blur. That blurring opens your psychic vision—your third eye. I know it sounds nuts, but try it a few times until you get comfortable with the sensation and can keep up that blurry focus for a few minutes.

When you're comfy, take a look at the oil or ink blobs in the water. What do they look like? Can you see shapes? Write it down!

BIBLIOMANCY

Bibliomancy is really cool for a quick answer. To do this, just grab a book, think of your question, open the book randomly, close your eyes, and point. Whatever word you point to is your answer. It's actually uncanny a lot of the time.

TAROT

Finally, my favorite part! I'm biased, I know, but Tarot is my absolute favorite form of divination. It works really well for me, and I love collecting decks, too. They're seventy-eight pieces of art (if you get a good one), and I never get bored with them. Tarot has been around for centuries, and many of the ancient cultures used the cards. Modern playing cards actully come from Tarot.

Tarot packs, as I just said, are seventy-eight cards divided into four suits (like playing cards), and these are called the Minor Arcana—the little secrets. Court cards (similar to playing cards; in Tarot, there are Kings, Queens, Knights, and Pages) represent other people, parts of yourself, or transitional situations. Then there's the Major Arcana, which playing cards don't have. These are twenty-two cards that represent universal or archetypal forces and the major human experiences.

Tarot also incorporates numerology—using numbers to interpret the cosmic flow. If you pull the Ace of Wands, for example, you'd read that card according to its suit (Wands) and its value (1). So, since Wands are Fire, this card would represent an active force (Fire) that's just beginning to make an impact. Or it could be a message to actively start working on a project. Or it can mean the beginning of summer, since summer is the fiery season and Aces are beginnings. Or . . .

When you first start reading Tarot, it can be pretty overwhelming to try to memorize a card's traditional meanings, since these can be pretty obscure. It's more important to look at them with your intuition. What colors are in the card? What does the picture illustrate? What does it make you think of or feel? Then, look at all the other cards in the spread. Are there a lot of Major Arcana cards? Are there more than three cards from one suit? Does one number show up several times? Tarot spreads have a beginning, middle, and an end, just like a story, and you want to read that story by linking each card to all the other cards.

There are lots of great books on Tarot, and if you're interested in learning to read cards, you should start by getting one of them. Try *Tarot Made Easy* by Nancy Garen for a simple introduction, check out Tarot.com to browse through the decks and for some basic meanings, and also look for Tarot info on the web at your favorite Pagan sites. You can get a starter deck, too. The Rider-Waite deck is usually suggested (I don't really like it— the colors are pukey). Other starter decks are the Robin Wood deck, Tarot of the Old Path, Servants of the Light, the Celtic Tarot, and Tarot of the Cat People. You can also make your own pretty easily. It's a lot cheaper than most decks, and you'll really get to know the cards this way.

❄ MAKE YOUR OWN TAROT DECK ❄

Grab some card stock or other stiff paper. Cut it into three-inch by five-inch rectangles. Using a utility knife and a ruler is easier than trying to cut seventy-eight pieces with scissors. Use your Tarot book as a guide to the traditional meanings of each card, and either do a collage of pictures that relate to that card or draw them. To make your own deck, compile as much info as you can about one card at a time from your sources. It would be great to start with the first Major Arcana card (The Fool) and work your way through the deck. See which symbols recur most often for each card, and look through magazines, old books, and other sources for images that relate to the card you're working on. Cut the images out and glue them on to the card stock (Mod Podge glue—available at arts and crafts stores—

works great for this; coat the cards with a layer of the glue after you finish to seal them), or you can draw your own pictures. It's also helpful to include a few of the card's keywords so you can start to remember them at a glance. You'll have to shuffle these delicately, but that's fine. Try spreading them facedown over your table and then grouping them together again.

TAROT SPREADS AND TIPS

There are lots of Tarot spreads, and each one has its benefits. There's the past, present, future spread (remember what we did with the runes?), and that's good for a simple answer. Just shuffle, pick a card, lay it down, and that's the "past." Shuffle again, and lay the next card to the right of the first; that's the "present." Shuffle one last time, and lay the third card to the right of the second card. That's the "future," and you can get your answer by interpreting these three cards.

The most popular spread is the Celtic Cross. It goes like this:

The positions are as follows:

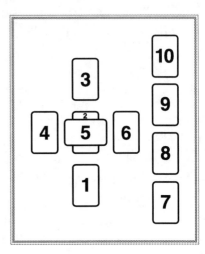

1. The root of the matter. These are the decisions or forces that brought you to the situation about which you're asking.

2. The heart of the matter. This represents you, your reactions, and the underlying emotion of the situation.

3. The best you can hope to attain. This is the highest ideal or benefit that you can expect if you stay on the same course.

4. The recent past. This card represents an energy or situation that's on its way out but still has an effect on you.

5. What crosses you. If this is a card with a negative meaning, it represents what is working against you. If the card is positive, it tells you what forces are in your favor or what strengths you'll be able to call on.

6. The near future. This card represents events or energy that's on its way in a few hours or days.

7. How the near future will evolve. This clarifies the last card and clues you in to the way you can expect your path to turn.

8. Other people. This can give you a hint about how other people will affect you in the next few days.

9. You in the near future. This card tells you a little about what you'll be doing or experiencing in the near future.

10. Final outcome. This card sums up the reading and your answer.

CHAPTER TWELVE

SPELL CRAFT

So, what is magick? Lots of people have tried to define magick, and I'm not nearly as knowledgeable or poetic as most of them. I can't give you a "scientific" definition of what magick is, and I can't prove it to you the same way I can prove that a pound of dirt is exactly a pound. All I know is that the human mind is capable of extraordinary power, and we don't even use all of it! In my opinion, magick is the ability to tap into your own mind's vast resources, find out about the way Nature works, and use your mind's symbols to find the connection between you and the rest of the Universe. Once you realize that all things are connected, you'll start to see that your thoughts have a real impact on your reality. Take it a little further, and you'll see that your imagination is as boundless as the Universe, and you can use your imagination, your mind's symbols, and what you've learned about the way Nature works to help bring to you what you want and need.

Now, get a few things straight. First of all, you won't be able to stop time and fly through the air . . . unless you're a specially trained Buddhist monk. I hear they're supposed to be able to do that type of stuff. Second, even

> "Magick is to feel, magick is to be. It is a means of changing your reality—not because you feel powerless and long for control over the uncontrollable—but because you are powerful and refuse to be a helpless victim. Magick is a celebration of life, death, and rebirth, both physical and psychological."
>
> —ATHENA, AGE 17

though your imagination has a huge part in magick, that doesn't mean it's all in your mind. And third, spells don't always work exactly the way you want them to. It's really important to be specific and to take all the possibilities

> Casting an excellent spell means blending a few key ingredients to get the desired result:
>
> · Use the right tools for the job.
> · Create sacred space.
> · State your desire clearly.
> · Raise and direct energy.
> · Ask the deities for help.
> · Act in accord.

into consideration before attempting a spell. Check out the astrological correspondences, check your divination to see if this is a good time to do the spell you want, and, most important, listen to your inner voice. If your conscience says that your timing is off or that you're imposing your will on someone else, refrain! I'm not going to lecture you about morals in magick. "Black" or "white" Witchcraft is a big lie. Witchcraft's energy isn't "good" or "evil," but your *intention* certainly can be. It's a completely subjective issue. HOWEVER—I can tell you from personal experience that karma happens.

There are two basic Witchcraft methods that fall under the heading *sympathetic* magick, which is the idea that images or representations of actual objects influence each other because they are similar. Similarity implies a relationship. Those relationships are an expression of connection, and Witchcraft is the art of finding connections and applying that relationship to use specific energy. For example, if you wanted to do a spell with lunar energy, you could use moonstone—called moonstone because its color and peculiar sheen resemble the Moon's light—to draw that energy down. Or you could use jasmine, because jasmine flowers at night, implying a connection between jasmine's energy and lunar energy.

Sympathetic magick includes *contagion* magick and *homeopathic* magick. *Contagion* magick assumes that objects that were once in contact with each other—the way fingernails and hair are attached to a person—will always have an effect on the object or person to which they were connected. This also includes the idea of drawing energy from another object, like a stone or tree. *Homeopathic* magick works on the theory that representations of actual people or things—like the infamous voodoo doll—will affect the person or thing at which you aim your magick. It's the old draw-the-stag-on-the-cave-wall-to-kill-a-real-stag principle.[1]

The spells here are candle spells (to aid your focus and use the properties of color, oils, and symbols), knot spells (to bind something to you or to keep it from you), or Elemental spells (to use the energy of a certain Element to get what you need). Some contain all three, and some have more than one part. When you do a spell, remember to take action in the "real" world, too, called "acting in accord." Witchcraft is effective, but it depends on your putting all your energy into your goal. That means working it in everyday life. You can do a spell for money, but you're more likely to get money by doing a spell to get a job and then working!

I've kept the spells basic and have explained each step of the way, so you'll be able to apply the techniques to writing your own spells. Something that comes from your mind and heart will work much better for you than something I suggest. For example, I usually use rhymes and sort of archaic language when I'm invoking and casting. You may prefer to use really simple language or total silence. If that's what turns your mind on, that's what you should use! Take another look at the How to Use This Book section before you dive in so you can get the most out of the spells here.

ABOUT THE RECIPES . . .

You'll find some recipes in this chapter for potions, incenses, oils, and creams. I tried my best to make sure all the stuff you'll need is really accessible, but if you can't find some of the ingredients, just substitute them with ideas from the variations, or take a look at the chart in the Appendices on page 283. Again, when you're trying new stuff—either to eat or to use on your skin—test a little bit before you drink or slather! For creams and oils, put a little bit on the inside of your wrist or elbow. You'll know if it's irritating in a day or so.

What do creams and oils have to do with Witchcraft, you might ask. It's not all about ceremony and elegant tools! First of all, when you take the time to know what powers herbs and spices have, you can use their energy to boost your magick. The simple act of making oils, potions, or anything else gives you an opportunity to charge and empower your creation with your own life force and intentions, in addition to the ingredients' own power. Herbs and essential oils have *evocative* properties. *Invocation* is calling on forces that are somehow outside you; *evocation* is calling on forces that are within you. Scents evoke emotions, and that energy is definitely useful in Witchcraft. Witchcraft is about opening your mind, remember? Use everything you've got!

Here's a little info about the ingredients. . . .

ESSENTIAL OILS

Essential oils are the *only* oils you can use to anoint candles or to put in incense. Perfume oils that are sold at stores usually contain synthetic ingredients, and they smell disgusting when you burn them—not to mention the fact that they release chemicals that are less than healthy. Never use essential oils directly on your skin because they are *powerful!* They need to be diluted in carrier oil, which I'll talk about in a second.

Essential oils tend to be a little expensive, so I figured out which oils were the most versatile and used those in the recipes. Essential oils will keep for over a year in a dark place, and you need only a few drops for each recipe. These will last a long time! To avoid blowing your budget, scan through the recipes and pick one or two that you really want to try. Buy those ingredients, and get the rest when you can.

INFUSED OIL

There are a couple of ways to use herbs in

Speaking of incense, I realize you may not be able to burn any in your house. My mom couldn't *stand* the smell of certain incenses, and she would bug out if I burned it in my room (mostly because she thought that meant I was smoking pot, for some reason). You can still make the recipes here, then put them in a bowl and use them as potpourri. Or you can simmer them in an aromatherapy diffuser—check out your local dollar store—or in a pot with a bit of water on the stove. You can also put incense in a pouch that you wear; give it a light squeeze when you want its energy.

Another option is to put a few drops of essential oils or fresh herbs into a bowl of very hot water. The vapors work just as well as incense.

If you can afford only one or two oils at a time, that's fine! Check out the Appendices for the oils' properties, and find the one that's best suited for your Witchcraft needs. Look carefully at the blends and recipes in this chapter, and choose one or two that will work for a few of the spells you want to try. You can use a single oil diluted in a carrier to get the effect you want.

Witchcraft, and making yummy (or not so yummy, depending on what you need) massage oils, body creams, healing salves, and perfume oils are all good ways to start.

You can make infused oils for your Witchcraft needs. It's really simple. All you have to do is gather a bunch of the fresh herb(s) you want to use. Make sure there's no moisture on them, gently heat some carrier oil, and pour it over the herbs. Let this steep for a day or two, then strain the oil and repeat the process with new herbs if you want a stronger scent. You can use dried herbs, too, like the ones you find at the grocery store. Cut the amount in half if you're using dried. I prefer fresh herbs, only because they have a little more life force in them.

You can also use the cold extraction method, which takes a lot longer but keeps the herb's properties better than heated oil. Gather a few handfuls of your herbs (one herb per infusion), preferably at noon, so they're dry. If you can't gather at noon, let them dry a little bit in a sunny window. Give them a light pinch before you put them in the jar. A little squeeze helps to release the herbs' essential oils. Put them in a jar and cover them with carrier oil. Let this sit on a windowsill for two to six weeks.

Whichever method you use, gently shake the jar occasionally while the herbs are infusing. Check it to see if the scent is strong enough for you. If not, strain the herbs and repeat the process with new herbs until you get what you want! Label it clearly, and list each ingredient.

Mind you, infused oils aren't as strong as essentials, and you won't

Making bath and body stuff is a great way to practice your Craft, especially if your parents aren't happy about all this Witch talk. Making oils and creams is pretty innocent, and you can pack a powerful magickal punch into your creations—without alarming your parental units.

be able to use them in incense—the carrier oil you use to extract the plant essence will smell *wretched* when you burn it. However, you *can* use infused oils in a diffuser or in a pot of simmering water, and they're perfect for blending into creams, adding to an herbal bath, or putting in body oils. When a recipe calls for any of the carrier oils, you can use one of your infused blends to add another dimension to your craft.

Infused oils will keep for three or four months in the refrigerator. Give them a sniff before using them; if they smell funky (or have visible mold on them) they've gone rancid. Make another batch.

Your best bets for carrier oils are:

· Jojoba, which is *excellent* for your skin and hair. This is my favorite for creams and body oils that get used all over the body, and it has an added benefit: It doesn't go rancid. Actually, although this is often called jojoba oil, it's not oil at all. It's the stuff that comes out of the jojoba plant, so even though it *looks* like an oil, it's really just jojoba. Because it's oil-free, it's great for people with oily skin or acne.

· Grapeseed, which has a very light texture and is pretty cheap.

· Avocado, which is also a good moisturizer, but a little thick.

· Sweet almond oil, which is perfect for massage oil—although some people are allergic to it, so be cautious—especially if you're allergic to almonds or other nuts.

· Olive oil—believe it or not—is really good for your skin, and it's a good choice for healing salves. However, you might *smell* like olive oil, so . . . don't use it for love spells!

MAKING YOUR OWN BLENDS

Smell each oil by itself first. Notice what your reaction is. Is it soothing or invigorating? Put one drop of each essential oil into a clean bottle, roll

Some of the recipes here require a double boiler. You don't need to go buy one, although they're pretty cheap, and you can find them in any store that sells pots and pans. In the meantime, make your own by finding a bowl that fits into a saucepan or two saucepans that fit together (the top one has to be smaller than the bottom one). You could also float an empty coffee can in a pot of boiling water; be sure to use a pot holder or oven mitt when you take the can out because it'll be really hot!

the bottle between your hands to mix them, and give it a sniff. To make essential oil blends to burn on charcoal, simply use the recipes or create your own and don't add a carrier.

At the very least, you can infuse one herb in oil and use that to make an anointing oil, or you can steep one herb in a bath for magical work. You can use a single herb as incense or potpourri, or you can mix three together.

A BLUEPRINT FOR SPELL CASTING

There are as many different ways to cast a spell as there are Witches and reasons for doing them, and you'll get better results from a spell you create yourself, always! I included spells of my own here so you can get familiar with the techniques, and if you look through each one carefully, you'll find several different methods for charging, invoking, channeling energy, and releasing it. Take the methods, apply them to whatever you personally enjoy and relate to, and you'll have a lot of fun getting what you need.

Notice I said "need." If you really play with this, you'll find that spells work pretty often, but the *way* they work isn't always what you *wanted*. If you cast a spell for love, you may get a kitten (my friend Johnathan has had this very experience). No, the

"The actual act of performing a spell is only a part of the spell craft process. Magick begins with defining your desire. If you'd like to cast a spell, you will want to specifically state your need. Once you've determined your goal, get more in depth. Are you looking to create, increase, or banish?"

—GWINEVERE, AGE 16

Universe isn't telling you that inter-species dating is the way for you. Maybe the message is that you need to find out a little more about what love *is,* so here's a friend with whom to learn. See?

In general, there are several tech-niques I like to work with: ritual spell casting; oils and creams; tonics and potions; and talismans, charms, or

> Keep in mind that esoteric symbols are cool and mysterious, but if you don't relate to them or understand their meaning, they won't work for you! Modern sym-bols, like hearts for love and peace signs, are just as magickal as ancient ones if they make you respond with emotion.

amulets. Ritual spell casting is great, but making all the other stuff is spell casting, too—if you do it with that intent.

Another part of good spell craft is choosing your props and your time wisely. If everything works together, you'll get much better results because the energies will fuse in a big powerful hunk of mind-opening symbolism that reinforces your intention. If your intention corresponds with the Moon phase, the Sun's position, the colors/stones/symbols you work with, and the objects or recipes you make—well, you've got yourself some mighty mojo.

Speaking of astrological corre-spondences . . . you can make your-self nuts trying to figure out all the astrological intricacies. Your inten-tion is always more important than any correspondences, so don't worry if the Moon is technically five minutes past full. Check the Appen-dices for other correspondences, such as colors, stones, deities, and alternative ingredients to the ones used in the recipes.

Work on one type of spell at a time, preferably one in a month.

> "While casting a spell, you might be asked to visualize. Visualization is the mental projection of a specific goal or result. When visualizing during a spell, it's best to convey the end result. For example, if I were doing a money spell, I'd visualize myself counting a bundle of money or depositing a check. Try not to visualize the process of how you'll obtain your goal because mapping it out could impede the progress or restrict the spell. Each spell will manifest in its own place and time."
>
> —GWINEVERE, AGE 16

That way, you'll be able to concentrate fully on one particular need at a time and not get jumbled. I also think it's good to work a banishing/cleansing before each spell, to get rid of anything that opposes your goal. Then, when you're ready to work on the invoking part, you should phrase your intention in positive terms. Instead of saying, "I desire not to fight with my parents anymore," you would say, "I desire a peaceful relationship with my parents." You can also state your intention as though your goal is already reached, like: "My parents and I have a peaceful relationship."

WRITING AND USING INCANTATIONS

To write your own incantations, keep it short and sweet (two, four, or six lines), and make them rhyme. To write invoking incantations, be sure to use only positive phrases, like "I will," "I am," and so on. Here's an example:

"All the powers are in place,
  Here inside my sacred space
  I will win my victory,
  By the power of three times three."

For banishing incantations, use negative words to pull the energy away from you, such as "Never will it," "nothing remains," and the like. Here's an example of a banishing invocation:

"Nothing can withstand this mix,
  The power of Nothing is what I fix.
  Back to the vortex and nothing remains,
  I banish back into the Spiral all bane!"

You don't have to be a great poet; don't be intimidated! Do be sure and mention each herb, symbol, or other ingredient that you're using in the spell. You're calling on their power, after all. Recite incantations while stirring potions or making incense, to shift your consciousness for meditation, or to raise energy during a spell.

SEAT-OF-YOUR-PANTS SUBSTITUTIONS

There will be times when you want to use the energy of certain Elements but don't have them readily available, and if your parents absolutely won't budge on the "no incense and candles" rule, you may feel as if your spell craft is lacking Elemental luster. Never fear! You can *always* substitute and be creative in finding a solution.

To invoke Fire without any Fire:

· Charge a quartz point, tiger's eye, obsidian, or garnet by letting it hang out in the Sun for a while. Use this whenever you need Fire, and recharge it occasionally.

· Use a small hand mirror or other reflective surface to shine light on whatever you're blessing/charging/consecrating. You can use the Sun as your light source, or even a lamp or flashlight.

· Incorporate Fire colors into whatever you're doing.

· Use Fire herbs to get that kick of heat. Ginger, cinnamon, pepper, wasabi, hot sauce, chilis . . . they're all fiery.

To invoke Air without burning incense:

· Use your breath. Blow gently on your items to bless them with Air or use concentrated breathing to summon Air.

· Go take advantage of the breeze outside!

· Create a breeze by spinning or twirling a cord with a crystal or key tied to the end.

· Sing! Singing is a powerful combination of your sacred breath, forceful intention, and sound waves—all readily available from your voice box.

HEALING SPELLS

Moon Phase: from new Moon to full Moon

Moon or Sun in: Virgo, Taurus, Capricorn

Sun amulet: *Use an image of the Sun and charge it with Solar energy while the Sun is high (noon), preferably when it is in Virgo, Taurus, or Capricorn.*

Earth talisman: *Since your body is an expression of Earth's energy, using a symbol for Earth is appropriate to charge yourself up, and trees are great energy amplifiers. Scratching the image with a twig into a clay talisman would be nice.*

REV-UP-YOUR-HEALTH SPELL

This spell is for getting rid of the blahs. Use it when you feel a little under the weather or as an occasional routine cleansing. If you're really sick, go to the doctor! Hello! This one's a two-part spell: First, you *banish* any energy zappers, and then you *charge* yourself with healing. Start this one while the Moon is waning or new, and continue to work it until the Moon is full again. Hey, even Witchcraft takes time! I included healing spells first, since you should always be in good health before doing any other kind of Witchcraft. If your body is run-down, you won't have the energy to put into spells or anything else.

INTENTION

Giving health to your body

TOOLS

Green votive candle.

White votive candle.

Black votive candle.

Bowl of salt.

Chalice filled with water.

Dish filled with dirt.

Charcoal tablets.

Frankincense and/or sage.

Cranberry juice, or Monkey Sweat (see page 145 for recipe) either in the bottle or in a cup.

Bread.

> What's the difference between talismans, charms, and amulets? *Talismans* are magickal objects used to draw something to you (like a necklace with symbols that express your need), *charms* are everyday objects (like lip gloss or a ring), on which you cast a temporary spell to put up a glamour (for invisibility or to attract a love, for example), and *amulets* are often natural objects (like herbs or a leaf from your favorite tree) used to protect you.

ALTAR LAYOUT

GO FOR IT

Cast your Circle, using whatever method you like best. State your intention out loud very clearly. For this spell, your statement might be: "I cast this spell to cleanse my body of anything harmful and to boost my health."

Add some more frankincense and sage to your charcoal—those suckers will burn for a good half hour or more, so you've got plenty of time. *Smudge* yourself thoroughly, imagining the smoke lifting any illness from you, dispersing it into harmless smoke. If any particular spot is bothering you, stay there awhile and concentrate on it.

Light the black candle, hold it a few inches from your breastbone, and imagine the flame burning away any unhealthy energy. Put it back on the altar. Meditate on the flame. Now, collect any unpleasant emotions, physical pain, or stress by concentrating on moving your energy through your blood around your body as if it were a bright light chasing away your gloom. Move your energy and any psychic gunk you collected into your dominant hand. Wrap your hand around the black candle and transfer your vexation into the wax. Let it go. Imagine the flame burning it away. Let it burn out completely—that's why I chose votives for this one! The black candle will continue to burn for several hours, so don't leave it unattended. Put on some music and relax while the candle does its work.

Drink the water in your chalice. Feel it working down your throat, into your stomach, into your cells. The water will cleanse you, too. Fill the chalice with cranberry juice, Monkey Sweat, or whatever you're using for a tonic.

Now that you've gotten rid of your funk, you can raise a little positive energy with which to recharge. Do what you do when you do that voodoo! Raise the energy however you like, and remember to *pull* energy from the Earth. When you've got some going, grab the chalice and hold your dominant hand over it. Move your hand clockwise over the chalice, repeating your intention or an incantation over it until you feel that it's charged. Put it down, and do the same thing with your bread and your green candle, filling them with energy. Plop yourself down, and eat, drink, and be healthy!

Light the white candle. Imagine that it casts white light around you, a protective shield. As soon as you sense that shield come up, snuff the candle. Any time you feel the need for that shield, light it again.

Release your Circle and you're ready to go. Bury the black candle stub. For the next few days—as long as the Moon is waxing—light your white and green candles for a few minutes each day, strengthening your shield. Keep drinking cranberry juice, too. It helps cleanse your system and keep it clean. You'll see that immediately when you have to pee every twenty minutes!

DETOXIFYING BATH

Charge this up during the ritual, and soak in if afterward. Use this for three days after you do the healing spell, or whenever you need it. Keep it in a jar or small box with a tight lid. Makes enough for 4 baths.

1 cup sea salt, Epsom salts, or a mix of half and half
2 drops frankincense oil
3 drops tea-tree oil
2 drops bergamot oil

Add the oils to the salt, and mix thoroughly with a fork. Keep this in a jar with a tight lid, out of direct sunlight.
    Or

¼ cup sea salt or Epsom salts
5 tablespoons dried sage
5 tablespoons dried rosemary

Bundle the herbs into a clean piece of cloth. Hang the bundle on the water spout as you run a hot bath, and stir the salts in right before you bathe. Makes enough for 1 bath.

MONKEY SWEAT

(Based on a recipe from Joyce)
I call this Monkey Sweat because that's what it tastes like. It really works, though! Don't kiss anyone after you drink it.

6 ounces tomato juice or V8 (fill the glass but leave about 2 inches at
    the top)
½ teaspoon black pepper
3 dashes tobasco sauce (more if you can stand it)
Juice of 1 lemon
1 clove garlic, smashed or pressed in garlic press

1 tablespoon apple cider vinegar or white vinegar
1 teaspoon horseradish
Small pinch salt (omit if using V8)

This recipe makes 8 ounces but you can make a bottle of it and keep it for a few days in the refrigerator—a good idea, since this mix will help you fight off infection, especially a cold. Change the measurements by figuring out how many glasses will fit in your bottle and adjust the amounts. For example, if you want to make a 32-ounce bottle of tonic, multiply all the measurements by 4.

Mix all the ingredients together, and as you stir—counterclockwise first, then clockwise—recite a little incantation.

When you make a magickal oil, there are several points on your body you should anoint to get the most energy out of the ingredients. These are your pulse points—the places where your heartbeat is most noticeable—and the chakras, as well as a few others for good measure.

Start at the topmost point and work down for banishing oils, and reverse the order to charge yourself.

- Between your eyebrows
- At each temple
- Behind each ear
- At the base of your throat
- On the back of your neck
- Inside each wrist
- Inside each elbow
- On your breastbone
- At the base of your spine
- Below your belly button
- On both sides of your groin (where your thigh meets your hip)
- Behind each knee
- Behind each ankle
- On the soles of your feet

PIMPLE BANISHER

This can help mild acne; anything more severe probably needs antibiotics, so go to the doc.

1 cup water, boiled and cooled slightly
5 drops lavender, tea-tree, or sweet orange oil

Pour the water into a small bowl that isn't made of metal (your mini-cauldron from the Devotional Month would be great). Stir in the essential oils and put your face over the bowl to steam your skin. When the water has cooled to just warm, splash the mixture onto your skin, avoiding your eyes, or use a cotton ball to dab it on.

PIMPLE BANISHER ALTERNATIVE

You can also wash your face with rosewater, or make an infusion of lavender or rosemary in water (1 ounce of fresh herbs or ½ ounce dried herbs to 1 cup of water). Boil the water first, and add it to the herbs in a glass jar. If you use distilled water (from the grocery store), you can make a double or triple batch of this to keep on hand. Just be sure that you use a cotton ball to apply it, or pour some into a bowl. If you stick your fingers in this, you'll get germies in the mix.

ZIT-BE-GONE TONER

After you wash your face, try this simple toner.

1 cup water, boiled
1 teaspoon apple cider vinegar or freshly squeezed lemon juice (don't use lemon juice if you have sensitive skin)

Mix together and cool the water to lukewarm. Dab on with a cotton ball.

CHAKRA-CHARGING SPELL

If you're having a little trouble with one of your chakras, or you want to boost the energy in a certain spot, try a simple meditation with light to recharge yourself.

Pick a crystal that you'll use only for healing. It doesn't have to be expensive or big. Quartz points are the best choice for this, since they conduct energy and light very cleanly, and you can buy them for a few bucks, tops. Other good choices are obsidian, hematite, or citrine (yellow- or orange-colored quartz). Cleanse it well before the first use, and use it *only* for healing. Leave it in a window that gets bright sunlight.

When you feel down (physically *or* emotionally), take it from the windowsill and hold it over whatever spot is bothering you. If you're using a quartz point, go out into the sunlight and catch the rays in the crystal. Point the light onto your body. If you're using obsidian or hematite, *pull* the funk out with the stone during a meditation, and leave the crystal in the Sun to cleanse itself.

SIMPLE CLEANSING

Gather some fresh or dried herbs, like sage, cinnamon, pepper, or whatever you have on hand for cleansing (check the Appendices for suggestions). Measure several cups of water into a pot on the stove. For every cup of water you use, add one tablespoon of dried herb or two tablespoons of fresh. Heat the mixture over medium-high heat and watch the water come to a boil. As you're meditating on the water, think of what you want to get rid of (sadness, illness, anger, whatever). Hold your hands over the pot, and feel the warm steam come up to cleanse you. Move your energy around your body, imagining it cleansing you. Gather into your solar plexus (below your breastbone) whatever feelings you want to rid yourself of. Breathe the vapors in deeply. As you get ready to exhale, pull the negative emotions out of your solar plexus, up through your throat chakra, into your mouth, and spit into the pot. Gross, but effective. Do this more than once if you need to.

Let the water boil away.

SUCCESS SPELLS

Moon Phase: waxing to full

Moon or Sun in: Sagittarius, Leo, Aries

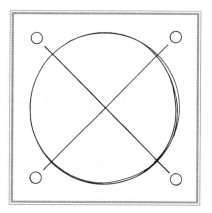

Seal of Jupiter: *According to Henry Cornelius Agrippa, this is Jupiter's seal—a powerful talisman to overcome difficulties.*

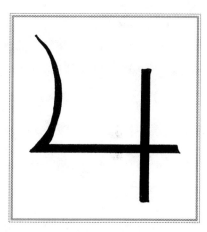

Jupiter's Astrological symbol.

UNSTOPPABLE SPELL

You've got to really need whatever you're doing this Unstoppable Spell for. My gram always said, "Be careful what you wish for—you just might get it!" Definitely check your divination tool before doing this one, and see if you're flowing with the Tao. This is a triple-whammy spell that includes just about every kind of magick. It'll take a lot of energy and a little bit of time.

INTENTION

To get what you want

TOOLS

Purple or gold taper candle. Carve this with runes for success, invincibility, etc., and anoint it with Secret-of-Success Oil (page 153). You'll burn it to release your will.

Paper and pen, ink, or paint (purple, gold, or black). You'll write your incantation on this, wear it on your body or in your pocket for nine days, and then bury it or put it in a stream or lake to release your will.

Dish filled with dirt. This time, you'll use your pentacle to capture positive energy and visualize your goal manifesting in it.

2 pieces of muslin, each about 2 square inches. Make a small pouch to carry . . .

One or more crystals or stones. Charge these with your intentions, and wear them in the pouch.

Purple and/or gold thread. To sew the pouch up, of course!

Needle. What do you think?

Purple cord or string (3). You'll braid these together, knot it to bind your goal to you, and wear it on your wrist. Or you can use this to hang your pouch around your neck.

Bean sprout or alfalfa seeds. You have to leave the Gods, the Universe, and the Elements some kind of thank-you, and growing a little plant is *very* nice . . . plus, you can charge the seeds. Save three to wear in your pouch.

A pot and some soil. Use these to plant your seeds in if you don't have access to the woods or if the ground is frozen.

Wand, if you use one.

ALTAR LAYOUT

Put the altar in the center of your room.

GO FOR IT

Cast a Circle however you can. This time, after you call all the Elements and deities (if any), go back around the Quarters with your wand and give the Elements a little instruction. Like this:

"Element of Earth, you are my bones and body. I truly need [your goal], with all of my being. I ask you to please let my desire take root and flourish quickly.

"Element of Air, you are my breath. I truly need [your goal] with all of my being. I ask you to please bring the winds of change to deliver my need swiftly.

"Element of Water, you are my blood. I truly need [your goal] with all of my being. I ask you to carry this to me like a quick and gentle rain.

"Element of Fire, you are the spark of my soul. I truly need [your goal] with all of my being. I ask you to burn fierce and bright to guide my desire to me."

Carve the candle with whichever runes you choose. Anoint it with Secret-of-Success Oil (page 153), plain olive oil, or your own blend. Anoint yourself. Anoint your fabric, cords, and your paper. Anoint anything that doesn't run away.

Draw a pentacle in the dirt, either with your wand or index finger of your dominant hand. Trace it three times. As you do this, say clearly: "The ancient power of the five-point star will materialize what I invoke. By the power of three, it comes to me."

Start moving around the Circle slowly, wand in hand, chanting something powerful. Start soft and slow.

When you feel the energy around you is powerful enough, lift the wand and imagine it filled with power. Pass it clockwise over your entire altar setup, still chanting. Aim the energy into each object.

Now, sew your pouch together. With each stitch, imagine your goal coming closer to you. You don't have to be a great seamstress; a simple over and under stitch is fine. Just place them very close together, so your stuff won't fall out. Put all the stuff in the pouch. Put the pouch in your pocket or hold it in your receptive hand.

Raise the power again. When the power is raised, put it into the dirt. Stick your wand or index finger into the center, and plant your seeds in the ground or the pot.

Raise the power again. Last time, I promise. This time, hold your pen in your dominant hand, and use it as an athame, directing all your energy into your words on paper. Write your intent very clearly on the paper. Fold it into three sections, like a letter.

Light the candle. As you light it, hold an image of what your life will be like when you get what you want. Drip a little of the wax onto the back of the paper. Say: "My will is sealed. It is done."

Meditate on the candle flame for a few moments. Ground your energy by sending it into the candle to release the power. Release your Circle, and go take a nap! You must be exhausted. . . .

One more thing: Burn the candle a few minutes every night for nine nights. Visualize yourself as successful in your intent. As soon as you get distracted or lose the image, snuff the candle. On the ninth night, burn the paper (if you can; if not, tear it into shreds and bury it). Bury the pouch and candle stub. Leave the alfalfa or bean sprouts outside as an offering. If you don't hear any news about your objective by the end of the ninth night, stop. There's a reason why you're not getting what you asked for. Consult your divination tool or ask for some guidance.

QUICK VICTORY

Get a fresh bay or lemon leaf. Mix Secret-of-Success Oil (below) or plain olive oil with a little dirt. Dip your index finger (dominant hand) into the oil and trace a rune for victory on the leaf or another symbol that works for you. Carry it with you until you feel that your energy has built enough power, and then bury it or float it down a river.

SECRET-OF-SUCCESS OIL

When you do a success spell, chances are good that you'll get what you *need* out of a situation, and that's not always what you *want,* so before you go casting, be sure you're groovy with all! Use this oil to anoint candles, pouches, and yourself.

10 drops bergamot oil
3 drops patchouli oil
½ ounce olive oil
½ cinnamon stick, crushed, or ½ teaspoon powdered cinnamon

Mix the essentials in the bottle first. Simmer water in the double boiler's bottom pot. Pour the olive oil into the top pot and add the cinnamon. Heat for one minute. Take the olive oil and cinnamon off the heat, let it cool slightly, and pour it into the bottle with the essential oils.

SECRET-OF-SUCCESS-OIL VARIATION

3 sprigs rosemary
½ cup mint leaves
3 cinnamon stick sticks, or 1½ teaspoons powdered cinnamon
9 cloves, slightly bruised
1 cup olive oil

Dry the herbs for a day or two by spreading them out on a clean towel in a dry place that gets a little Sun. Then put the dried herbs, cinnamon, and cloves into a jar, pour the oil over them, and cap tightly. Let them infuse for at least a week or two. Done!

CONCENTRATION OIL

Use this when you need to keep your mind focused. This is great for tests, job interviews, public speaking, or any other situation when you need a little mental energy.

5–15 drops bergamot oil, lavender oil, peppermint oil, or a combination
1 ounce grapeseed, jojoba, or olive oil

Make this during the day, noon or dawn would be best. Put the essential oils in the bottle first, and then add the carrier oil. Go outside, hold the bottle up to catch the Sun's rays, and draw down the energy into the bottle. Roll it between your palms to mix. As you roll the bottle in your hands, focus your mind completely on the oil. Send that intense concentration into the mixture, and each time you wear it, remember how easy it was to keep your mind focused.

You can try an infusion of rosemary, lavender, or mint in oil, too.

PROSPERITY SPELLS

Moon Phase: new to full *or* full to new (you'll see why)

Sun or Moon in: Cancer, Scorpio, Pisces, Virgo, Capricorn, Taurus

ABUNDANT BLESSINGS SPELL

Do this when you can wait a little while for the money to come. A waxing moon in Cancer is the best time for this, but waxing moon in any of the above signs will do the trick!

INTENTION

To plant the seeds of prosperity

TOOLS

Alfalfa seeds. You'll charge these with prosperity, let your spell take root, and harvest abundant blessings. (You can use any seeds you have lying around, in a pinch!)

A green candle. Charge this with your energy and burn it to release the vibes.

Dish filled with dirt. Pentacles drawn in dirt draw and concentrate energy, and they're also good in money spells.

Prosperity Oil (page 158) and/or Prosperity Incense (page 159). Charge it, burn it, wear it, get stuff!

Three coins. You'll charge them, plant one, keep one, and toss one. We're bending the no-metal-except-athame rule here, but that's okay. You'll use the coins to direct energy.

An amulet. Make this out of clay or use a pouch to draw abundance to you.

Wand, if you use one.

ALTAR LAYOUT

Put everything in the center of the floor or put your altar table in the center of the room. You're going to dance like mad and take it outside! Or you can just *do* this outside.

GO FOR IT

Cast a Circle and invoke Earth in particular. Hold the candle in your dominant hand and the coins in your receptive hand. State your intention clearly, and be very specific about *how* you want prosperity to manifest. Talk about the kind of job you want (be reasonable), and go into as much detail as you possibly can. Decide when you want the job, too. Carve runes or words into the candle that describe your goal. Anoint the candle with Prosperity Oil. Put the incense in the middle of your pentacle and light it. Pass the candle through the smoke, and ask the Universe or deities to please hear your request. Light the candle.

Raise the energy with movement and whatever other methods you use. When you feel the peak, hold the seeds in your dominant hand and raise them above your head as an offering. Plant them. Plant one coin somewhere near the alfalfa. When you ground the energy, do it by directing the energy through your wand, or hands, directly over the planted seeds. Move your wand, or hands, in clockwise circles over the seeds while you concentrate the energy.

Anoint the amulet (or make it in the Circle and then anoint it) with oil, and wear it someplace out of sight until you get what you need. A pouch anointed with Prosperity Oil (page 158) and filled with Prosperity Incense (page 159) and a coin is a good one, or you can make the amulet out of clay. Make a small square for Earth energy, and push a coin into it. Dimes would work best for this, since they're thin. Cover it with another square of clay, and pinch the two squares together lightly. Use green, gold, or silver paint to draw symbols on it.

Release the Circle and throw the other coin as far as you can. Let your intention fly with it, and let go of the need. It'll come back to you! Light the green candle every night while you envision your goal, and snuff it as soon as you lose the image. Replace the candle when it runs out, if you don't see a surge of abundance happening. If you can't light it, just meditate on it. Harvest a little of the alfalfa when it sprouts, and leave the rest as an offering. Switch to the Poverty Rots Spell during the waning moon.

POVERTY ROTS SPELL

This is a tad yucky. Oh, well. Do this when the moon is waning. It's a prosperity spell, but it works by banishing poverty. Notice that I spun the spell's purpose to fit with the moon's phase.

INTENTION

To banish poverty

TOOLS

An apple. Slice this across the middle (horizontally) so you can see the star in it.

Back-to-the-Vortex Incense (page 170) or another banishing blend.

A black candle. Inscribe this with "banishing," "diminishing," etc. Anoint it with banishing oil or frankincense oil.

Charcoal tablets.

Dish filled with dirt.

ALTAR LAYOUT

Do this one outside, if you can. Make the altar away from any trees. You don't want to bother them with a bunch of negative vibes. Set the apple on the ground and put the black candle in front of it. With a banishing oil (Protection Oil, page 171, can double as a banishing blend, or create your own recipe using the Appendices. I have faith in you!) trace a pentacle on a rock, and put your charcoal on that or on a pentacle drawn in a dish filled with dirt.

GO FOR IT

Cast a Circle, and invoke Earth in particular. Light the incense and the candle. This time, when you raise energy, you have to imagine that you're collecting your poverty into the Circle. Then scrunch it into a ball and put it into the Earth. Imagine the incense and candle flame burning any remnants away.

Leave the apple out there, and let it rot. As the worms, bugs, and Earth take the apple away, your poverty is banished.

QUICK-AND-DIRTY PROSPERITY SPELL

If you're really in a bind for some quick cash, take a dollar bill, anoint it with Prosperity Oil, and carry it around with you for a day, rubbing it occasionally. Don't spend it! Every time you rub the dollar, ask the Universe for a little prosperity. Throw the dollar to the wind at the end of the day, preferably in a public place where someone else can pick it up. What goes around comes around!

DRUM UP A LITTLE CASH

Put some cinnamon in a bowl with as many coins and dollar bills as you can muster. Each time you pass the bowl, shake it or bang it gently with your wand or something else to generate a noise, and try to put a penny in it.

Keep an eye out for a sudden opportunity to make a few quick bucks, like baby-sitting a neighbor's kid or shoveling a driveway. It's not a career, but you just might get what you need!

PROSPERITY OIL

1 ounce olive oil
½ cinnamon stick
5 drops bergamot oil
5 drops patchouli oil

Mix all ingredients together in a clean bottle. Remove the cinnamon stick after 6 weeks.

PROSPERITY OIL VARIATION

1 teaspoon powdered cinnamon
1 teaspoon powdered ginger
Several cloves, crushed
½ ounce olive oil

Pound the spices together, and stir while concentrating on prosperity. Put the herbs in a clean bottle and cover with the oil. Let it steep. Alternatively, you can use straight-up basil.

PROSPERITY INCENSE

3 cinnamon sticks, powdered, or about 3 teaspoons of store-bought
*   powdered cinnamon*
3 drops patchouli oil
5 drops bergamot oil

Pound the cinnamon sticks into a powder. Add the oils, and mix well with a fork. Keep this in a jar with a tight lid, and mix often.
    Or

Cinnamon
Ground ginger
Cloves

Use equal amounts of each herb. Pound them together.

LOVE SPELLS

Moon Phase: waxing to full

Sun or Moon in: Taurus, Scorpio,
    Pisces, Cancer

COME-TO-ME LOVE SPELL

The best way to cast a love spell is to cast it on *you*, called putting up a glamour. By charging yourself with love, you will draw love to you. Besides, you don't want to manipulate anyone. In fact, if you have a target in mind at all, wait until you can be neutral about it before you cast any love spells. The thing is,

Venus: *This is the astrological symbol for the planet Venus, which influences love. Make this talisman when Venus is in Pisces, Scorpio, Cancer, or Taurus.*

Ankh: *This is the Egyptian symbol for the life force and sexual energy.*

you may not *say* you're trying to catch this particular person, but somewhere in your deepest heart, your *intention* will be to turn that person's head.

INTENTION

To call a lover. (I'm using the word *lover* in its true sense—someone who loves you. It's not all about sex.)

TOOLS

2 red or pink candles. One represents you, and the other your lover.

White candle. This represents the purity of your desire.

6 pieces of rose quartz, clear quartz, moonstone, or other stones. Charge 'em up!

Claddagh: *The claddagh is an Irish symbol for love, loyalty, and friendship.*

Sankofa: *An Adinkra symbol for undoing mistakes, this symbol is useful when you've had an argument or otherwise made an error that hurt a relationship.*

Essence-of-Love Oil or another blend. Charge it, wear it, and anoint your candles with it.

Wand, if you're using one.

ALTAR LAYOUT

GO FOR IT

Cast your Circle. You can call on a specific Element according to what kind of love you're looking for. To do this, place objects that relate to that Element inside your main Circle (red candles for Fire, glasses filled with Water, plants or dirt for Earth, feathers for Air). After you call the Quarters, simply ask the one Element you want to work to be your guide and help. Call Fire for passionate love, Water for a deep emotional love, Earth for a friend and companion, and Air for an intellectually stimulating relationship. Heck, call all four, if you want! The more specific you are, the better it'll turn out for you. If you find yourself thinking about a specific person during the spell, STOP, drop, and roll. That is, stop doing the spell, drop the energy, roll it into a ball, and ground it. Wait until you can control your intention before you try the spell again.

Carve the white candle with symbols for "pure," "male or female," and "unity." Carve the candle representing you with symbols for "magick," "love," and so on. Carve the other with symbols for male or female, love, and so on. Place the white candle in the center, with the other two on either side.

Raise the energy. Direct it into the candles, oil, and stones by passing your wand or dominant hand over them as you chant:

"Lover, you must come to me,
   If in truth a lover you be.
   Harming none, for good of all—
   Feel my need and hear my call.
   Let your heart beat as does mine
   So we may our hearts entwine."

Anoint yourself and all the candles. Light the white candle. Let the white light remind you that your heart is pure. Using the white candle, light the candle that represents you. Move these to one side of the altar. Use the white candle to light the other one that represents your lover. Place this in the center of your altar.

Set five of the stones around your lover's candle, in the shape of a pentacle (you'll have one stone left. Hold it in your receptive hand). Draw a pentacle by moving from stone to stone with your wand or index finger. This is to draw your lover's attention to your call.

LOLLIE'S LOVE BUTTER

If you pick only one recipe to try, make it this one! This stuff is awesome! Here's how it works: First of all, it opens your heart and makes you receptive to love—all of the ingredients stimulate your psyche and make you feel euphoric. The anise will actually make your skin feel warm because it stimulates blood flow to your skin—which gives you a rosy glow, which signals to other people that you're looking for love. Second, you'll smell like a gourmet chocolate bar, and chocolate is an aphrodisiac. Last, but not least, it's great for your skin! Don't use this on your face, but use it everywhere else. . . .

Before you mix the ingredients, make sure that the jar, lid, double boiler, and beaters are really clean and bone dry. Even the tiniest bit of water will make this separate. For the same reason, when you pull this off the double boiler, do it quickly and take the top away from the steam! Store the butter in a warm, dry, dark place. If it gets too cold, it'll get waxy—which is fine, it still works. Alternatively, you can nix the beeswax and make this a body oil.

1 ounce cocoa butter
1 ounce jojoba oil
shaved bits of amber resin
1½ teaspoons beeswax
2 drops anise oil—ONLY TWO! More will make your skin burn!
5–10 drops sweet orange oil

Put the cocoa butter and jojoba oil in the top of your double boiler. Heat the water until it's just simmering. Take the amber and shave little bits off it with a knife—carefully! Let them dissolve completely, stirring constantly. Add the beeswax, stir, and let it dissolve.

Swirl the pan clockwise, and imagine a warm, golden glow around it—not hard, since the oil is a beautiful golden color. Take the mixture off the heat, stir it clockwise with a whisk or your wand and recite an incantation over it. Here's a sample to get you going:

> "As below, it is above—
>   As I stir this, I bring love.
>   Orange sweet, anise to warm
>   No one will be hurt or harmed.
>   As my own love gleams and glows,
>   So my lover's heart will show.
>   When he [she] sees my hand and shoulder,
>   His [her] sweet love will kindle, smolder."

Add the oils in the order I've listed in the ingredients. Beat this with a hand mixer until it's cool, thick, and creamy. Scoop it into a nice jar with a wide opening so you can get in there and scoop it out! When it cools, you'll have a fabulous body butter that will help you draw a warm, gentle, happy love!

ESSENCE-OF-LOVE OIL (UNISEX)

This is good for guys or girls. It's really simple to make; it's great for attracting a passionate love; and it looks exactly like fresh blood. Weird visual bonus!

½ teaspoon chunks of dragon's blood resin, pounded[2]
1 ounce jojoba or grapeseed oil
5 drops patchouli oil
10 drops frankincense oil
½ vanilla bean, sliced down the middle
3 peppercorns; bruised (optional)

Put the dragon's blood in the top of your double boiler, and heat it over direct heat. Hold the pot an inch away from the flame, and move it away if you hear sizzling or see the resin bubbling away. It'll get gummy and—well—bloody looking. When it's fairly soft, add the jojoba or grapeseed oil. Cook this for a few seconds, stirring constantly. Put the mixture on the double boiler, with the water boiling rapidly. Stir constantly. The dragon's blood won't dissolve completely—there'll still be some solids in the bottom.

Pour the oil into a nice clear bottle, and add the patchouli, frankincense, and vanilla bean. For something a little "spicier," lightly bruise 3 peppercorns and add those to the bottle.

ESSENCE-OF-LOVE OIL VARIATIONS (SUPER SIMPLE)

Add rose petals, a cinnamon stick or ½ teaspoon powdered cinnamon, two drops of vanilla extract or a vanilla bean, and a few bruised peppercorns to a bottle with vegetable oil (not olive).

APHRODITE'S ELIXIR

This is a romantic little cocktail to share with someone you're already dating to strengthen your bond. Ask your lovey before giving him/her this little love potion. It's not a passion potion, so don't worry that you'll break your vows of chastity. This is a heart-warming potion, and it would be extra nice served with homemade cookies on Valentine's Day. Okay, so it's not a Wiccan holiday, technically speaking.

If you're looking for a warm love companion, mix this during full Moon, drink it yourself, and do a ritual love spell.

*2 cups plain or vanilla rice milk (if you hate rice milk, regular milk will
    do, but don't burn it!)*
2 tablespoons honey
*½ teaspoon freshly ground cinnamon stick—you can do this in a coffee
    grinder, or use 1 teaspoon of store-bought powdered cinnamon—
    or whole stick (see below)*
1 vanilla bean
2 tablespoons rosewater
A wee sprinkle of freshly grated nutmeg

Heat the rice milk over low heat. Add the honey and let it dissolve. If
you're using a whole cinnamon stick, add that now, too (doesn't work
quite as well, unless you make this in advance and let it hang out in the
fridge for a few days). Slice the vanilla bean down the middle, and scrape
out all the gooey black stuff. Put the gooey stuff in, and then add the bean,
too. Add the rosewater. Heat all this for just a few moments, stirring constantly. Pour into glasses, and grate the fresh nutmeg over each glass—
only one little sprinkle, since more will give you a wretched headache and
a rotten stomach. Trust me, I tried this a few ways.

This tastes better cold, but it works better warm. Go figure.

HOT-DATE SPELL

You need a date for the prom, for a party, or just for fun. First of all, be
nice and flirt! That's the best way to get a date. Use your witchy ways—
responsibly, of course. Anoint yourself with Essence-of-Love Oil or another
blend. My friend Ronnie used to wear straight-up vanilla extract, and she
always has a hot date, so give it a go if you can't get your hands on other
Essence-of-Love Oil ingredients! Wear red or pink clothing (not you, boys
. . . go for red or black) that you've charmed. You can also charm a pair of
earrings, a necklace, or makeup. Lip gloss works especially well, and body
glitter would be groovy, too. Go easy on the makeup and glitter, though.
Subtlety is very sexy.

Guys, you can charm a necklace or bracelet, or take three pieces of
red and black or gray and black cord, braid a glamour into them and wear

that around your neck or wrist. Or, you can put on some chapstick that you've charmed, or charm a box of mints. Sweet breath is always a good thing.

To set up a glamour, light some sweet-smelling incense if you can (vanilla, cinnamon, Nag Champa, rose, frankincense . . . whatever you like). Trace a clockwise spiral in the air. Pass the object through the smoke. Try this out:

"Glitter [red lip gloss, etc.] is sexy and so am I,
  Let this glamour charm the eye.
  Cute boy [girl], call me and don't be late.
  Bring to me a really fun date."

IRRESISTIBLE SPELL

Use Fire instead of incense to charge yourself with supersexy vibes. Pass a red or pink candle around your body, imagining a warm glow surrounding you. Move the candle in clockwise spirals to generate positive, glowing energy.

Make incense with Fire herbs—especially cinnamon and pepper, cut with a bit of amber to sweeten things up. Hold a favorite piece of clothing over the smoke as you recite your incantation. Put the clothes on. Create clockwise spirals with the incense as you dance and chant to draw glowing, Fiery energy to you.

You can also use Water to charge yourself with a soft and subtle glow. Draw a warm bath. Infuse the water with essential oils or herbs like patchouli, lavender, or anise. As the tub fills meditate for a moment, breathing in the scent of the oils or herbs. As you breathe, fill yourself with energy. Pull the energy down into your dominant hand, and plunge it into the water. Stir it in clockwise spirals, chanting your incantation. Step into the water, and bathe thoroughly. As you smooth the water over your body, imagine that you're smoothing a glowing light around you.

In either case, make yourself a charm with the herbs or oils that you used. Do this in a small bottle or pouch. Carry this around with you in a pocket or purse, and reapply as necessary.

CALL-ME SPELL

You have to give someone your number for them to call you, right? When you write down your digits, draw a little symbol on the paper, either with the pen or by tracing your finger quickly over it. Try something like "mysterious," to pique the person's interest.

Take three quartz points and tie each one to a yellow cord. Tie the cords together and hang them on a tree branch or nail outside. Take your athame or wand and lightly knock them together like wind chimes while you say, "Hello, [whoever]! Call me!"

I hate to tell you this, but if the person really doesn't want to call you, he or she won't. Sorry. It's a free-will thing.

PROTECTION SPELLS

Moon Phase: new, full, or waning

Sun or Moon in: Aries, Scorpio

Musuyidee *(mo-soo-yee-day): This is an Adinkra symbol for strength and spiritual balance.*

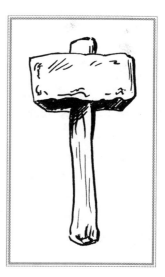

Thor's Hammer: *This is the Norse God Thor's weapon. Imagine his mighty power keeping watch over you.*

WHITE-LIGHT PROTECTION SPELL

Use this to charm a piece of jewelry, talisman, or stone that you can carry in your pocket. It needs to be recharged occasionally, as all charms do!

☀INTENTION

To charm an object with white light for protection

Eye of Horus: *An Egyptian symbol for protection, this is also called an Utchat. Draw it in an ascending triangle for added protection.*

☀TOOLS

An object to charm. Pentacles work very well, but you can use whatever you like.

White candle. Carve this with a rune or symbol for protection and/or light.

Athame or your index finger with a ring on it.

A dish filled with dirt, charcoal tablets and Protection Incense (page 170) and Protection Oil (page 171), or your own blend. Use these to charge and anoint your charm.

Salt. Use this to consecrate your charm with Earth.

Chalice and Water. Use these to consecrate your charm with . . . you guessed it.

ALTAR LAYOUT

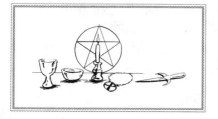

GO FOR IT

Cast a Circle. Anoint the candle with Protection Oil and light it. This is the source of your white light. As it burns, visualize white light radiating from it. Pull the white light in through your receptive hand, run it through your body, and gather it in your dominant hand. Draw a pentacle in the dirt. Light the charcoal tab from the candle and place it in the center of the pentacle. Throw some Protection Incense on the charcoal and smudge yourself.

Now, pass your charm through each of the Elements to consecrate and charge it. Start with the incense (Air), hold it over the flame (Fire), sprinkle it with Water (guess), and sprinkle it with salt (Earth). Hold it in both hands at your heart to infuse it with Spirit.

Put the charm in front of the candle. See the white light radiating from the candle. Hold the visualization and focus on the light. Take your athame or index finger, and catch the light on the metal. Concentrate on the light. As you hold the visualization, bring your athame or finger to the charm, and see the light surround it, soak into it, and be infused into the charm.

Wear this on your body. If you make a talisman yourself, measure the cord so it's long enough to wear at your breastbone.

QUICK TIPS

· Dispose of incense and candle stubs in a formal way, and never reuse a candle for another spell after you've consecrated it for a specific purpose.

· Always remember to pull energy from the Earth or the Elements and to run it through your body . . . it helps to keep you from spacing out.

· Be sure to ground and release any extra energy that's floating around after a ritual.

· For a quick psychic shield, simply lower your eyelids, put a vague smile on your face, and repeat the word *blank* in your mind or draw circles around your head with your dominant index finger to balance your thoughts and protect you.

BACK-TO-THE-VORTEX INCENSE

Make this at the new Moon, if you can wait, since the new Moon is best for banishing. This is enough for about two uses. It doesn't smell pretty, folks. That's the point! When you want to get rid of something—negativity, anger, fear, whatever—you want to dispel that energy, right? Well, could *you* withstand the stench of burning pepper? Speaking of which, don't inhale this directly, and don't get it in your eyes—OUCH!

6 cloves
6 chunks of frankincense, or 3 drops oil (or substitute sage)
1 cinnamon stick (break this into a few pieces before trying to pound it)
12 black peppercorns

Grind up all ingredients! Pound the heck out of them, and really put your energy into it. As you're pounding, recite an incantation over it. *Yell* an incantation over it, if you can. You want a strong, warriorlike energy in this. When the ingredients are relatively small—you'll have some chunks—stir it counterclockwise with your pestle (or spoon). As the ingredients go around and around, imagine that spiral as a vortex, where you will send any unfriendly energy as it burns.

PROTECTION INCENSE

12 chunks frankincense, or 6 drops oil
1 tablespoon dried sage
6 chunks dragon's blood

Crush, pound, and stir all ingredients together. Charm it with white light. Burn whenever you need a little help from your herbal friends.

Or, you can simply use any of the ingredients on their own. They all work!

PROTECTION OIL

Again, make this at the new Moon. This mix includes a few ingredients that you might find irritating—I know cinnamon bothers some people, and anise can burn, too. Go easy on it. If it's irritating, simply transfer it to a larger bottle, add a bit more oil,

> "Spell casting is a hard-earned skill. If you're not sure where to start, find a protection spell and try it out! Practice creates valuable experience."
>
> —GWINEVERE, AGE 16

and take the solids out. Interesting note: Anise masks the human scent. It's useful for invisibility spells and to heighten your psychic awareness. You can also use any of the ingredients by themselves for protection.

6 chunks frankincense, or 12 drops oil
2 tablespoons grapeseed oil
1 drop anise oil, or a pinch of ground star anise (optional)
6 black peppercorns
6 cloves
1 cinnamon stick

Infuse this! Heat the frankincense (if you're using resin) on direct heat over a low flame in the top of your double boiler until you can smell it and it looks a bit gooey. Add the oils, and put the pot over boiling water. Add the rest of the solid ingredients and heat for a minute or so. When you can smell everything, pick up the top of the double boiler (carefully!), and swirl it gently. Hold a whisk or your athame up to a light, and see the light pouring onto it. Collect that light onto the whisk or athame, and direct it into the mixture as you stir.

INVISIBLE LOCKER

When you have a moment alone with your locker (as in, there's no one else in the hallway), stand in front of it and take a few quick deep breaths. Conjure some white light and move it into to your dominant hand. Smooth your hand over your locker (as if you were polishing it), and cover it with the white light. "Blend" your locker into the ones next to it by rubbing your white light into it, as though you were flattening their edges together. Voilà! An invisible locker that'll keep your nosy neighbor from peeking over your shoulder the next time you open it.

BETWEEN-THE-WORLDS ENCHANTMENT

(Based on a protection spell taught to me by Joyce)
Use this spell to keep your tools or anything else from being invaded by nosy folks. You don't need a formal Circle, although you could certainly do this while in Circle.

A candle, some other source of light, a Fire-charged crystal, or some protection incense

Gather all the items you want to protect. Put them in a pile, if possible. Breathe and meditate for a moment, getting centered and drawing in energy from either the candle or the incense. Draw light into yourself and run it through your dominant hand. Visualize the light pouring out of your finger or the crystal. If you're using incense, put your hand over it and draw the smoke around the objects by using your fingers to grasp and concentrate the smoke.

Draw a vertical circle around the objects, sounding a long note like "AHHH." When you feel that the circle is very vivid, do it again—this time, going around them horizontally. Sound a slightly different note. Do this a third time, circling around the opposite ends of your pile, using another note. Then, recite something like this:

"Three times circled and thrice protected,
 Around my tools a shield projected.
 Between the worlds these items stay,
 Hidden every night and day."

GET-OFF-MY-AURA SPELLS (SETTING UP WARDS)

Putting up *wards,* psychic energy guards that protect you and your personal space, is a key skill for a Witch to have. There are lots of ways to set up effective wards. You can use images like gargoyles, dragons, or animals, charge them with protection, and carry them around with you. Or you can use symbols, like a pentacle or a necklace with a small silver dagger, and charge those.

PSYCHIC PENTAGRAM WARDS

Conjure light (white, bright blue, or red are a few choices to consider) and move it into your dominant hand. Use your index finger to trace a pentagram over every window, wall, and door in your space, or over your stuff or your body. As you trace the symbol, imagine that it's a psychic stop sign that will force all unwanted energy or prying eyes to keep off the grass. See the light soak into whatever you're protecting, and see that object glow with light for a moment. You have to recharge these pretty regularly, say, once a week.

CRYSTAL GRID

Use several quartz points together to create a psychic energy grid that lets in only the energy *you* allow. You can put a quartz point in each corner of your room, placing them so their tips point to one another. Hang a quartz point from the top of your locker.

A good way to charge up your personal shield is to lie on the ground or floor with quartz points at your head, hands, on your breastbone, between your legs, and at your feet. Meditate for a few moments as you imagine the energy from the stones as the light hitting them weaves a strong web of protection around your entire body.

THORNY-ROSE CHARM

Cut three roses from a bush (say "please" and "thank you"), leaving as much of the stem and thorns as you can. Carefully wrap the ends with white cord, knotting protection into each twist. Hang these upside down in your locker, in your window, over your door, over your bed—wherever you like. This is nice and low key; it just looks like you're into dried flowers.

DEFLECTION DEVICE

Get a piece of plywood or very stiff cardboard and cut it into a triangle. Paint it black or silver. Now, smash a few CDs that you don't listen to anymore, or carefully break a few bottles. Carefully glue the broken pieces onto the base. If you're using CDs, face the shiny side (without any writing) up. Hang the triangle (point down) on your wall or in your locker with double-sided mounting tape to deflect and break up any negative energy. Remember to cleanse this device occasionally with incense or by taking it down and leaving it under a full Moon.

Mercury: *This is the astrological symbol for Mercury, which rules communication. Inscribe this on a talisman in yellow, light blue, or gold to increase your powers of communication.*

COMMUNICATION SPELLS

Moon Phase: waxing

Moon or Sun in: Libra, Sagittarius

HEAR-ME SPELL

If you're having trouble getting your point across or don't express yourself well in general, try making one of the talismans or oils (or both) and empowering them with this ritual. Wear the oil or talis-

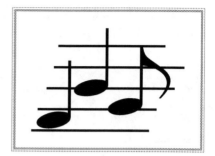

Musical notes: *Music is definitely a form of communication. If you're musically inclined but can't seem to get your ideas across in words, keep a talisman with a short musical phrase from your favorite piece close to your throat. Keep the side with the notes turned toward your body. Whenever you're at a loss for words, play that musical phrase in your head and relax!*

Alphabet: *You can use the regular old English alphabet as a talisman for flowing speech. Write the alphabet from A to Z on one side, and then write it backward on the other side. Wear the backward side against your throat, and each time you speak, imagine that the mixed-up letters pass easily through your throat chakra and come out correctly.*

man when you need it, or wear it constantly from full Moon to full Moon to work on communicating more effectively.

INTENTION

To get your point across in a particular situation

TOOLS

A picture of an ear. Didn't expect that, did you?

Incense. Anything you like will do, or you can burn a few drops of Communication Oil (page 176)—without a carrier.

Pen and paper. If you can get yellow-colored ink or paper, that's great, but plain blue pen is just as good.

ALTAR LAYOUT

Prop the ear up on the table in front of you, and put the incense in front of it. Stash the paper and pen nearby where they're handy.

GO FOR IT

Think very carefully about what you want to express. Write it carefully, with your best handwriting. Reread it. If it's garbled or has any rough spots, rewrite it. Do this until you express yourself perfectly.

Concentrate on the person you need to communicate with. Imagine it's his or her ear sitting on the table. Light the incense. Whisper your letter into the smoke. As the smoke rolls over the picture of the ear, your words will be carried to that person.

COMMUNICATION OIL

A small quartz point
1 ounce grapeseed, olive, jojoba, or almond oil
10 drops peppermint oil
5 drops lavender oil
5 drops bergamot oil

Do this at noon. Cleanse the crystal with running water (the tap will do). Hold it in your dominant hand as you say a poem perfectly. You can go slowly, just make sure you say it to the letter. If you screw it up, rewash the crystal and start over. Put the crystal in a small bottle. Add the oils, cap the bottle, and roll it between your palms. Take it outside and hold it up to catch the Sun for a moment. If you can light some incense, pass the bottle through the smoke.

COMMUNICATION INCENSE

1 tablespoon dried mint
1 tablespoon dried lavender
A few drops of bergamot or frankincense oil

Pound and mix together all ingredients.

HEAR-ME SPELL VARIATION

Use this variation to communicate with a friend or loved one who's far away. Do this outside. Set up a big rock, use a tree stump, or just plunk on the ground. Clear the area of any leaves or sticks, so they won't catch fire.

INTENTION

To express yourself to a friend or loved one

TOOLS

These will actually vary, depending on what your feelings are. To communicate with a lover, use tools that reflect that.

Pen and paper. This is to write your letter on, like the original spell.

Rock or crystal. You'll charge this with your emotions and cast it into a body of water or throw it.

Incense. Lots of it. The smoke will bring your thoughts and words to your friend.

Candle flame. This is to burn the letter, if you can. Be careful, of course! Have a big jug of water handy, along with . . .

A big pot. As soon as the paper catches, put it in here to burn out completely.

ALTAR LAYOUT

Incense in the center. You'll use this more than anything, and it's a good place to focus your mind.

Candle behind the incense. You'll burn the letter and use the incense smoke to carry those words to your friend.

Rock or crystal in front of the incense. Charge this with your words and cast them away.

Pot and water jug wherever they're close. You want to put the letter in the pot as soon as it catches, so have it very close by. Of course, you want the water handy in case anything goes haywire. Oh, your parents are going to *hate* me. . . .

GO FOR IT

Cast the Circle. Make sure the incense is lit. If it burns away while you're working, just throw some more on the charcoal. Write your letter the same way as in the original spell. If you have something of your friend's, like a piece of jewelry, some clothing, or a photo, wear it or hold it while you raise the energy by chanting your friend's name. Start slowly and softly.

When you've got the flow going, add more incense to the charcoal while calling your friend's name loudly and forcefully. Read your letter into the smoke. When you read the closing, say your name loudly. Put the corner of the letter into the candle flame, and quickly put the burning letter into the pot. Your words are released.

Hold the rock in your dominant hand, and bring it to your heart. Charge it with feeling. Bring the rock to your lips, and whisper whatever those feelings are. Bring it to your forehead, and picture your friend. Cast it into a lake, the ocean, or a running stream, and ask the Elemental to bring your words to your friend. If you don't have a large body of water handy, throw the rock away from you as hard as you can.

SWEET-SPEAK MOUTHWASH

1 cup water, boiled and cooled
2 drops peppermint oil
1 drop tea-tree oil

Mix together ingredients. Swish and gargle before you have an impor-
tant conversation. Don't swallow this! Alternatively, you can chew a few mint or sage leaves before you need to express yourself clearly.

Cinnamon gum is another quick communication fix. Chew a piece and recite a little affirmation to the effect that your words will come out true.

CHAPTER THIRTEEN

BOOK OF SHADOWS

Sounds creepy, but "Book of Shadows" originally referred to the book that Gerald Gardner kept all his rituals and liturgy in to pass down from High Priestess to High Priestess. The Initiates in the coven hand-copied the book, and it was kept very mysterious. Your Book of Shadows will be the place where you keep your spells, recipes, divination readings, thoughts, dreams, and visions. It's your personal grimoire and a collection of your knowledge and experiences, and it's a very individual thing.

Depending on what you "major" in, you have *lots* of options for putting this together. Maybe you'll get really into herbalism. In that case, you might want to have a whole section about herbs, with descriptions and drawings of herbs you grow and use, and lots of recipes. Maybe you're really into crystals, and you want to have a section about them. Whatever you choose, be sure to leave plenty of room! Your Book of Shadows will grow like mad. I learned a little trick from my friend Ronnie: never write on the first page of your book until it's filled. That way, you can go back when it's all done and make a really good cover page that represents the whole work.

FIRST BOOK

Three-ring binders are a really good choice for your first Book of Shadows because you can move stuff around, add pages whenever you need them, and keep little bits of things, like business cards from your favorite suppliers, in folders or pockets. You can divide this type of notebook into

Theban script is attributed to Honorius, an old grimoire author. Some Witches use this alphabet in their Book of Shadows. It will force you to concentrate on your words, giving them extra magickal energy. Simply write the letters of our alphabet underneath each character to figure out what each symbol means. The Theban character for "I" is also used for "J," and the one for "U" is also used for "V" and "W." The last character marks the end of a sentence.

sections, too. A sample Table of Contents for your Book of Shadows might look like this:

Your self-dedication or initiation ritual, if you did/had one

Your favorite Circle-casting ritual

Elemental work: meditations, drawings, poems, rituals for calling them, or Elemental spells

Esbat rites: Include bits of folklore and mythology, and how you celebrated each full Moon for a year

Sabbat rites: Myths and traditions, how you celebrated each Sabbat for a year, and recipes (see Chapter 15 for info on the Sabbats)

Recipes for lotions, potions, incense, and oils

Divination: Include interpretations for runes, Tarot, I Ching, etc., and any particularly weird readings.

Spells: Keep each spell that you cast in your book, with plenty of room for notes, responses, and how it all turned out. Be sure to note the Moon phase, where the Sun and Moon are, and any other astrological correspondences for each spell that you cast. You may want to make a separate section in here for spells you use all the time. Divide them into categories.

DISK OF SHADOWS

It's the twenty-first century, after all. There's so much good witchy stuff on the Net—and some not-so-good stuff, too. When you're surfing around and happen on a few good sites, put them in the "favorites" folder of your browser, and go directly there next time. You can save whole sites as a PDF file, or copy and paste them into Word documents. You might have to reformat a little. Don't plagiarize anything, and be sure to keep track of what info came from where. It's great to keep online catalogs for Pagan supplies, too . . . that way, you can compare prices, check out inventory at your leisure, and make wish lists. Make a bunch of different folders so you can organize your disk into different categories, like spells, recipes, and all the rest. . . .

The Appendices include a list of recommendations, but I'm sure you want to explore on your own. When you're putting together your disk, you'll want to make sure that the sites you're working from are reliable sources. Poke around the entire site to get a feel for it. If you come across anything that's racist, sexist, or elitist, take it off your list. Chances are that a person who writes stuff like that isn't very spiritual at all. If they're wrong about that kind of thing, they're probably wrong about Witchcraft, too.

CHAPTER FOURTEEN

SOLITARY WORKS
AT FULL MOON

The full Moon has always been associated with Witchcraft. Some rumors are true, I guess. Many Witches celebrate the full Moons, or Esbats, with their covens or by themselves. I love getting together with my friends for full Moon, but it's not always possible. Besides, full Moon is a great time for Solitary work, and I make every effort to do *something* special. Full Moon is definitely a time of power, and if you want to attune to Nature's cycles and walk the Witches' Path, observing full Moon is the best place to start.

This is the best time for Goddess worship, working on psychic abilities, making oils and incense to use for the month, performing healing rituals, and having prophetic dreams.

PSYCHIC VISION SPELLS

Moon Phase: full, or up to three days before full Moon

Sun or Moon in: Scorpio, Cancer, Pisces

The full Moon is *prime* time for psychic power. Make oils and incense on the night of the full Moon, and they'll be charged with extra energy.

VISION INCENSE

⅛ teaspoon freshly grated nutmeg
3 chunks dragon's blood
3 chunks frankincense
½ stick cinnamon, or ½ teaspoon powdered cinnamon

Pound all ingredients together with a mortar and pestle, or whatever you're using instead. This smells kind of bad (the nutmeg doesn't smell too great when it's burned), but the last time I made this on full Moon, I dreamed of the Norse Gods! If you can't find frankincense and dragon's blood (definitely pick them up sometime soon!) simply omit them and use nutmeg and cinnamon, or use anise and oregano.

POWER INCENSE

2 parts dragon's blood
1 part frankincense
1 part sage
2 or 3 drops lavender oil, or 1 part dried lavender

Crush the dry ingredients up, add the oil, if using, and get ready! This is the stuff I mentioned that had me seeing auras. Actually, what I made included mullein (another herb), as well, but that's optional. Use any of these ingredients by themselves.

OPEN-UP OIL

Make this at the full Moon, and try to do it when the Moon is in Scorpio, Cancer, or Pisces—the most psychic signs, in order. This recipe is great for opening up your psychic awareness and for meditation. Rub a little bit on each chakra point, starting at the root chakra and working up to the third eye; move your finger in small circles on the third eye while you concentrate on awakening your powers of intuition.

1 ounce grapeseed oil
1 teaspoon dragon's blood resin, melted
1 teaspoon frankincense, or 10 drops oil
½ cinnamon stick, or ¼ teaspoon powdered cinnamon
⅛ teaspoon grated nutmeg

Crush together, infuse, and enjoy!

FULL MOON MAGICK

PRAYER BUNDLE (FROM JOYCE)

The full Moon is a great time to do spells to get what you want, but it's also nice to offer prayers without asking for anything in return. My good friend Joyce offered this suggestion for a full Moon prayer ritual:

Sit outside where you can see the moon, and meditate on all the blessings in your life. Write each one down and say "thank you," saying something like this: "For abundant food, I thank you. For a loving family, I thank you . . ."

When you've counted all your blessings, roll up the paper and tie it with a ribbon or cord. Offer it to the Goddess, and leave it somewhere outside.

MOON WATER

Boil water or use distilled water for this. Fill your chalice and take it outside. If you live by the ocean—lucky!—gather some ocean water (you can't drink this!). Let the Moon shine on it as you meditate. Pour the water into a very clean jar with a tight lid, and never let sunlight touch it. Use the charged water for spells during the rest of the month, especially when you're working with Lunar Goddesses.

SACRED HARVEST

Full Moon is a great time to harvest the herbs in your Witch's Garden. Do this with some ceremony, asking the plant if you can have a little and saying "thank you." Actually, you should do this slightly after the Moon is past full. If the Moon is completely full at 10:45, for example, then you can harvest any time after that. Check *The Old Farmer's Almanac* or your local paper for the exact time.

CLEANSE AND CONSECRATE

Bring your tools—especially your scrying tools—out under the Moon's rays to recharge and consecrate them. Frankincense, sage, and dragon's blood all work very well by themselves, and you can also blend them together in equal parts with two drops of lavender oil for a consecration blend. Wash your tools in blessed water or Moon water, pass them over a white candle flame, sprinkle them with salt, or bury them in dirt for a day or two. Of course, if your tools are metal, you'll just sprinkle them with water and salt, and make sure you wipe them clean. Salt and water can ruin metal!

SEND HEALING TO A FRIEND

Full Moon is a good time to send psychic energy to other people, and it's especially nice for sending loving, healing vibes to someone you care about. If you intend to do a healing ritual, you need to get your friend's permission first. Even though it's a gesture of love, it's still a magickal gesture, and you have to have the go-ahead from the person for whom you're working. Frankly, I don't recommend that you attempt any healing rituals that are meant to pull sickness from another person. First of all, sickness is sometimes necessary for someone to learn or grow. You can't choose someone else's karmic lessons. Second, healing rituals like those require a lot of experience and training. You can sometimes make yourself ill doing it.

Instead, try sending your friend comfort by working with light. Different colors are good for different things, so listen to your intuition and let that guide you. Another nice way to send healing energy is to keep a candle altar for remembering people who are sick or having some troubles. Simply assign a candle to each person, and light them every night or on each full Moon.

INTENTION

To send comforting energy to a sick or troubled friend

TOOLS

Candle. This can be white, green, light blue, gold, or any other color that speaks to you. I prefer white, light blue, or gold. Carve your friend's name on it.

Something personal of your friend's. This is optional, and you can create a charm or talisman for them instead. It's just an object to focus your energy on.

Essential oils to blend for your friend. Making a perfume blend for your friend to wear is a lovely gift, and you are comforting just by the fact that you care enough to take a minute to make something. If you have a chance, bring your oils to your friend's house and let him or her sample all the different smells. Put the ones your friend likes aside, and incorporate them. Even if they aren't the right oils for healing, the fact that they give your friend pleasure will have a healing effect.

Quartz points or other crystals. Get enough to make a circle around all the other stuff, and then four more to make a square around the circle. The crystals are totally optional, but I like them.

ALTAR LAYOUT

Put everything in the center, and make a circle around them with the quartz. If they're single terminated—only one perfect point—aim the points toward your other tools. Then, make a square with the four other crystals, each one pointing to the next.

GO FOR IT

Cast your Circle. Breathe and meditate. Put a circle of white light around yourself. Light the candle. Focus on the flame, but don't stare. Blink normally; let your eyes relax. Put your dominant hand in front of the flame (not too close), and see the light glow around your hands. See the light extend beyond your hand in rays. Send that light through your hand to your friend.

Now, focus on the flame again. Look at the base of the flame and concentrate. Visualize a little sphere of light forming in the candle, whichever color appears. Watch the sphere roll and turn around, and pull it out with your recessive hand. Put your hand near the candle, and just pull it. Imagine your hand is like an energy magnet (it is). Then, visualize the sphere in front of you. Either whisper your intentions to it or send comforting energy into it through your dominant hand. Bring it down to the charm or the oil and watch it melt in. Anoint the charm, and give the oil and charm to your friend next time you see him or her.

I did this once with a yellow candle to send yellow light—for intellect and vision—and the sphere started out the color I wanted it but turned to a deep green—healing and growth. I guess the situation needed green light. Go with the flow.

Be sure to cleanse all the stones you used for this ritual, and it's a good idea for you to have a soak, too!

LOVE-APPLE SPELL

Use this when you want to call a lover. Repeat the spell every full Moon as part of your Esbat celebration

INTENTION

To call a lover over time

TOOLS

An apple. Cut this in half across the middle (horizontally) to see the star in it—a natural pentacle.

Honey. Cover both halves of the apple in honey to draw love.

A really clear idea of the kind of person you want to draw. Don't concentrate on looks. Think about the qualities you want in a companion, like humor, spirituality, or kindness.

ALTAR LAYOUT

You don't need a formal altar for this, but if you have one set up for an Esbat, just place these items somewhere on it.

GO FOR IT

Cut the apple in half across the middle so you see the star. Use this as a pentacle to draw love to you. Pull the seeds out, and scatter them to the wind. Recite the qualities you're looking for in a lover. Cover the apple in honey. Eat one half as you meditate on your love, and leave the rest outside as a symbolic act of sharing with the person you're calling to you.

SPELL FOR WORLD PEACE

You can repeat this spell every full Moon when you feel that you have some extra energy to give.

INTENTION

To encourage world peace

TOOLS

A globe or map of the world. Use this to concentrate your energy.

A candle, either white, light blue, or light green. Also to concentrate your energy, and you'll light this often. Carve this with runes for "magick," "peace," or "unity." Anoint it with Peace Oil or another blend.

Peace Incense or whatever blend you like.

ALTAR LAYOUT

Set up your altar however you like. A formal altar with all the working tools would be good here, and then you can set these items in the center.

GO FOR IT

Cast a Circle, and invoke whichever Goddess seems appropriate. Light the incense, and pass all the items through the smoke to consecrate them. Raise the energy. You can then take the energy back into your body and release it through your hands as you pass them over each area of the globe or map, concentrating on the thought of peace and joy. Move slowly over the entire globe.

Pass the objects through the incense again, this time saying a prayer or repeating "peace and joy" over and over. Or, you can raise a cone of power and direct it straight up, imagining it bursting like fireworks and raining peace all over the planet. Light the candle; the flame symbolizes your commitment to working for peace. Replace the candle every month.

PEACE INCENSE

Dried lavender
Frankincense
2 or 3 drops sweet orange oil

Mix the dry ingredients in equal parts, and crush together with the orange oil.

Or

Dried lavender
Dried sage
Star anise

Crush together equal amounts of each ingredient.

PEACE OIL

1 ounce olive oil
5 drops lavender oil
10 drops frankincense oil
5 drops sweet orange oil

Or

1 ounce olive oil
Lavender
Sage
Orange peel

Vary the amounts of the ingredients according to your preference. Dry the herbs for a day or two. Peel the orange very thinly (a zester would be best) and chop into thin strips. Pour the oil over the herbs and let infuse.

DEDICATION RITUAL

Self-dedication is a totally valid form of initiation, and even if you decide to be initiated into a coven, I recommend that you do a Self-Dedication before you start looking. You won't have the same experiences as a Witch in a coven does (we'll talk more about that in Chapter 19), but Self-Dedication is a powerful experience. Initiation means that you'll be a part of a coven and probably have some kind of formal teacher, but Self-Dedication means that you're accepting Life and Nature as your most important teachers. It's making a promise to live in harmony with yourself, human and animalkind, the deities, and the Universe. Seriously think about what that means to you before you Dedicate. How will Dedication change your life? Only you will know! Do you want to choose a God/ess to be your patron—or has one already chosen you? Self-Dedication can be as simple as sitting on the ground outside and declaring that you are a Witch. That's really all it takes, but we creative types usually want some kind of exotic ritual to declare our Path. I say, go for it! Have a blast!

It's really nice to make yourself something to mark the occasion, like a necklace or armband, so you can look at it and wear it as a reminder of your faith. Traditional Wiccan High Priestesses often wear a necklace made out of amber and jet beads, and Wiccan Priests often wear a torque, an armband that fits above the elbow. The pentacle has become a traditional symbol of Wiccan faith,

"I have no qualms about going to synagogue and reading aloud the prayers that I've known since childhood. This is because, basically, I have no animosity toward the Jewish religion or community. 'Why be Pagan then,' you ask? Well, because I prefer to call the spirit my family calls 'God' the Goddess *and* the God. I feel comfortable in the Pagan community and with the rituals and meditations commonly associated with Paganism. I also believe some Pagan beliefs that are not embraced by Judaism. Sometimes I wonder if, according to pure Reconstructionist beliefs, I am a Jew. I believe in a divine presence, I follow all the Reconstructionist ideals that I have been taught, and I do not see the ceremony when I became a bat mitzvah as any sort of lie. In that ceremony, I declared that I was old enough to live according to my own ethics, and that's exactly what I did. It is *connected* to my bat mitzvah rather than a *denial* of it that I became Pagan."

—MARJORIE, AGE 13

and so is the Triple Goddess symbol. Something as simple as a sun or moon is totally appropriate, too. Choose whatever you like, even if it's not "Wiccan." Write your Dedication vows, explaining what you think Dedication means, and use these in your ritual.

Some Witches choose a new name when they're initiated, and some choose several over the course of their lifetime, depending on what they feel expresses their magickal nature or the energy that they want to work with. Their magickal, or Craft, name is sometimes used only in Circle, only among other Witches, or kept totally secret and only used by the Witch alone. Native American people, as well as African people, often have several names throughout their lives, and they're given or choose a new one at each rite of passage or initiation. Witches also use Craft names to distinguish between their magickal life and their mundane life. It's a symbol, and it's a tool—much like our other tools—that signals the Witch's mind to flip the magickal switch. I never chose a Craft name because I prefer *not* to make any distinction between my witchy self and my regular old self. It's up to you.

If you decide to use a Craft name, you'll also have to decide when and how you use it. Frankly, you'll probably really freak out your family if you decide that your new name is Mercury Light Feather and that they should only call you that from now on. You'll also have to pick your name, of course! You can do a "vision quest" type of meditation and see what name comes to you, or you can simply choose something that feels right. You can work out the numerical value of your given name and choose a new name that has the same value, choose something that describes your magickal personality, or take on the name of a God/ess to whom you feel a connection.

One last word, and I promise to get on with it! After you Dedicate, please refrain from flapping your gums about being a Wiccan High Priest/ess. You're not. A High Priest/ess, in traditional Wicca, has been initiated three times, which is called Third Degree. A High Priest/ess is the head of a coven, either active or retired, and a High Priest/ess (we hope) has an enormous amount of life experience to help him or her with the enormous responsibility that comes along with being a spiritual leader. However, you certainly *do* have the right to call yourself a Witch, and if you continue to act in a way that backs up your claim, a Priest/ess. We'll talk more about Priest/ess Craft in Chapter 21.

INTENTION

To dedicate yourself to the Witch's path

TOOLS

A candle. This represents Diety and Spirit on your altar. You can pick any color you like. I think white, silver, gold, purple, or light blue are good choices, and white is the best. White light actually contains all the colors of the spectrum, so it makes sense in this case.

Incense and charcoal tablets. This represents Air on your altar, and it's also for consecrating your tools. If you can't burn incense, use your breath to consecrate your tools. The Ritual blend that follows would be perfect, but you can make your own, of course! Frankincense, sage, dragon's blood, rosemary, and lavender are all appropriate, either by themselves or in combination.

A flat, round rock. This will represent Earth on your altar and you'll make a pentacle with it as part of your Dedication.

Your chalice or cauldron. This represents Water on your altar, of course!

Whatever working tools you have. You'll bless these and dedicate them, too.

An amulet or other symbolic token. Consecrate and charge this during your dedication to have a lovely reminder of your faith.

Your dedication vows. Pretty obvious!

Salt. To make blessed Water.

Oil. To anoint yourself and your tools. Ritual (page 197) is a good blend, but feel totally free to create your own. Make a full ounce of this, so you can use it as your signature anointing oil. If you don't have any essential oils or herbs, just plain olive oil is perfectly good for anointing. Be sure to write the recipe down, if you make your own; you'll want to be able to make it again!

Music (optional). I like having music on when I do ritual, but that's up to you!

ALTAR LAYOUT

If you can do this outside where you can see the Moon, that's the best way! Set your altar up in a formal, traditional pattern for your Self-Dedication with your working tools set in their traditional directional correspondence. Face the altar to actual East, where the good old Sun comes from every day, and set up your altar with as many tools as you have.

By the way, take a ritual bath before doing your Dedication. Use any of the cleansing recipes, Ritual, or make up your own. I put this note in the Altar layout section because your body is absolutely an altar. Wear something that's both nice and comfortable.

BLESSED BE

Cast a Circle. Breathe, meditate, and get into the magickal mode. Bless and charge the salt and water in your chalice. If you're calling specific deities, do it now. Explain what you're doing and why. Light the deity candle.

Dip your hands into the chalice, and say something like:

"Blessed Be my hands that they might always work in Love."
Take some blessed Water and touch it to your eyelids, saying:
"Blessed Be my eyes that they might always seek Truth."

Now put some Water on your forehead and say:

"Blessed Be my mind to remain strong and clear."

Touch your lips with the Water and say:

"Blessed Be my lips to speak the sacred words in Truth."

Touch your heart with Water and say:

"Blessed Be my heart to always give and receive Love."

Girls, touch your abdomen (right below your belly button) with Water
    and say:

"Blessed Be my womb, where all Life is nourished."

Take more Water to the spot where your hips and thighs meet (the
    groin) and say:

"Blessed be my loins, the start of all life." (Oh, get over it!)

Anoint your feet and say:

"Blessed Be my feet that I might joyfully walk my Path."

Repeat this ritual with each of the Elements, using the incense, the candle, and the oil (you've already used salt in the Water, although it'd be good
to sprinkle a few grains around the Circle).

One at a time, take each tool in your hand and bless it with each Element, saying something like: "I consecrate this tool with [the Element] in
the name of [whichever deities you're working with or simply the Goddess
and the God] and by my will. Let it always serve the highest good and never
turn against me."

Pour some Water over the charcoal (if you use some) and mix it together to form a paste. Add a few drops of the oil to this. Dip your finger in
it and draw a pentacle on the rock. This will be your Pentacle to use in ritual from now on. Present it to each Quarter.

When you've consecrated all of your tools, go back around the Circle.
At each Quarter, say something to this effect: "I hereby dedicate myself to
the Witch's Path [or the Wiccan Path, or the Pagan Path, etc.], and from
this moment onward I vow to walk in Truth and Love . . . [read your Dedication vows now]. I present myself, [your name—if you're using a Craft
name, state it now], to You as a Witch and a Priest/ess."

Take your charm and hold it above your head. Say something like:
"Goddess and God, all of the Elements, please bless this token that it will

always remind me of the vows I have spoken tonight and of Your blessings."

Raise the energy however you like, and put it into your charm. Relax, ground, and meditate for a moment. When you close the Circle, say something to each Element and the deities, like: "Thank You for Your blessings tonight and every night; this Circle is open but never broken."

RITUAL INCENSE

Frankincense
Rosemary
Lavender
Sage
Dragon's blood
Rose petals, dried
Vanilla, scraped from the bean

You can use any or all of the above herbs to make an all-purpose ritual blend. Crush together.

RITUAL OIL

Dragon's blood, crushed
1 ounce jojoba or vegetable oil
Frankincense oil
Lavender oil
Vanilla bean

Heat the dragon's blood in the top of your double boiler. Add the jojoba oil. Add the essential oils (equal parts). Split the vanilla bean down the middle and add.

RITUAL BATH

1 cup Epsom or sea salt
1 cup rose petals, fresh or dried
5 drops frankincense oil
5 drops lavender oil

Mix all ingredients together. Give an additional stir each time before using. This makes enough for 8 baths.

CHAPTER FIFTEEN

HOLIDAYS
AND
CELEBRATIONS

The Wiccan holidays are called Sabbats, and there are eight of them: four High Holy Days and four Lesser Holy Days. The four High Holy Days are Samhain, Beltane, Imbolc, and Lughnasadh. These are based on the Celtic Pagan traditions and are called fire festivals because fire was—and still is—a Pagan representation of divine presence, power, and magick. The Lesser Holy Days are the equinoxes and solstices, and those dates change each year depending on the astronomical calculations. You can easily find out the dates by checking an almanac, an ephemeris, or your favorite Pagan web site. The Sabbats are based on agricultural happenings and the Sun's Cycles; the changing of the seasons and the rhythm of the Earth make up the Witches' Wheel of the Year.

The Pagan Wheel of the Year is the single best summary of Pagan spirituality: that Life and Death are a grand cycle, without an end. When you celebrate the Sabbats, you'll find that your connection to Life's cycles becomes incredibly strong. Living with a profound connection to Earth and Nature can be a potent source of divine inspiration, and it's key to your magickal practice!

There are lots of ways to celebrate the Sabbats, and in many cases you can incorporate Wiccan symbolism and ideas into your family's holiday celebrations. Heck, that's exactly what the Christians did in the first place. Ever notice the strange little symbols that go along with some Christian holidays? What do Easter eggs and chocolate bunnies have to do with the resurrection of Christ? Nothing. However, eggs and bunnies have plenty to do with the Pagan holiday Ostara, which used to be celebrated right

around the same time as Easter. Notice the similarity in the names? Is it a grand coincidence? I think not! When the medieval church converted Europe to Christianity, it found that the country people (Pagans and Heathens) still celebrated their old holidays. No problem, thought the Christians. We'll just throw our holidays in with the Pagans, use some of the same symbols, and call it a day! Remember in Chapter 1 I explained how, when one culture dominates another one, the new culture melds their gods with the old ones? It's the same deal with holidays in this case. Consider Yule. Pagans decorated evergreen trees, gave gifts, and lit fires to encourage the Sun to come back—the same way Christians do now at Christmas, except a Pagan probably wouldn't have killed a living tree and kidnapped it into his living room.

Some Pagan holidays are specific to our traditions and don't have direct parallels in the Judeo-Christian or Muslim faiths. Those times can feel lonely for the Solitaire, but rest assured that somewhere other Pagans are celebrating right along with you. Simply acknowledging these natural days of power connects you to the wild world, and therefore with your own witchy energy. Recognize them and take a minute to do something special. If your family insists that you have to go to church or synagogue, don't feel like less of a Pagan.

"You know what's funny? I was thinking about two Jewish holidays, the celebrations of Tu B'Shevat and Sukkot, the celebration of the coming of spring and the harvest festival. On Tu B'Shevat, we praised nature and every different kind of fruit and vegetation, and somehow this related to our moral values. On Sukkot we were meant to sleep outside under the sukkah that had no top but only branches. The starlight would shine through them as we slept. It was all about God in Nature. It's not so different from Paganism. Isn't that kind of cool? I can easily see Pagans and Jews sleeping under the sukkah, lighting candles and meditating. Who knows?"

—MARJORIE, AGE 13

Go to the service, remember that divinity has many faces, and consider it an exercise in comparative religion.

Cooking seasonal foods is a simple way to celebrate a Sabbat, for two reasons. First of all, preparing symbolic food is an ancient way of connecting with friends and family on holy days. Second, eating seasonally—eating only those foods that are in season—is one of the easiest ways to connect with the Earth's energy by accepting Her abundance. Spring a yummy cake on your family and wish them a happy Spring Equinox. They may not know what you're talking about, but they'll enjoy the cake! If you feel comfortable enough with your beliefs, you can celebrate whichever holidays your family observes right alongside them, adding your own unique twist to their traditions. It's all good! It's just one more reason for a party. If you have a few friends who are into this, too, you'll have a great time putting together bashes.

SAMHAIN: OCTOBER 31–NOVEMBER 1 (PRONOUNCED "SOW-EN")

More commonly known as Halloween, Samhain is often considered the most important of the Witches' Sabbats. Despite the title of this book, we *don't* go flying about on broomsticks, although a broomstick ritual was indeed part of European folk custom—on Beltane, though. Leave it to mainstream media to get it backward! Anyway, Samhain is often referred to as the Witches' New Year because it's the official end of the Light Half (and beginning of the Dark Half) of the year when we harvest the last of the crops and get ready for winter. Since Samhain marks the *end* of the fertile harvest season, it also represents the *beginning* of the year to come.

Some Wiccans express this time of the year with the metaphor of the Oak King (the young and virile king of summer) being overcome by the Holly King (the lord of the underworld and winter). The Oak King loses the battle and temporarily leaves the world while the Holly King rules until he is born again at Yule.

While the rest of the world is parading around in superhero costumes, scaring the hell out of one another and begging candy from their neighbors, the Witches are usually cooking delicious foods in honor of Earth's bounty and getting ready for the most magickal night of the year. (All right, we're parading around in costumes, too. We're a fun-loving bunch, for the most part, and Samhain is the one day of the year when we can get *really* Witched out and totally fit in!) Samhain is traditionally associated with mystery, magick, and otherworldly beings. The veils between the worlds are thin on this night. Mexican people celebrate the Day of the Dead on October 31, and the traditions behind their festival are closely related to Wicca's worldview. In Mexico, special feasts are made for deceased friends and relatives so they can visit us and be refreshed and remembered. Food and gifts are left for the ancestors at their graves and in their families' homes. It's a very cheerful, beautiful festival that celebrates death as a natural part of life. Since many Wiccans believe in reincarnation, Wicca includes the idea that death is just a part of the cycle and not something to be frightened of. It's another rite of passage.

Wiccan myth and metaphor include the idea that the Goddess, who rules the Light Half of the year, is leaving the world to be replaced by the God, who rules the Dark Half of the year. The myth of Demeter and Persephone (or Inanna's descent—same symbolism, different culture—see Chapter 2) is often reenacted at Samhain rituals. Samhain is the best time for divination, spirit work, getting rid of things you don't want in your life, and laying the groundwork for future endeavors. It's also a great time to play in the shadows, confront your fears, and cackle with gusto.

FUSE YOUR FAITH

This is one of the easiest Sabbats to incorporate into American customs. Like I said, you can be as witchy as you please tonight, and no one will look at you cross-eyed. Throw a party—costumes required! Set it up with some of the traditional American decor, like jack-o'-lanterns, cobwebs, and spiders—all that good stuff. It's totally appropriate to Samhain. Dress as a Witch, of course. Have Tarot card readings, go on a ghost hunt, rent *Bram Stoker's Dracula,* and generally ghoul it up.

· Set up an altar in honor of your ancestors. Leave them offerings of fresh water and food, and light a candle in their honor, if you can.

· Do a divination for the coming year. Cast a card/rune/hexagram/ whatever for each month, and be sure to write it down. Keep this and refer to it throughout the coming months.

· Scry to communicate with the spirit world.

YULE: DECEMBER 20–23 (A.K.A. WINTER SOLSTICE, MIDWINTER)

Right alongside Christmas and Hanukkah, the Witches have their own holiday that's all about good cheer and lighting the darkness. Christmas trees have their roots (sorry about the pun) in Pagan traditions, as I mentioned earlier. Evergreens were decorated because they retained their life through the cold of winter, and they're a symbolic "light at the end of the tunnel"; Yule customs, like burning a Yule log or bonfire, are to honor the Sun God/esses. Yule is celebrated on the Winter Solstice, the longest night of the year. During this time of ultimate darkness, fires are lit to give strength to the Sun, and Solar and Fire deities are asked to return light to Earth.

Wiccan mythology includes the rebirth of the Sun today; since Winter Solstice is the darkest day of the year, it's *also* the time when the Sun's powers begin to strengthen.

FUSE YOUR FAITH

Give handmade gifts for Hanukkah or Christmas. Freshly baked bread, cakes, cookies, or homemade chocolates are all easy to make, and gifts of food are very traditional Yuletide presents. You could make bath salts, add a few drops of food coloring, and put them in a pretty jar, or make personalized body oils for everyone. Make or buy scented candles, get some pretty paper, and write a lovely prayer. Wrap the paper around the candle and tie it with a silk ribbon. Whatever you do, enjoy the spirit of giving from your heart.

If your parents keep a real evergreen in the house for Christmas celebrations, ask them if they could buy one that has the root ball attached so you can replant it when it's done with its Christmas duties. This takes a little planning. First of all, depending on where you live, you have to dig a hole for the tree in October, before the ground freezes. Take good care of the Christmas tree while it's living in your house. Keep it watered. After Christmas, take the tree out to the garage or a covered porch for a few days, to get it used to the cold. Then, plant it in your predug hole, cover it with hay or peat moss to keep it warm, and—voilà! You've saved a tree, kept to your Wiccan ideals, and still celebrated along with your family.

WITCH WAYS

· Make potpourri out of pine needles, orange rind, a vanilla bean, cinnamon sticks, and cloves. Simmer this over low heat in a pot with a little bit of water, and fill your house with Yuletide cheer.

· Decorate an evergreen outside with cranberries, orange slices, and stale bread cut into different shapes with cookie cutters. Cover the bread shapes in peanut butter and then coat them with birdseed. String your decorations together and hang it on the tree. The birds will really appreciate the treats, and you won't murder an innocent tree! (This is an idea I got from Martha Stewart's show, of all people!)

· Do a ritual to welcome the Sun God/ess back into your life. Make a Solar talisman and charge it at noon on Yule. Hang the talisman above your bedroom window to greet the Sun and encourage its return.

IMBOLC: FEBRUARY 2 (PRONOUNCED EE-MELC, A.K.A. OIMELC, CANDLEMAS, BRIGID'S DAY)

Imbolc is the Witches' Festival of Lights. It's the beginning of spring in our Wheel of the Year. Although *actual* spring is a couple of months away,

Imbolc represents the beginning of the end of winter, if you catch my drift. Brigid is the Goddess traditionally associated with Imbolc, the Goddess of healing, inspiration, and fire. Some Wiccans mark this Sabbat by putting a single lit candle in every window to honor Brigid and encourage the Sun's light to grow stronger.

The God is said to be a young child now, and the Goddess is recovering from childbirth. The Sun is gaining its strength, and the natural world is waking up. Plant the psychic seeds of success for future endeavors.

WITCH WAYS

· If you can light candles, put a white taper in your window or on your altar. Meditate on the flame and scry. Write a poem or paint a picture in honor of Brigid's inspiration.

· Give your room and ritual tools a thorough cleaning and cleansing in honor of the new season. Clean out your own mental cobwebs with a day of deep meditation: brew some ginger tea and drink it throughout the day to rouse your spring spirit. Cleanse your chakras.

· Do a generic healing spell, putting your energy out there for anyone who needs it.

OSTARA: MARCH 20–23 (A.K.A. SPRING EQUINOX, VERNAL EQUINOX)

This is the first official day of spring on the Pagan Wheel of the Year, the time when animals start their mating season—especially sheep, which were very important to the ancient Celts. The traditional Goddess for this Sabbat is Eostre (which is where the name "Easter" comes from . . . hello!). Eostre is the Anglo Goddess of dawn, rebirth, fertility, and new beginnings—all the good things about spring! This holiday falls around the same time as Easter, remember? It's still traditional to eat lamb on Easter in lots of places, and Easter's date is calculated according to the first full moon after the Vernal Equinox . . . hmmm, I wonder why?

Wiccan rituals might include blessing seeds to plant later. On the Spring Equinox, day and night are perfectly balanced. The Goddess and God are in perfect accord and fall in love, ensuring that the world will regenerate during spring.

FUSE YOUR FAITH

It's really easy to incorporate Ostara into an Easter celebration. Color some eggs—I know, you're too old for that, right? Hell, I still do it. It's fun, for crying out loud! Put the eggs on your kitchen table and surround them with fresh flowers to encourage fertility in your home. Chocolate bunnies taste good, and they're definitely appropriate to Ostara. Stock up on little yummy bunnies and give them away to anyone who wants one, along with little cards hand-painted with spring colors and a poem to the joys of re-birth. Eggs and bunnies are totally Pagan symbols that were borrowed. We don't mind sharing, but at least give us credit for our own stuff!

WITCH WAYS

· Find the exact time of the Spring Equinox by looking in an almanac or ephemeris. Prepare your entire day around that moment; to feel the amazing impact of perfect balance, be sure that you're alone in a peaceful place at that time. Take that power deeply into yourself to gain equilibrium and cosmic joy with All.

· Wake up before dawn on Ostara and go outside to watch the Sun rise. As it comes up over the horizon, experience each color of dawn. Take those colors deeply into yourself. Watch how each tree stretches to meet the Sun. It will be a moving experience.

· Meditate on a yin and yang symbol. Try to balance an egg on its end at the exact moment of the Equinox. It'll stand up straight! Invite your parents to your egg balancing act, so they can see exactly what all this Witch stuff is about.

BELTANE: APRIL 30–MAY 1 (A.K.A. MAY DAY, ROODMAS, WALPURGISNACHT)

The other most famous of the Witches' Sabbats (next to Samhain), Beltane is a joyous fertility festival. This festival celebrates virility and Nature's explosive reproduction. Handfastings (Pagan marriages) are often performed at Beltane, and the infamous broomstick was a part of old country customs. Brooms are phallic symbols (hello, think about it), and parading around on the phallic broom to "fertilize" the Earth's womb was a method of sympathetic magick. The country folks would hop around on their broomsticks and jump high in the air to encourage the crops to grow tall.

The maypole is a common part of Beltane festivals. A pole with colored ribbons tied to the top is sent into the ground. A circle of people dances clockwise around the pole, each holding a colored ribbon, while another circle outside the first dances counterclockwise, each of them holding a ribbon as well. Members of each group weave their ribbons around the pole by raising and lowering them as they circle the pole. This ceremony is done to weave blessings and happiness into the coming year, and to marry the God (the pole) with the Goddess (the ground).

WITCH WAYS

- Find a running stream or waterfall near your house. Gather some water in a bottle or jar. This is a great day for making tonics, and it's a wonderful Beltane ritual. If you're concerned about the quality of the water, use it symbolically. Wear it in a small vial around your neck or carry it in a pocket to infuse yourself with the bright energy of Beltane.

- Bless wildflower seeds and "scatter plant" them anywhere outside, sprinkling them all over the ground. With each handful, make a wish out loud. Or plant a flower garden with your parents.

· Invite your friends over for a bash—including an equal number of guys and girls. Make it dressy. Serve romantic food, like chocolate-dipped strawberries. You may help a few couples get together!

MIDSUMMER: JUNE 20–23 (A.K.A. LITHA, SUMMER SOLSTICE)

The Sun is at its peak today, so remember to spend some time with Solar and Fire deities. Everything is in full bloom, and summer fruits are ripe and luscious. In fact, midsummer is the absolute peak of fertility. Everything is full of life. This is an excellent time to work magick of any kind, but it's *especially* good for playing with the faeries and nature spirits, and for love spells.

The Goddess and God are radiant and powerful today. They have plenty of energy to give you for your magick. Play and be mischievous. This is one of the Lesser Holy Days, but I love Midsummer.

Try baking this Midsummer cake for your family:

Chop 2 cups of strawberries and put them in a bowl with 2 tablespoons of sugar. Let them chill in the fridge while you bake a double layer vanilla cake (from a box). Cool the cakes and cover them with a thin layer of French vanilla icing (store bought). Stick the cakes in the refrigerator until that thin layer of icing sets, about 20 minutes. Put the strawberries in the middle, grate some chocolate over them (optional), and put the top layer on. Then, finish frosting both layers with a generous amount of icing. Add a few whole strawberries to the top, and you've got a delicious midsummer treat that your whole family will dig.

WITCH WAYS

· Do an ecstatic ritual early in the morning, and get yourself deeply into a magickal mode. Cast an utterly enchanting glamour on yourself and spend the entire day walking between the worlds. Encourage faerie madness in the rest of the world. Leave cryptic messages in random places, like writing bits of poetry or mystical symbols in gold and silver ink on small stones. Toss them around wherever you go. Go someplace public, like a park. Bring glitter and toss it around at intervals, just for the fun of it. You'll get some strange looks, but you're probably used to them by now.

· Tonight is the night to call a lover, more than any other night of the year. Break out every witchy move you have and really go for it. Work yourself into an ecstatic frenzy as you call your true love to you. The more impassioned you are, the more quickly your love will come. Be careful what you wish for, because you just might get it!

· Throw a party! Everyone loves random party days . . . make it a costume ball with a faerie theme (boys can come as elves or wizards). Make sure there's plenty of glitter to go around, and go trouping through the local supermarket, the local park, library, wherever!

LUGHNASADH: AUGUST 1 (PRONOUNCED LOO-NAH-SAH; A.K.A. LUNASA, LAMMAS, HARVEST HOME)

Lughnasadh is the beginning of the end of summer. It's the first harvest festival, and the days are getting shorter already. Lugh is a Sun God in the Celtic pantheon (and the origin of this Sabbat's name, but you can work with any of the Solar Gods—or Goddesses—to whom you feel connected. Did I say "Solar Goddess"? Yup. In fact, Patricia Monaghan, author of *The Book of Goddesses and Heroines,* reminds us that there were many Sun Goddesses in other cultures).

Bread baking is a traditional Pagan way to celebrate this Sabbat, since grain is harvested around this time of year. The Goddess has prepared abundance, and the God (the grain) is sacrificed to ensure that the people will grow.

WITCH WAYS

· Apples are in season now and are very appropriate to Lughnasadh rituals. Pick some of your own, if you're lucky enough to have an orchard nearby, and make something good to eat with them in a Kitchen Witch ritual. Remove the seeds from your apples and reserve them. Make yourself a pouch. Carry the seeds—along with some cinnamon, cloves, and nutmeg—as a reminder of divine abundance. Wear it when you feel lonely or worn out to connect with the constant flow of energy that's there for you to call on.

· This is a great time to harvest your wand! Apple wood would be perfect, but any wood is good. Go for a long walk outside and enjoy the scents and sights of harvest time. Find yourself a nice tree and talk to it. I'm very serious. Telepathic or otherwise, really make an effort to have a little conversation with the tree. Ask the tree if you can have a small stick, and look around the base for fallen twigs. Say thank you, for the wand and for abundance.

· The ancient Irish Celts used to have the Tailltean games in honor of Lugh's foster mother, Tailte. Throw a bash with a contest theme, like a poetry slam or a race.

MABON: SEPTEMBER 20–23 (A.K.A. FALL EQUINOX, AUTUMNAL EQUINOX)

This is the second harvest festival, a Pagan Thanksgiving. God/esses of hunting and abundance (like the Ashanti Goddess, Akuba) are welcomed into Witches' Circles and thanked for their graces.

The Sun is losing strength rapidly, and the God is still giving up his life for us to eat; the Goddess is saddened by the God's death, although he will rise again after winter. The days and nights are balanced again on Autumnal Equinox, but now darkness will reign. This is a time for introspection and gathering up your energy to keep it for the coming winter. Slow down and get ready to hibernate! Harvest and dry herbs now to use later.

WITCH WAYS

· Find a fallen leaf outside. Thank the tree it came from. Write down something that you're grateful for and would like to keep in the next year. Float the leaf on a river, lake, or stream, or leave it outside to be carried by the wind.

· Find a large rock outside. Make an altar of nuts, berries, and leaves as offerings of thanks for all the good things in your life. Whip out the yin and yang symbol yet again, but when you meditate on balance this time, concentrate on looking inward to see the aspects of yourself that you want to strengthen. Leave a small crystal or other token as a symbol of your willingness to give back to the Universe.

· Go to the grocery store with your folks and pick up a turkey breast on the bone. Rub it with 2 tablespoon of butter. Stick it in a roasting pan, cover loosely with aluminum foil, and cook one of the most delicious meals ever: a Pagan Thanksgiving feast! Include squash, sweet pota-toes, cranberries, apples, and other seasonal food. Set your family's table beautifully, with large bowls of fresh fall fruits and nuts and fresh flowers, and celebrate Nature's bounty with your family.

PART V

CHAPTER SIXTEEN

COMING OUT OF THE BROOM CLOSET

Do you want to run through the halls at school screaming, "I'm a Witch, I'm a Witch, I'm a Witch, Witch, Witch"? Or would you rather read your Tarot cards in the dark, under the covers, with the doors locked and the curtains drawn? Maybe you fall somewhere in the middle: you want to tell your friends and family about your newfound sense of Pagan pride, but you don't want everyone at school to annoy you with incredibly lame questions. ("Hey, did you ride your broomstick to school today?")

It's up to you to decide how public you want to be, but you should be aware of several things before making your decision. First, please know that being "in the broom closet" does not make you less of a Witch. In fact, magick performed in secret has a particular power to it, and many Witches choose to practice in secret because they find it to be a very effective way of concentrating their energy.

Many Witches keep their pentacles under wraps for fear of persecution; while America is a free country, we are also predominantly Christian—at least in the ruling majority's eyes. I'm not knocking Christianity, but some translations of the Bible state, "Thou shall not suffer a witch to live" (Exodus 22:18). Some argue that in this instance "witch" is a mistranslation for "poisoner," but the idea has had an enormous impact on our culture, regardless. Many people raised in the Christian religion have a genuine fear of Witchcraft and for a Witch's immortal soul. If you find yourself in the middle of a Christian Youth Group meeting and you feel the need to vocalize, you might try using a word other than "Witch" to describe your beliefs,

> "I don't have any regrets. I am proud of my religion. I refuse to give in to the ignorance and oppression of others' beliefs. It isn't easy, but it isn't supposed to be—that's life!"
>
> —ATHENA, AGE 17

like "nature worshipper." Even then, you can expect opposition from people who want to save you from hellfire and damnation. Take a deep breath, nod in the appropriate places, and continue being exactly who you are—quietly. You probably won't be well received if you stand up at midnight mass on Christmas Eve and declare that Yule was stolen from the Pagans and you want it back. If someone comes at you with a pile of sticks and a lighter, run! Run fast and far!

I was kidding with that last bit, but only partly. While Witches are no longer burned at the stake (or mutilated, tortured, drowned, and all the rest), the fear of persecution still runs deep, and with good reason. In our glorious Republic, you absolutely have the inalienable right to practice whatever religion you choose, but persecution still exists in more subtle forms. Just ask anybody who's gay, Jewish, black, Spanish, or female (we will talk more about protecting and asserting your rights in Chapter 21). This may range anywhere from patronization ("Isn't she cute? She's a tree-hugging hippie/misguided feminist/mentally deficient tribal throwback"), to outright fear and isolation ("Don't cross her; she'll put a curse on you"). Do yourself a favor and practice self-restraint when you encounter ignorance. There is very little to be gained by standing on a desk in English class and denouncing the imperialist patriarchal regime in dire tones and with performance art–type drama. Besides, hardly anyone will get it.

If you feel that your community will be outright hostile to your beliefs, then it is preferable to keep quiet about your Pagan ways. If you're only into Wicca to cast the occasional spell here and there, then it doesn't make much sense to wear a big shiny pentacle to school. Doing so will certainly bring you plenty of attention, but you may not necessarily want to deal with the subtle (and not-so-subtle) prejudice that lingers around that symbol.

Philosophical debate is great, and I encourage you to engage people in discussion at every opportunity. Sharing thoughts and ideas is one way to become closer to the people in your life. However, there is a very fine line between intellectual discourse and argument. When discussing controversial issues like religion and politics, it is best to begin the discussion knowing that the person you're talking with probably won't agree with you on all accounts. Keep your tone pleasant, and end the discussion if you sense that it's getting too heated.

ANONYMOUS ACTS OF PAGAN MAYHEM FOR THE BROOM CLOSET WITCH

- On Ostara, write "Happy Spring Equinox" on the bulletin board in your local grocery store. (You can do this for any of the holidays!)
- Replace "In God We Trust" with "In Goddess We Live" on a dollar bill, and leave it on the ground. (Okay, this is slightly illegal, so make a fake dollar bill and do the same!)
- Write "Blessed Be" in chalk on a sidewalk.
- Paint an ankh, a crescent moon, or the zodiac symbols on a big rock, and stick it somewhere public.
- Buy a little fairy doll, tie it on a string, and hang it from a tree. Take it down after a while, so you're not littering.

> "It usually is best to keep your mouth shut. I know how tough it is. But in places where you have to go every day, especially school, you don't want to be discriminated against. To be picked on every day is something that can break your spirit. Many teens have become depressed just because they can't fit in. You don't want to be all alone, have people stare and point, and be feared."
>
> —KRYSTLE, AGE 14

DEBRIEFING THE PARENTAL UNITS

For many people, the most difficult aspect of "coming out" is talking with parents and other family members, especially if they are devout in their particular religious beliefs. Gauge your family's response before announcing your heathen heart to them. Are they strict or liberal? Do they require you to attend their own house of worship or let you do your own thing? Are they devout in their practice but open-

> "Wicca is a hidden religion, one that isn't widely known by the public. Slowly and carefully, Wiccans are emerging, growing, and educating others. So if you do choose to come out of the broom closet, your job starts by explaining what Wiccans do and why we do it! Other teens you talk with might know about the magickal Path because of movies or TV shows, but most parents don't have a clue. During your conversations about Wicca, the picture you paint, the information you provide will have a serious impact on the reaction you receive. Specifically for this reason, you need to do research and be thoroughly prepared."
>
> —GWINEVERE, AGE 16

minded to other ways of life? Decide what and how much you want to tell them about your spiritual persuasion. You may be pleasantly surprised at the way your family relationships deepen when you go out on a limb and reveal your true self, or you may find that you'll have to work at a close connection with your family. Either way, being honest feels fabulous.

If your relationship with your parents is somewhat lacking, look at the reasons why. Are you screwing up in school? If so, try to get your act together a little bit before springing the "W" word on them. This will help you to gain their confidence in your ability to make good decisions for yourself. Do you run out of the house every night to hang out with your friends, leaving them to eat dinner by themselves? Try to spend a little time with them and let them in a little; smooth the way for discussing the big issues by letting them know you better in every way. Are they the ones who don't have time to spend? Ask them specifically for a day or night that you can get together and do something fun, like shopping or cooking dinner or anything else that you all like to do.

It's truly grand to have a close relationship with your family that allows each family member to be respected, enjoyed, and applauded for his or her unique personality, but sometimes this just isn't the case. If your family isn't close, then maybe you don't have to worry about revealing your deepest thoughts. It's unfortunate, but sometimes that's the way life is. If that circumstance is unacceptable to you, then this is an opportunity to build that closeness. It's great to respect the Gods who made you, but your parents feed, clothe, and comfort you in everyday life. Give them a chance to show you how good they can be, and let them see how great you are.

There are a couple of different strategies for starting The Talk:

THE GUERRILLA METHOD

One night at dinner or while you're gathered around the TV watching vapid sitcoms, spring a surprise attack on their brains, like asking them what they think God looks like, or what they think happens to us when we die. Watch the popcorn fly as they twitch! Don't impart your views yet; listen to them first, and see what their reaction is. If they ask why you asked, then jump in and speak your piece. Be prepared for the inevitable questions, and know your subject very well. Answer to the best of your ability, offer your opinions in a pleasant way, and present your parents with a completely mature, rational, passionate-yet-calm, obviously well-thought-out explanation of your basic beliefs. Offer to let them read your books. Expect to have this conversation repeatedly as they try to understand you.

> "My parents were completely unreceptive to what I believed. My dad and stepmom really didn't care about me or my spirituality. They screamed 'Satanist!' and in a sudden, dramatic move became representatives for the Christian community—despite the fact that my father hadn't attended church in years and my stepmother was just as devout."
>
> —ATHENA, AGE 17

THE CRAFTY TACTIC

Leave a book on Wicca (hey, this one would work!), a pack of Tarot cards, a crystal, or other witchy objects on the kitchen table, coffee table, or some other communal place. Wait for their reaction. If your parents ask what all this stuff is, give a matter-of-fact, concise, literal definition. Wait some more. If you get no further response and feel the need to push the issue, revert to the first tactic. Be ready for a million questions! Again, know your subject, and expect to have this conversation often!

Explain what you find attractive about Wicca/Paganism. Is it the Goddess? Is it the connection to Nature? Expound on your connection to

Divinity as a beautiful Goddess, or your love of the Earth as a living creature. Talk about how meditation helps you to relax and stay healthy or how you find crystals and rocks interesting and beautiful. Whatever you find divine in Wicca, share that passion with your family. You may want to leave out the spell-casting bit for now, or you may want to really lay it out there.

AVOIDING SOCIAL DISASTER AND TEENAGE TORTURE

The other arena for coming out is at school, that swarming pit of hormones, cliques, and cruelty. I don't know why, but teenagers are often unbelievably nasty to one another, and anyone who is perceived as "different" is a target for bullying, teasing, and general mental torture. On the other hand, teens are usually willing to embrace anything that is rebellious or provocative. It's a weird paradox. You have three choices: tell your close friends and swear them to secrecy (it'll probably get out eventually), tell no one and be a silent Wiccan, or tell everyone and duck the fallout.

Keep it simple when you're talking to friends who don't know what Wicca is. Depending on the person, you may want to keep your focus on the Earth-as-a-living-being aspect, rather than the chanting/spell-casting/astral-projection part. If they're antagonistic about your spirituality, then just don't discuss it further. If they're indifferent, then you haven't lost anything, and you have gained a sense of your own integrity. If they're intrigued, then you may have found yourself a study partner!

When you "go public," be aware that you are taking on the responsibility of representing Wicca and Paganism with your actions and words. While you and I know that there is infinite variation within the general heading of "Wiccan" or "Pagan," most people tend to lump us all

> "Once you tell someone, you can't take it back. So this first step involves you and only you. It's sort of an internal conversation. Ask yourself the following questions: Are you serious about this Path, or is it just something you do for fun? What is your motivation for coming out? What do you hope to accomplish? Is another Wiccan person pressuring you? Are you 100 percent sure this is the correct time?"
>
> —GWINEVERE, AGE 16

together—usually under the heading "Satanic." If you run around telling people that you'll curse them for gossiping about you, not only will you lose friends, but you'll also damage the Pagan cause (and you'll get a dose of wretchedly stinking karmic retribution, too). Besides, if you're looking for like-minded people to practice with, or teachers, or want to be initiated into a coven, you'll come up against closed doors if spewing negative press tarnishes your reputation.

Decide how important it is for you to be Pagan at school. Perhaps you find the history surrounding the Salem murders truly horrifying, and you feel the need to speak out in social studies class. Saying what's on your mind, without labeling yourself as Wiccan, is standing up for your beliefs. If you feel strong enough to take the heat, go for it and claim your heritage. Again, it's up to you, and, again, it's best to really know your subject before you speak out about it. There's nothing worse than being cross-examined by your peers and having nothing intelligent to say in return.

You don't need to bludgeon the world with your religious viewpoint, and always keep in mind the way you feel when someone is trying to "save your soul." It feels totally rotten to be told that your views are wrong, so don't get zealous and go damning every other religious philosophy. Tolerance is the order of the day, and if you crave respect and open-mindedness in others, then generate that by being tolerant and open-minded yourself.

"Going to a Catholic all-girls' school is not easy for a Witch. In fact, it's downright hard. I learned the hard way that you can't tell everyone the truth. When I was in grammar school, I brought a Wiccan book to school to show a friend who was interested in Wicca. I let her borrow it, but as I gave it to her, one of my 'friends' saw it. 'Don't you know that all Witches go to hell,' was the first thing she said. This launched us into a huge fight. I told her the truth, that Witches weren't the old hags that she thought we were. But, in the end, she didn't believe me, and she said that all Witches are evil. I never really talked to that girl again. Because of this fight, I learned that had to be careful with whom I shared my faith."

—KRYSTLE, AGE 14

> "Most of all, I am out of the closet for those who cannot be, and for those who are discriminated against. Each morning as I don my pentacle and start to school, I think, This is for Wiccans everywhere. We may walk quietly in the night, but the Goddess is everywhere."
>
> —ATHENA, AGE 17

If religion comes up in class and you really feel the need to profess your undying love for the Great Mother, go ahead and say it. (I'm sure She appreciates being stood up for, nowadays.) If one of those narrow-minded monkey types tells you you're stupid for thinking of God as a woman, turn around and ask: "How many men do you know who can give birth to a seven-pound baby, much less an entire Universe?"

You can also remind the instigator that many ancient cultures revered goddesses along with gods, and the title "Mother Nature" wasn't made up by Hallmark just for laughs.

Just know that you might be harassed for it, and if you get the feeling that your fellow students are truly hostile, then I suggest that you keep it a little more vague and conversational. You certainly don't have to proclaim yourself as Wiccan or Pagan to be Wiccan or Pagan, and nobody in the greater Pagan community wants to see you get beaten up, isolated, or otherwise disturbed for speaking out in high school. High school is a relatively small part of your entire life, and it will be over sooner than you think.

Being purposely confrontational doesn't solve very much (although I do love the warrior spirit!), and it can cost you a great deal. Instead, when you hear somebody spouting ignorance, smile, say a little prayer under your breath, and feel good about the fact that you know better. And tell them to get off your aura.

BLATANT ACTS OF PAGAN MAYHEM FOR THE PUBLIC WITCH

· Refuse to buy products that use harmful packaging (like Styrofoam), and write to the company you have boycotted, politely expressing your dismay at the murder of your Mother. Be sure to sign the letter "Blessed Be," and scrawl a pentacle under your name.

· If someone tells you to be quiet, settle down, or otherwise stifle your creative flow, tell him or her it's against your religion.

· If somebody says "God bless you" when you sneeze, respond by saying "And Goddess bless you."

· Anytime you would say "Thank God," say "Thank the Gods" instead!

· Tell your teachers that you will be taking Halloween off for religious observance. Then do it!

· At your class Christmas party, tell everyone that Christian holidays have their origins in Pagan festivals. Back it up by explaining the symbolism of the Yule log and decorating evergreen trees. Don't be surprised if no one believes you.

CHAPTER SEVENTEEN

WICCA IN THE WORLD

So what's a Witch to do when the Circle is opened and the candles burn out? Do you leave your witchy self out in the woods? The answer is a resounding *No way!* You're still a Witch after Circle and if you really feel a connection to this way of life, you'll want to express your spirituality beyond wearing a sparkling pentacle necklace.

Being a Witch is so much more than casting spells and burning incense, as fun as those are. You can take the power and joy that Witchcraft brings you and put the philosophy and practice into your daily grind. You'll find that Wicca's peace and enchantment will blend beautifully into your schoolwork, your home life, and everywhere else you need the sparkle of magick—without tattooing WITCH across your forehead.

DO IT LIKE YOU MEAN IT

It's all well and good to talk about the joy of Nature and the occult properties of herbs, but how will you *use* your knowledge in the rest of the world? First of all, you use it to evolve into the best person you can be. I'm not talking about being "perfect," I'm talking about being the best person you can be at any given moment. Strive for mental, physical, and emotional balance. Put your best effort into everything you do. When you screw up, acknowledge and move on. Forgive yourself, forgive others, and learn from every mistake.

Talk is totally cheap, but actions blaze trails—in your own soul and in the world.

WICCA AT SCHOOL?

A lot of the teens whom I spoke to while I was writing this book had some concerns about being out of the broom closet at school. A few had experienced some discrimination from teachers and other students, and we'll talk more about defending yourself in Chapters 20 and 21. For now, I want to give you some constructive ideas about incorporating your witchy life into your (usually pretty boring) school day.

When you have to write a report on something for English or social studies, tie it into your witchy interests. You could write about European folk customs in a social studies report, examine their roots, and compare them to Neo-Pagan customs. For an English paper, you could study William Butler Yeats's poetry (he was a brilliant poet and a member of the Golden Dawn) and detail the occult references in his work. You could write a paper about how many religions' holidays are similar in theme, and how some holidays originated with Pagan customs (not recommended for a Catholic school!). You could also give a presentation and call it "cultural anthropology."

USE YOUR TALENTS

Contribute to your school's literary or art magazine. A beautiful poem about Athena or a drawing of a goddess among the stars isn't anything that would get your school up in arms. Write an article for the school newspaper about the Open Circle you went to last full Moon or about how your spirituality helps you get over life's rough patches. Maybe that's geeky, but who cares? It'll look great on your college applications. I'd avoid any spell-casting references, only because people who don't understand how spells work will probably either make fun of you or freak out.

GET ORGANIZED

Put together an Earth Day festival at your school. You could invite guest speakers from the ACLU, have a table from the local health food store, and so on. You'll have to get permission from your administration to do this, but you can work it out if you have a solid plan. Check out Earth-Day.org for some ideas on getting started. You'll need some money to cover costs, but I know you Witches are resourceful enough to pull it off! You may even be able to get some funding from your school. Talk to a teacher or administrator whom you respect.

OUTSIDE YOUR OWN BACKYARD

Being a Witch means . . . well, what does it mean to you? If your own definition includes being a Pagan Priest/ess, then how will you walk that Path? What does a Priest/ess do in other religions?

Volunteer at a hospital, nursing home, or soup kitchen in your town. I cannot stress enough how vitally important that type of Priest/ess craft is! When you take the time to care for other humans, when you open your heart to them, you're truly acting as a Priest/ess does. You're healing, you're helping to build and strengthen your own community, and you're adding your mark to society. That's real magick, too. Think about this: If you volunteer your time in a soup kitchen—even if you can squeeze it in only once a month—you're helping people with a basic need: nutrition. If one person whom *you* helped to feed is able to live healthily, then she'll be able to contribute her own talents to society. In turn, maybe the person she helps will help someone else, and yet another human being will be healed. Think about that ripple effect spreading through the world.

The only downside to this type of Priest/ess craft is that it can be emotionally draining. You have to be sure that you've got the time, energy, and a real commitment to seeing this stuff through. Make sure

> "Growing up Jewish, I had a strong view of right and wrong. The most important thing I have ever believed in is that everyone is equal, and everyone deserves to be happy and fed and safe. I think it's about time that Pagans thought about this. I'm sick of seeing books all about how to improve your magick abilities. We have magick. It's important to us. We *need* magick as a community . . . but, you know, it's not all we need."
>
> —MARJORIE, AGE 13

you keep yourself emotionally balanced, too. Ritual is great for your mental health! Decompress when you need to, pray, know your limits, and be sure to balance it out with some lighthearted humor. Other options for walking the Priest/ess's path could include working at an animal shelter or a day care center, donating old clothes to charity, and so on. Any action that starts with feeling compassion and taking responsibility for being a part of our global community is the act of the Priest/ess.

CHAPTER EIGHTEEN

OTHER VOICES

I'd like you to meet a few of my good friends and coven mates: Laine, Joyce, and John. They've all been practicing Witchcraft for a long many years, and they're all smart, groovy people with some solid advice for you as you start on your Path.

HELAINE LUBAR

Just because you are a Solitaire doesn't mean you lack a teacher. You become your own teacher. And just as you would trust your teacher, you have to trust yourself. This is the hardest lesson for a Solitaire. We are not solitary beings. People thrive on contact with others, and the perspective and information (either in the form of praise or otherwise) that we receive from trusted advisers are things we use in our learning process.

But in Magickal Spirituality, there is no clear-cut road to enlightenment, no formula to soul ascension. And I really wanted a formula. I wanted someone else to have the answers, but once I began the Solitary Path, I realized quickly this was not going to happen. This is about making your own Path for the enhancement of your spiritual self. This is about helping you change yourself and, in turn, changing the things around you, I hope, for the better. Trusting that you are up for the task is 50 percent of the job.

Actually, you are up for the task or you wouldn't even be thinking about it. One thing being a Solitaire taught me was that I could trust my senses to tell me what was happening in my world; I realized that I had backup; either my own inner resources, or the Goddess. Most often, they work together.

To start a solitary journey, a person needs first to develop a keen sense of awareness, and this comes from introspection and perspective. Weird things happen when you're watching. I spend an hour a night writing in my journal and always carry a small notebook (I mean small, like a notepad). A diary can be the Solitaire's best friend. I have three—one is a journal of everyday life, one is for magickal studies, and another is a dream diary. Since the Solitaire has no one to discuss ideas with, diaries and journals can provide perspective.

Sometimes in magick, things don't make sense or look like isolated events. When the Solitaire looks back over the journal entries, what seemed like an isolated event will usually fall into place as a series of events leading up to a specific result. Have you ever been thinking about a specific person whom you haven't seen in a while and met that person later in the day? Or have you ever heard a song in your head only to turn on the radio and hear it playing? This is called synchronicity, and it happens often. It's another tool that the Solitaire can become accustomed to using. It's also a tool that helps develop self-trust. If intuition is giving you a little nudge to do something, and you're not sure you want to follow that intuition, looking for synchronicity can help.

Suppose you were caught between two good choices: a great job in a nice warm southern state (assuming you love sunshine) and another great job in a northern state for twice the money. Your intuition says stay north, but you really like the idea of year-round sunshine. As you're thinking about this, you pass by a man putting up a billboard that happens to be a tourist ad for the state in which the northern job is located. And then, a few minutes later, you hear a song with lyrics about this state. Finally, you go into a convenience store to get some chocolate, and you hear another customer talking about his relative who lives in that state. Is it by chance? Or is synchronicity trying to validate your intuition? This is where paying attention can help. And by working alone, you can concentrate your efforts more toward developing these skills, as opposed to learning how to work in magickal groups.

The concentration of energy toward definite goals is very different between solitary practitioners and coven members, which is why, in order to serve balance, you should try to experience both in your magickal lifetime. But experiences come as you need them in life and it's a well-known fact that the Universe will provide you with what you need regardless of whether you want it or not.

One last note, one that is important to and for younger Witches. There are many different traditions in Paganism and Wicca. Some of these traditions require participating in a set process in order to be considered knowledgeable and experienced. All traditions have value; however, this should not discount your experiences as a younger Witch. Remember to own your magick and know when to stand up for yourself and your experience and when to back down and add to your experience. I can say from what I've learned that what you do carries much more weight than what you say, and it's important that younger Witches validate themselves by not backing off their own truth in favor of something that may be "older."

JOYCE VALENZANO

Growing up in the '60s was a challenge to a woman's will. I've always been one of those girls who didn't want to toe the mark or behave in the "acceptable" way. I dance to the beat of my own drummer and weave the fabric of my life with a magickal heart. As a teen, I spent countless hours in the woods, finding my solace in their stillness, and I believe that those hours spent in the company of the living Earth were my saving grace.

It would have been helpful to have someone tell me that I was experiencing a budding psychic awareness coupled with hormonal surges. Don't underestimate the power of hormones! Study your cycles and learn how they affect you. That advice isn't just for the young women; guys, your cycle runs amok about every forty to forty-five days. For those of you who were gifted with naturally strong clairvoyance or clairsentience—and for those of you who want to develop your abilities—my advice is to remain centered through daily meditation. Breathing exercises and daily meditation are essential to maintaining balance. Those tools allow you to pull your inner resources together and work your will more effectively. That's good advice for anyone, but it's especially important if you have or want to attain a high degree of psychic awareness and are opening yourself up to a spiritual path like the Craft.

I can sympathize with you regarding the strict discipline required to practice meditation. Sitting still can be torture for me. Training my unruly mind to achieve a state of deep focus as second nature seemed like a great work, indeed. It was a great work, one that I joyfully celebrated the doing of, because I knew it would lay the foundation to claim my own power as a Witch. I had always possessed the tools and raw materials to work with, but it was meditation that taught me how to use my abilities rather than be used by them.

As a Witch, I consider myself to be, first and foremost, a healer. That healing had to begin within myself. You know those black moods and dismal times when you have no clue how you got to such a dark place or how to get out? Been there. It's unfortunate that those experiences have become the norm in today's society. I believe they're the by-products of a culture without roots. For the sake of the children of my children's children I want more. Because I want more, I work at changing my own life, knowing that as I change my interaction with the world, so, too, does the world around me change.

I use the energy that once fueled my dark moods to fashion a brighter reality for my life. I've learned to channel that energy in a manner that yields concrete results instead of illness and anxiety. We are the masters of our own fates, and the choices we make create the world we inhabit. I've learned that instead of blaming circumstances or other people for the sticky situations I've often found myself in, if I accept my responsibility for my own part in it, I can affect a more positive outcome of events. That is my power as a Witch! I understand that the energy of life is available for each of us to use responsibly. I hold the power to direct the course of my life, to make of it the best I can, and to inspire others to reach for their highest good.

Witches are artists who bend energy, shaping it into the form *we* want it to take, always mindful of the consequences and spiritual implications. As Einstein said, "For every action there is an equal and opposite reaction." Another law of physics states that energy never dies, it just changes form. The most powerful magick you can wield will be in regard to yourself. By focusing on making changes within yourself, you'll find that your work ripples out to affect the world you live in.

From a veteran's point of view, I know that practicing Witchcraft will change your life in many ways. If you approach the Craft with an attitude of sincerity, you can expect to feel a sense of responsibility to yourself and to others, and your self-esteem will rise with every success. Working consciously and responsibly with your will sets up great energy around you that replaces the feeling of having no control over your own life. Slowly, with dedication, honesty, and patience, you'll find that others notice the positive changes you're making. Your relationships with others will change, too. Some will erupt and be left behind as you change and grow, but that creates room for other connections to bloom and develop.

As you continue to grow and shine, the world will benefit from your enlightened interaction with those around you. When you create a positive image of what it means to be a Witch, you'll draw those folks to you who are genuinely curious about this ancient path. And you'll help remove the stigma that has caused so much pain and injustice to a group of people who only wish to heal, feel joy, and harm none.

JOHNATHAN ARCHIE

Being a man in Wicca is not like being a man in any other religion. In Wicca, men and women are equal partners. We celebrate this equality in our worship of the Lady and the Lord. In many other religions, and in many cultures, women do not play an equal role.

As men, the worship of the Goddess has changed the way we perceive ourselves and the world around us. When the patriarchal religions took over, they emphasized worship of one god who was separate from ourselves and all life on Earth. It is easy to destroy that which we do not feel connected to. Ultimately, this has worked to destroy the environment and disrupt the balance of all life on Earth. As a man, I need a great deal of courage not to follow that pattern. Wicca gives me that courage.

Women everywhere are turning to the Goddess, recognizing Her as being alive and existing in all things. Men are also discovering that the Goddess is alive and growing ever stronger within us.

And so the men of the world are challenged, not just by women, but by the Goddess. Men are no longer in control of everything. How does this make us feel? Do we strike out in fear of losing our illusion of control, or do we journey forth and realize that all we are really in control of is ourselves and our actions? Scary stuff, which is why it has taken us decades to get this far. True power comes from within, not without. Men have made the mistake of seeking power over others. That is an unbalanced way to live. I find that there is power in unity, and true unity can only be achieved through equality.

It is not only the image of the Goddess that has suffered, but also the image of the God. Men have lost touch with our primal selves, the part of us that ran in the wilderness. We lost our connection to the Horned God, our primal Father. We must take a deep look within to find our connection to Him. Who is He? To find the answer, we must discover who we are.

I thank the women of Wicca who have held up a mirror so that I may see the Goddess within, who leads me to rediscover the God within. There is no all-powerful God who punishes, controls, and dictates living inside of me. Nor do I see that kind of God reflected in Nature. In perverting His image, men have lost touch with who we are supposed to be. In losing touch with who we truly are, we have lost our connection to Nature. We have lost our balance within. We are learning to heal the image of the God, and we are rediscovering what it means to be a man. We learn that, not only is it okay to have feelings, but it's also healthy to express them rather than repress them. We find that it's okay to be nurturing and caring and expressive. Men in Wicca, along with our sisters, are reclaiming the image of the God.

In working together with women to reclaim our Gods and Goddesses, we are healing ourselves. We are reclaiming our inner power as we learn to reconnect to the Universe. We discover that interconnectedness exists to all living things, and that we're all ultimately one living symbiotic system. As we heal ourselves, we are healing the Earth and vice versa. I urge men everywhere to learn about both the Goddess and the God. In order to achieve balance in our souls, we must learn to get in touch with both our feminine and masculine sides. Both exist in everyone. A good way to do this is to become aware of the Lunar cycle to connect with your feminine side and the Solar cycle to get in touch with your masculine side. When you do rituals to the Moon, do so knowing you are working together with the Goddess. When you do rituals to the Sun, know that you are working together with the God.

The Gods of Nature have taught me to live responsibly in accordance with the Earth. As men, we need to understand this. Let our knowledge and connection to all living things guide our decisions and change how we live our lives. Wiccans have been taking action for decades to hold politicians and corporations responsible for the destruction of life on this planet. We look to you to continue in the fight to save our planet and to free Her from the binds of patriarchal abuse. We look to you to help secure a better future for generations to come as has been done for you.

We are healers, and one of the most important things we can do to make this a better world and heal the planet is to heal ourselves and one another. When we so much as pick up litter, or plant a tree, we heal both Her and ourselves. We are a part of, not separate from, Nature. The God and Goddess exist in all people and all things. Witchcraft continues to evolve, like the Earth Herself. As a friend once told me, true magic is the balance of the soul. We live in a constant state of learning, a constant state of change. Wiccan men strive to seek out the answers to who we are, where we come from, and why we do what we do. We may never know all the answers, but this journey has been more exciting that I could ever suppose. Unlocking the hidden secrets that exist deep within our souls as we learn to listen to our intuition, we let it guide us into the realm of natural and wild magick. That is true masculinity. And nobody can take that away.

CHAPTER NINETEEN

COVENS AND OTHERS

You've already heard my friend Laine's views on the virtues of being a Solitaire, so I won't go back over that ground, although I *do* want to make it perfectly clear that solitary practice is rewarding, fun, and *totally valid.*

However, there are benefits to working with a coven that you just won't get as a Solitaire. In a coven, you can bounce ideas off of people who've probably been doing this longer than you have, as well as learning alongside other people who are new to Wicca, the same as you are. That environment can be great for investigating your own powers, and the added bonus of other people's experiences, thoughts, and opinions can help speed you along in your understanding. If you're lucky and find a group that's well balanced and loving, you'll also have a wonderful new family. A coven won't replace your birth family, of course, but it can create the most amazing feeling of belonging, friendship, and love. My first "coven"—they'd probably tear their hair out if they heard me using the word, since we were wildly opposed to any labels—was a great mix of personalities. I'll never forget any of them, and even though we're no longer together (I'll get to that later), any one of them could still call me at 2:00 in the morning for help. I'd go running. My current coven is the same way, and we love one another pretty fiercely. Unfortunately, I live two and a half hours away from the rest of them, so I don't get to hang with them as often as I'd like to (sniff). So, how did I meet these groovy Pagan brothers and sisters? Fate, of course!

I *did* just sort of bump into them. I was at a club, and I saw some friends from school. I was talking to one guy in particular, and *he* had this other

" 'When the student is ready, the teacher will come.' I have no idea who said this, but I fear it has been taken far too literally. It all falls upon your definition of a teacher. To me, a teacher is anything that makes you think. This book is a teacher, questioning your faith is a teacher, and Nature is a great teacher. Open yourself up to the life around you, and that will be the greatest teacher of all."

—WYLD WYTCH, AGE 19

friend, whom I'll call Pan (because he totally was). We ended up talking that night and hanging out together a few days later. The first time we got to hang out alone, the subject of religion came up. I told him that I was interested in Wicca (I had been studying for about a year), and he just sort of smiled at me. He took me up to his room and showed me this awesome collection of crystals he had. He was a Witch! Well, he was more of an occultist/magician, but he was Pagan, at any rate. Then he introduced me to his other friends: Paul, an incredibly talented woodworker and crazy wisdom type, who analyzed everything; Rowan, a metal artist and herb enthusiast; and you've already met Joyce in the last chapter! We all ended up sort of living together. Pan and I moved into this house with a bunch of punk rock kids. Paul lived next door. Rowan would hang out whenever she was home from school, and Joyce spent whole summers with us. We would drum and dance around a fire almost every night, and I'll never forget those times. It was amazing. I was lucky. They gave me a formal Initiation because I really wanted that ritualized rite of passage, and it was a ceremonial dedication to one another and to Nature more than anything else. It was a powerful experience because we had powerful friendships, and we were totally dedicated to enjoying every second of life, learning about human nature and the natural world, and to living in this miniature community together.

I happened to fall in with a really great group of people. If you want to seek out a coven, there are a few ways to do it, and I wish you well. However, you need to sit down and think about exactly what you're looking for. Be really clear about whether you want to be part of an active magickal group or a study group, or whether you just want to hang around the edges of the occasional public Circle.

SHOP AROUND FOR A COVEN

If you're lucky enough to have a Pagan shop around, go check it out! See what the place looks like, and sort of feel out the energy. If you get a good vibe, start a conversation with someone who works there. Ask about their recommendations for books, or ask if they have the supplies on your list. Ask if the shop offers any classes—like yoga, meditation, or astrology—or if they do workshops there. If you see something you'd like to learn about, go for it! Since you're going to be meeting new people and hanging out in a new place, bring someone else with you. It's always a good idea to check out new situations with a friend or parent, and make sure your parents know where you're going. If you plan on being initiated into a coven before you're eighteen, you'll need parental permission, anyway.

LOOK INTO YOUR CUUPS

Covenant of Unitarian Universalist Pagans, that is! CUUPs is a nationwide group of loosely coordinated Pagan folks who meet at Unitarian Universalist churches all over the country. Call your local Universalist church, if you have one, and ask if there's a CUUP group there. Or, check out CUUPs's home page at CUUPs.org for local listings.

When you first introduce yourself to adult Witches, act politely. That goes for meeting anyone! Ask intelligent questions, and talk a little bit about why you're interested in Wicca. If you show that you've been doing some reading and learned a little on your own, older Witches are more likely to share their knowledge with you. You don't have to prove yourself to anyone, but if you're interested in finding a teacher, it helps to demonstrate your incredible intellect and passion for the subject!

A WORD OF CAUTION

One word of caution, and then I'll get on with it. I *did* have a really frightening, horrible experience when I ran into someone who claimed to be Craft but ended up being a lunatic.

If you happen on a "teacher" or a coven who tells you that you *don't* need parental permission, or if someone tells you to keep your new group a secret, *bust out of there*. They're not legitimate. In fact . . .

RUN LIKE HELL IF . . .

· **The group or person tells you to keep *anything* from your parents.** If you're not allowed to tell your parents about what you're doing, then you shouldn't be doing it. That's an attempt to control you. Bad mojo.

· **The group or person insists that you have to be naked/have sex/use drugs to work with them or be initiated.** Lies, lies, lies! Whoever hands you this line is trying to use you. No reputable Wiccan group or Witch will try to have sex with a teenager, and although ritual nudity is perfectly acceptable and valid, asking a teen to disrobe is *illegal*.

· **The person or group will only meet you alone.** This should really set off alarm bells. It's just shady if he/she/they won't meet you in a public place with plenty of people around.

· **The group or person insists that you give up all your other friends, family, or activities.** Again, this is someone who wants to control you, not someone who wants to help you grow!

· **The person or group claims to have "secret knowledge" that only they can teach you.** Malarkey! Anyone trying to impress you with their unsurpassed knowledge will also probably try to undermine your own self-confidence and wisdom. Who needs it? Not you!

· **You just feel like there's something wrong or off about the person.** Last but certainly not least, if you get any feelings about the person that are just uncomfortable, take these feelings seriously. You've been working hard to develop your intuition, and it pays off when you can avoid a bad situation.

Now that we've gotten that out of the way, you might want a few tips on what makes a good teacher. In general, a good teacher will:

· Honor your ideas, opinions, and experiences.

· Be respectful of your limitations and boundaries.

· Not ask you for money in exchange for teaching you. It's perfectly fair to ask you to pay a reasonable fee for a class, especially if it requires materials. You can offer a service to your teacher in exchange for her assistance, like working for a day in her shop, helping her to harvest or plant herbs, or contributing your own talents in some other way.

· Say "I don't know" every once in a while. Even the best teachers don't know everything! If your prospective teacher never says "I don't know," forget it. That's an egomaniac waiting to erupt all over you!

· Want to meet your parents. If someone is taking on the responsibility of instructing you in spiritual matters, don't you think he or she would want to talk with your family and explain what he or she's about? If your teacher *refuses* to meet and talk with your parents, run like hell.

· Be reasonably happy, secure, and well adjusted. If your teacher is a total emotional mess, how can she help you? I'm not saying she has to be perfect—we all have our moments—but she should be on an even keel most of the time.

· Encourage you to ask questions, do your own research, and debate your opinions! You don't want a fascist dictator who tells you that her

"A thing to be cautious about when trying to obtain a teacher would be how humble they are. If they take the slogan 'My way or the highway,' you're better off taking the latter."

—WYLD WYTCH, AGE 19

way is the only right way. How ridiculous. You *do* want someone who encourages your creativity and personal interpretation while she stands back and lets you learn.

WITCHES ON THE WEB

There are plenty of good web sites out there with message boards and chat features. Use that! You can certainly get a lot of info and help by writing to someone who knows his stuff. The Witches' Voice has a bunch of covens, groves, festivals, and other Pagan events listed by area, so you can just click on your state to find other Witches. Covenant of the Goddess's site also lists covens and Solitaires that are registered with them. For those of you in the tristate area (New York, New Jersey, and Connecticut), check out WaningMoon.com, a really cool Goth site whose webmaster also puts out the NYC Pagan Resource Guide. This is great for finding covens in the area that are open for students, as well as info on shopping and other Pagan yummies.

Start corresponding with people and check out local happenings. However, *never* give out your full name, address, telephone number, or any other personal information over the web! Duh! It doesn't matter if someone seems really spiritual and cool. The same rules apply to them as to other Internet buddies. There are some wackos who try and pass themselves off as Pagan and take advantage of our free-spirited and loving ways. That's why you need to be able to detect a fraud. Refer to the Run Like Hell section. Read, memorize, and wear comfortable sneakers with which to burn rubber if you encounter a fraud.

> "Before you accept a teacher, be sure to interview them. They may also interview you. You both need to understand what each person is expecting out of the relationship and what your interests are. It's helpful to get through the 'get to know one another' phase so you feel comfortable. This is a delicate relationship that you're trying to initiate, so move slowly and be completely honest with your new guide."
>
> —WYLD WYTCH, AGE 19

WHICH WITCH IS THE REAL WITCH?

· A real Witch doesn't talk constantly about his or her fabulous super-human powers.

· A real Witch doesn't act like a bitch. Simple, but true! A real Witch won't go around acting as if she's Queen of Everything.

· A real Witch doesn't speak in riddles. If someone doesn't answer your questions in plain English, steer clear. Mystical mumbo jumbo is exactly that.

INITIATION FACTS AND FANTASIES

In my opinion, the most powerful Initiations happen spontaneously or through acts of Nature. For example, being pregnant and giving birth to my daughter was the most astounding initiation into some of the Goddess mysteries—not that I recommend getting pregnant! On the flip side, taking care of my grandmother while she was dying of cancer was an honor and a privilege that gave me some penetrating insights into death and dying. "Nature-made" initiations come in so many forms. Any time you learn a deep lesson about the way Life works, that's initiation. Psychic experiences are initiations. Falling in Love for the first time is an initiation. Any time you feel as though Life has pulled back the veil between the worlds to show you some deep truth, the Universe has initiated you!

Initiation ceremonies vary wildly depending on the coven and even on the initiate. Standard Wiccan Initiations follow basically the same pattern. The Initiation consists of giving passwords, being challenged, and then being presented to the Elements and the Deities.

Initiation into a traditional coven is a matter of degrees—three degrees, to be exact. Candidates for Initiation are often called "Outer Grove," "Outer Court," or "Outer Circle." They are allowed at some rituals but not all, and they are usually accepted into the coven after studying with that coven for a year and a day, when they can become First Degree Initiates. I'm not Gardnerian, so I can't tell you what their training is about, but it seems that applicants need to have a good grip on Gardnerian ritual structure, mythology, and general principles.

The requirements for moving from one degree to the next are determined by the individual coven. Traditionally, Gardnerians required a male/female couple, preferably married, to be initiated together to represent the male/female balance in Nature. There are 162 rules that apply to Gardnerian covens, which you can read in *Lady Sheba's Book of Shadows*.

STARTING YOUR OWN COVEN

I've read a couple of books that discourage teens from starting their own covens, and I have to wonder why. It seems like a power trip to me; you know, that whole "I know something you don't know" attitude. Some people think that a teenager (or any other newbie) doesn't have the experience and training that's necessary to do ritual safely. If you keep things simple, I don't see what the problem is. By "keep it simple," I mean don't go trying to conjure demons or any other such insanity.

A traditional coven requires a High Priest and High Priestess to regulate the coven's activities and guide its members, but you don't have to adhere to that structure. My coven is totally democratic, and we don't have any "High" Priest/ess. All of us contribute our talents, ideas, and opinions, and all of us have exactly the same amount of input into rituals and other work. We don't always *agree* on everything, and when that happens, we debate into the wee hours of the morning until everyone is satisfied with the resolution, or we nix the entire project and do our thing separately.

We each end up doing certain jobs most of the time, only because that's what we're each good at! Laine is an excellent researcher and historian, so she compiles vast databases about different traditions and other cool information. John is into high ceremonial magick, so he gives us another perspective on creating rituals and spells. I'm the wild child who sparks the spontaneous Pagan mayhem. Joyce is the Crone in the group, and she often helps us to redirect our goal or focus our energy, but she's *not* the "leader." In fact, she absolutely balks at the idea of leading anyone, and we all agree that if you want to follow someone, you're already in trouble.

LOGISTICS

When you think about belonging to a coven, what comes to mind? My experience has been that covens are like a study group, only cooler, with an emphasis on personal growth and a deep family bond. Sit down with your friends who want to do this, and talk about what everyone thinks being in a coven means. Write everyone's answers down, and then read them out loud. See if everyone agrees on the basic idea. If not, go over those things that don't work and figure out a way to compromise. What you end up with is the start of your coven's manifesto: its statement of purpose.

Decide where you'll meet, too. Hopefully, all your parents will be totally cool and respectful and let you alternate from house to house. If not, find someplace outside that's safe, like a backyard, where you can be out of your parents' actual house but close enough that you know the area and feel comfortable being outside at night.

Come up with a name for your coven. Make it descriptive of your collective energy, the place you live, or your patron Gods. My coven is The Witches of Broome because most of us live in Broome County. We figured it was a cool verbal bonus that "Broome" sounds like "broom," and hence was appropriately witchy. Maybe your spot has a lovely willow tree in it; you could call yourself Willow Grove or Willow Circle. I'm sure you can come up with something good!

Then have each person write down what aspects of the Craft he or she is most interested in, like herbalism, ancient customs, making amulets or other magickal tools, shamanistic rituals, whatever. See if there are any answers in common. Make a note and include that information when you start planning your ritual structures and your training program.

Did I say "training program"? Oh, yes, I did! If you're going to make the commitment to starting a coven, you'll want to do it right, right? Pick a few books that everyone can read. You don't have to buy separate copies, if money is tight. Just get one of each and share. In my opinion, *Wicca: A Guide for the Solitary Practitioner* by Scott Cunningham is an absolute must-have. I recently bought a second copy, and I pick it up often when I want to get back to the basics or need some reference material. Pretty much anything Scott Cunningham ever wrote has a special place in my heart. Phyllis Curott's *Witch Crafting* is also an excellent guide to Wicca's methods and ideas, a perfect workbook for beginners that will take you through to more advanced techniques. Other good ones include *True Magick* and *Coven Craft*, both by Amber K.; anything by the Farrars; and *Wicca Covens* by Judy Harrow. The last one was written for adults who want to put a coven together, but the ideas and principles are dead-on. *The Woman's Book of Holy Mysteries* by Z. Budapest and *The Spiral Dance* by Starhawk are incredible books about hard-core women's magick. If you're going for a mixed-gender coven, you may want to stick with the other selections.

Speaking of mixed-gender covens . . . the reason my first group split up was too much sexual tension. I was engaged to be married to Pan, but I developed strong feelings for Paul, who was in love with Rowan, who used to date Pan . . . it just got weird, and the friendships eventually suffered. It's okay that we grew apart; most friendships change, and when you've learned the lessons you need to learn with a coven, it often naturally dissolves. Be very wary about starting a group with friends who are dating or who have an attraction. When you form that bond and start working with magickal energy, emotions and relationships get really intense. That's not a bad thing, but it can wreak havoc with the coven and your friendships. You might want to start a same-sex group first to help cut down on that kind of trouble. Besides, I find that same-sex groups often have a much more vibrant energy about their rituals, because there's a lot less shyness among "your own kind." Don't get hung up on the male/female polarity issue that's so prevalent among the British traditions. Every person has both male and female energy!

Back to the business of building a coven. I totally believe in the democratic type of structure, regardless of the coven members' ages. There *is* a need for people to take on certain jobs, though. You'll need someone to take care of researching, someone to keep track of any money the group puts together for rituals or supplies, and someone to write down what goes on at your meetings. You might want to rotate each job so no one gets sick of his or her role and so everyone gets to experience all aspects of covenhood. Let each person contribute to constructing the rituals; you may be better at picking out the appropriate symbolism for a ritual, another friend may write the actual poetry and invocations, and someone else may offer to cook or make the incense. Take turns hosting Sabbats and Esbats.

You'll also need to decide if, how, and when you'll admit new members. Try a two-references rule: two members of the original coven have to recommend the people you're considering, without any reservations. Then, invite your potential new Witch friends over to hang out with you guys outside the coven meetings. Hang out like that for a while. Keep everything low-key, and don't mention the coven right away. That way, if the group decides that some people aren't right for your coven, they won't have hurt feelings because they won't even know they were being considered.

Meeting at the full Moon for Esbats is a great way to keep the energy going. You'll also know exactly when every meeting is, so you can plan your schedule accordingly. You don't have to cast a Circle and do a ritual every time you meet, although that's a great way to start your magickal training. Talk, hang out, meditate, craft stuff, or just have a relaxing night out under the Moon.

When you cast a Circle or do a spell or ritual, make sure every single person agrees with the structure, wording, and intention. It's not fair to ask people to participate in something they don't feel totally comfortable with. It's their karma, after all.

You might also want to include community service in your coven's life. Set up a day for visiting a nursing home, working in a soup kitchen, cleaning up a park, or volunteering at an animal shelter. Even if you can only do it once in a while, I think you'll find that the spiritual benefit is well worth your time. You might have to enlist your parents' help to get around; what a great way to show them what Wicca is all about! They'll probably be very proud of you for being such a groovy citizen of the world.

When conflict arises—and it will—you'll need to have a plan of action for keeping the group happy and healthy. Well, not *you* alone: government by consensus. Disagreement within a coven can be a really minor thing—like one of your coven mates constantly interrupting when someone else is talking. In that case, maybe the group could gently tell the person that interrupting makes it hard to let all members get their ideas across. Then use a talking stick to keep everyone happy. When someone has the talking stick, everyone else is quiet. The only advice I can give you is to be sensitive to everyone's needs, have a sense of humor, be totally honest with each other, give criticism kindly, and be willing to take it, too. You should make a list of actions that are grounds for "firing" a coven mate. For example, if someone casts a spell that's deliberately hurtful or manipulative, he's out. You know, that sort of thing. The key is to make sure everyone agrees on the rules and everyone is perfectly clear about them right from the start. I hate to talk about harsh stuff like that, but you won't be able to grow a strong coven if there's constant negativity and no way to stop it effectively.

If you find that the group is seriously not working, dissolve, move on, and try again later. And please, don't let your coven be an excuse to be snobbish. That's not what it's about. Keep it out of school. Don't talk about your coven business there, and don't brag about how fabulously cool you are because you have your own coven. If the chemistry isn't quite right, don't get together in a coven. Try working together as a study group first, and take your time! These relationships will probably have a profound impact on you. There's no rush. If you all feel confident that you can deal with all the details, I wish you all the luck in the world. (See why some adult Witches don't think teen Covens are a good idea? It's hard work!) Be sure that you love and trust one another enough to keep it real and be mature. If you feel that the ingredients are all there and you're ready to take on the challenge, go ahead and do . . .

A COVEN DEDICATION RITUAL

Do this on a full Moon, on Beltane, Lughnasadh, or one of the equinoxes or solstices.

INTENTION

To bless your new Coven!

TOOLS

Everyone's working tools, if any.

A working candle to see by.

Two candles, one to represent a God and one to represent a Goddess. Inscribe Their names on each one, or use symbols for the energy you want to invoke, like a Sun on the God's candle and a Moon on the Goddess's.

A white taper candle for each coven mate, plus one more candle to represent the entire coven.

White satin cords for each coven mate. Measure the length of cord by stretching it from the top of your head to your feet.

A coin from each coven mate.

Bread and juice. For your first cakes and ale with your new coven.

Chalice with water in it. Use one person's chalice or make a special one for the coven.

Bowl of salt. I assume you know what this is for by now?

Red candle. Use this to represent Fire on the altar, or use a fiery stone, like obsidian or tiger's eye.

Incense and charcoal. Frankincense, sage, lavender, or any blend you like. Nag champa (the brand in the blue box) is one of my personal faves, and rose, vanilla, sandalwood, or jasmine would also be appropriate. If you don't use charcoals, regular sticks are perfectly fine.

Oil. Ritual oil is an option. You can use anything that everyone likes or just lovely, plain olive oil! If you use a blend, make several ounces so your coven can use it during rituals. If you're going with olive oil, put it in a nice bottle and use that for each gathering.

A flat rock. Use this for your pentacle, and dedicate this one just for coven use.

ALTAR LAYOUT

If you can do this outside, use a flat rock as an altar and put it in the center of where your Circle will be. If you're indoors, use whatever's handy and set it up in the middle of the room. Before you cast the Circle, burn some frankincense, sage, lavender, or a cleansing blend you like to smudge the entire room. Have everyone take a ritual bath before they come over, and decide what you want to wear. Will you all use robes, or will you wear street clothes? Determine what you want the ritual to include. Will you invoke a specific God and Goddess? Who will do each part of the ritual? Definitely let each covener have an active role; if you have four members or more, you may want to have each person or a pair call one Quarter and/or consecrate the Circle with one of the Elements. Will one person read the invocations, or will the group do it together? (I like the second idea.) You may want to write the entire ritual out on a piece of paper and keep a copy in your hand.

GO FOR IT

Mark the perimeter of your Circle by laying all your cords on the ground. Everyone in the coven should stand at the altar before casting the Circle, and each person should smudge himself or herself with the incense and anoint himself or herself with oil. Light the working candle. Take turns passing any tools you all have through the incense and the candle flame.

All the coven mates can hold their hands over the chalice and move them in clockwise circles while you all say together:

"Peace, Love, and Light now flow into this Water. Blessed be." Repeat this until you feel the Water is charged. Do the same thing over the salt, and have each person put a few grains of salt into the water, stirring it clockwise with a finger, an athame, a wand, or a stick. Don't worry, you're not going to drink it!

Cast the Circle outside the circle of white cords. If one coven mate or a pair will call each Quarter, everyone should face toward that Quarter as they're invoking it. If you all want to do it together, stand at each Quarter and say the invocations together. Choose one person to carry the Elements around the Circle (three times each!), or you can all take a turn carrying each Element. Either way, pass each Element to the person standing next to you and let him or her bless himself or herself with it. You may want to agree on a simple blessing phrase to use for each Element, like: "By Air [Earth, Fire, Water, Spirit—the oil!], I am cleansed and blessed."

Or you can let each person improvise. When you're done with each Element, put it back on the altar and stand behind your cords, next to your tools and candle.

Now the Circle is cast, and you can invoke the deities. Ask Them to come and celebrate with you, and tell Them that you're gathering in Their honor. If you want to recite the invocation together, make it short and sweet. Try something like: "Goddess and God (or Their names), we are here tonight to celebrate Life, Nature, Love, and Your presence. Please be with us and bless this Circle." Light the deity candles.

Start the traditional challenge by having one person turn to another and ask: "How do you come to this Circle?"

Response: "In perfect love and perfect trust."

Questioner: "It would be far better for you to turn and leave this Circle now if you have any fear in your heart. Do you have fear in your heart?"

Response: "I have no fear."

Questioner: "Do you stand here of your own free will, and are you willing to abide by the rules that all of us have set down?"

Response: "I am here by my own free will, and I am willing to abide by the rules that all of us have set down."

Questioner: "You may leave this Circle at any time for any reason without any ill will. You come to this Circle with perfect love and perfect trust, you have no fear, and you are here by your own free will, so I welcome you as my coven mate and true friend!"

The two kiss each other on the cheek, and the person who was just questioned turns to his or her left and asks the next person the same questions. Keep going around the Circle until you end up with the person who started. After each person has answered, he or she can tie their own cords around their waist.

Have one person start the ritual by blessing himself or herself with water the same way I outlined in the Self-Dedication ritual in Chapter 14. Then, have that person turn to his or her left (so you're going clockwise) and bless the person next to him or her. Have that person turn and do the same, and keep going this way until everyone is blessed with each Element.

Let everybody take their working tools to each of the Quarters and bless and dedicate them. Do this one person at a time, and bless each tool with all the Elements. Decide beforehand if you'll all use the same words or individual phrases.

Have each person walk over to the deity candles, one at a time, and light his or her taper from them. Go back to your spot in the Circle. Read your coven's statement of purpose together or have one person do it. At the end, have everyone reply with "So Be It" or some other affirmative phrase.

Douse the incense with some water, add a little of the oil, and have each person trace a Pentagram on the rock. This is your coven's pentacle! Carve your coven's name on the coven candle, along with any symbols you want to incorporate. Have each person trace the letters. Put the coven candle back on the altar, and have everyone come up to light it with their flames. Stick your taper in the ground behind your spot in the Circle.

Whoop it up! Raise energy by dancing, clapping, hooting, whatever. You're a coven! Hold your coin in your hand while you dance. When the energy is peaking—you should all make eye contact to be sure you're on the same wavelength—throw your coins into the bowl of salt with a release word, like "yeah" or "go." Then shout: "Blessings, Growth, and Prosperity for [your coven's name]!"

Have a snack (cakes and ale) and enjoy the night. Before you open the Circle, have each person write his or her name in the Book of Shadows, if you have one.

Best wishes to you!

PAGAN-FRIENDLY COLLEGES

Lots of teenagers consider what religious life a campus has to offer when they're looking at schools. If it's really important to you, then be sure to check out your prospective alma mater's web site to see if there are any Pagan groups that meet on a regular basis. I bet you'll be surprised!

Check out About.com's Pagan/Wiccan site for a few links to colleges and universities with established Pagan groups. Witchvox.com also has links to college groups that you can search by state. Go to your potential school's web site and look under Religious Life to see if there's anybody out there. If not, you can always start one yourself. Someone has to be first! Take a peek at Prism.gatech.edu for some advice on starting a Pagan group on campus, as well as some practical tips about being a Witch in college, like sharing a dorm room with a non-Wiccan and other helpful hints.

Go to the web site for the Coalition for College and University Pagans (CCUP) members.tripod.com/ccup_org to get a complete list of schools that have existing Pagan organizations on campus. CCUP's idea is to link all the college Pagan bunches into one virtual "Circle" to exchange ideas.

CCUP's site also has links to each college organization, so drop the crew a line, tell them that you're thinking about attending, and give them a quick interview.

CHAPTER TWENTY

REPELLING NEGATIVITY

"**M**ama said there'd be days like this . . ." Sometimes it feels as if the whole world is against you, and you just want to crawl under the covers and die! Cheer up, take heart, and act like a Witch: stand up for yourself, protect yourself, and send that negative energy back to the vortex. There are a few ways to repel negativity, and none of them have to include harming someone else. Don't be a doormat. Work it!

When you're doing spells to dismiss nasty energy, remember to keep your intentions very clear (as always). You do not ever want to send harmful vibes out to anyone. Remember the Law of Threefold Return. Even if you're willing to take on the consequences, it's a big black mark on your aura, and it's not worth it. Having said that, there are plenty of witchy ways to keep yourself from soaking up psychic or physical bullying.

Essentially, there are three spell-casting methods for getting rid of the uglies. You can choose from *banishing, binding,* and *redirecting.* Banishing takes the energy out of your environment, while binding keeps energy or a specific person from being able to affect you. Redirecting involves sending whatever is bugging you back to its sender. Most of the spells below are a combination of techniques.

Before we go any further, I want to say that you should always take action in the "real" world before, during, and after you use magick to protect yourself, by acting in accord. If you really feel unsafe—if someone is threatening you with physical violence—then *you need to tell your parents, your school officials, and everyone else.* Keep talking to someone until you get the protection you need.

If you're feeling totally low and miserable and it doesn't get any better in a week or two, *please* talk to someone! Again, magick is great, and it works, but if you're overwhelmed, *talk about it!* Take it from a survivor of depression: it's an illness, it can be overcome, and you need help to kick it. There's no shame in visiting our modern-day shaman, the therapist!

If you're dealing with something a little less serious and you want to womp it with some juju . . .

TOOLS OF THE TRADE

Several common objects are quite handy for repelling negativity, so keep them on hand at all times:

· Mirrors. Use one in your bedroom to protect your personal space. Save old compacts and get some craft mirrors from a large arts and crafts store near you. In the same vein, you can use anything that's shiny or reflective the same way you'd use a mirror. Silver or silver paint, water, and glass will do the trick, too.

· Black and white candles. Black and white both have protective color vibrations. Black is better for absorbing energy, and white is good for restoring peace.

· Salt. Sprinkle some around your room for protection, including around the windowsills and doors (remember Chapter 4?). You can also add salt to water, make blessed water, and use that.

· Cords, especially black, gray, and white ones.

· Actual Elements like candle flames, bowls of water/ice/snow, herbs to burn as incense, and dirt.

· Nails, safety pins, straight pins, staples, and other sharp stuff. You can use these to make defensive talismans, to seal a spell, or to poke holes in someone else's astral ego trip.

· Rose water, a sage or rosemary infusion, orange water (made from orange flowers—get this at a health food store), water with lemon juice, or salt water in a spray bottle. Spray a wee bit in the air around your room to cleanse it.

BANISHING SPELLS

Moon phase: new or waning

Moon or Sun in: Aries, Leo, Scorpio

BANISHING BASICS

If your foul mood is due to a specific person, like someone at school spreading rumors, you need to keep in mind that you're banishing the energy—not the person! Do these spells at noon, when the Sun is at its peak, or at midnight, when the Moon is high. Instead of stirring or dancing clockwise in a Circle, you'll move *counterclockwise*, *widdershins.* Clockwise motions reflect the Sun's pattern and are used for increasing or invoking, but counterclockwise motions go against the Sun's natural path and are used to banish. Instead of positive phrasing for your incantations, use negations to pull the energy out of your life. Try to be calm when you do this type of spell; it's much easier to control your energy when you're calm, and you'll get better results.

The absolute best ingredients for banishing preparations are sage, frankincense, cloves, cinnamon, and pepper. Choose one or mix 'em in any combination. Hot sauce is good, too—dilute this and sprinkle it around outside your house to keep unfriendly energy out.

DISPEL-ANGER SPELL

If you're ripping pissed, do this for yourself before you cast any other spell. Anger is totally natural, completely healthy, and valid. It's *not* healthy to carry it around, though, and if you try to cast a spell when you're fuming, it'll likely backfire on you.

INTENTION

To harmlessly release major anger

TOOLS

A cucumber. Bizarre, I know, but cucumbers are *refrigerant*—they cool you down.

A black or white candle. Put your anger into the candle and let it burn away.

Water. Use this to wash your rage away. You can use your chalice or a bowl.

A lemon wedge. Add the juice to the water. Lemon is very cleansing.

Incense, if you can use it. This is to cleanse your aura and restore your inner peace. Sage is my favorite, and frankincense is excellent, too.

ALTAR LAYOUT

You don't have to set up an altar for this; your *body* will be an altar. Do this outside or when no one's home, because you're going to *howl!*

GO FOR IT

I'm assuming that you need to get into the mode pretty quickly, since you're fuming and spouting fire. Gather your gear, close your eyes, and breathe deeply three times. Visualize a Circle of white light around you, and clap your hands to snap the Circle into place.

Grab the candle in your dominant hand, and *scream.* Feel your anger, really let it absorb your being, and then move it down your arm, into your hand, *out* of your hand, and into the candle. Howl, freak out, and rage. Put that fury into the candle through your hand. Repeat this until you feel better. Light the candle and say something like: "I release my anger to burn away, no harm to anyone in any way."

Squeeze the lemon into the water, and stir it around counterclockwise. Say something like: "Anger dissolves, I quench my fury, anger can never control or disturb me."

Drink a few sips, then splash the lemon water over your hands and sprinkle a few drops all over you. Light the incense and pass it around your entire body, concentrating on the spots in front of your chakras. As you breathe the scent, feel your equilibrium return.

Cut the cuke into thick slices and, while lying down, put one over each eye and your third eye, your throat, your breastbone, and your stomach.

With your eyes closed (you have cucumber on them) visualize the flame, send your anger into the flame, and release it. Start breathing deeply. As you breathe in, feel calm and peace fill your cells; pause, hold your breath for a second, and gather any remaining emotional distress into your chest. Release your breath slowly and deliberately, pushing the anger out of your body. You should feel a little more reasonable! Let the candle burn out completely, if you have the time. If not, snuff it. Either way, ditch the stub.

BANISH A BAD ATTITUDE

Use this when someone is giving you attitude. This works for banishing stinky energy, too.

INTENTION

To banish negative vibes from someone else

TOOLS

A black candle. Black absorbs and dissolves, and you'll pull the psychic junk out of your body and put it into the candle. Carve the person's name in it along with symbols that say "stop" to you.

A mirror. Set your candle in front of the mirror, which will collect any negativity aimed your way and deflect it from you.

Banishing herbs. Obvious!

Something that represents the person you're banishing. A photograph would be good, but you can simply write the person's name on a piece of paper.

A bowl of water. You'll see . . .

ALTAR LAYOUT

Set up in front of a mirror. Do this in your bedroom if you can. You can do this in the bathroom, too, if that's the only place you can get some peace. If you can't light candles or burn incense, adjust the spell by taking it outside or substituting. I'll explain in a moment. . . .

GO FOR IT

Cast your Circle and meditate to gain a cool head. Light the candle and add incense to the charcoal. If you can't do that, simply put the herbs in a pile near your other tools. Think about the situation that's irking you. Imagine it in great detail, and let your emotions wash over you. Feel it completely, whether it be sadness, fear, insecurity, anger, whatever. Where do you feel it? I usually feel gross energy in the pit of my stomach. Let your emotions grow to a peak. Then, put your receptive hand over the spot where your emotions are rolling around. *Pull* those feelings out of your body by moving your hand counterclockwise around the spot. Make pulling motions with your hand, and picture the nasty energy collecting there. Put your dominant hand over your receptive one. Move your dominant hand counterclockwise, and visualize the energy coming together in a sphere, still touching your receptive hand. Then, say a banishing incantation over it.

As you say an incantation, visualize the sphere lifting off your hand so the energy isn't touching you anymore. Move it into the candle flame or into the bowl of water, if you can't light candles. Move the candle, bowl, and incense in front of the mirror (if you're not burning incense, sprinkle the herbs in a circle around your setup or throw them into the water). Any obnoxious energy will be deflected by the mirror, pushed into the flame or water, and disintegrated. Take the photograph or write the person's name (if you're sure who it is—if not, just write "Troublemaker") on a piece of paper. Burn it, bury it, or rip it up.

BANISH A BAD HABIT

Sometimes, it's your own quirks that get in your way. Try this on a new Moon to quit doing something that's bad for you, like lying, smoking, or overeating. As the Moon waxes, do another spell to bring you a new way of life.

INTENTION

To rid you of a bad habit

TOOLS

All the working tools you have, if any. Set these up in a traditional layout with each tool placed at its corresponding direction.

An image or representation of your habit. If it's lying, draw a mouth with a cartoon bubble that says "Lies." If it's smoking, round up your cigarettes. If it's overeating, try a picture of a doughnut or some other non-nourishing food.

A black or white candle. Use this to burn your habit away and release its hold over you. Write what you want to banish along with symbols for "decreasing," "death," or something along those lines. If you can't use a candle, write your habit in a descending triangle with your symbols in the corners and bury it.

Banishing herbs. Of course! If you can't burn incense, carry these around with you in a pouch and give them a squeeze when you need help.

Two black cords. You'll bind your habit by tying up the representation of your habit . . . your first binding! You'll knot a spell into the other cord and wear it to remind you of your power to overcome. Wear it high on your arm under your shirt or on your wrist.

ALTAR LAYOUT

Set your altar up traditionally. Ritual is great for reprogramming yourself to change your habits.

GO FOR IT

Cast your Circle as formally as your situation will allow. Ask the deities to help you. Tie the first cord around your image; if it's a piece of paper, roll it up and tie it. As you do this, imagine that your image *is* the habit. Try saying, "This is not a photograph. It is [your habit]." Carve your habit on the candle, light it (or write it on the paper), and say a banishing incantation.

Burn the herbs and repeat the incantation as you move your dominant hand counterclockwise through the smoke. Keep repeating the incantation until you feel the energy shift and the words take hold in your mind. Repeat the last line until you can't do it anymore. Feel the hold your habit has on you dwindling away.

Now you can knot some magick into your cords. This will remind you how powerful you are and that you made a commitment to yourself, the Universe, and the deities to do your best banishing. Hold the cord over the incense, if you're using any. Hold it up to the sky and present it to the deities. Ask Them to please help.

Tie the knots like this:

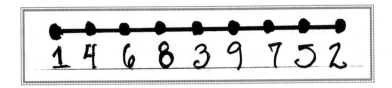

Recite:

"With knot number one, this spell is begun;
With knot number two, my will does come through;
With knot number three, I want to be free;
With knot number four, freedom I adore;
With knot number seven, I have help from the heavens;
With knot number eight, my habit abates;
With knot number nine, triumph is mine."

Tie it to your arm or wrist. Any time you feel the urge to relapse, spin the cord around a few times and visualize another way to act. Then, do it! Burn or bury the cord after you've successfully stopped your habit for twenty-one days straight.

CLEAN OUT YOUR SPACE

(based on a ritual from Tara and a spiritualist medium "house-cleaning" ritual)

Use this when you feel that negative energy has collected in your home or room, like when there's been a big argument or constant tension. This is great for times when your family's been bickering. You'll probably want to do this when no one's home, since you have to make some noise.

INTENTION

To cleanse your space of any energy beasties

TOOLS

Banishing herbs, charcoal, a bowl, and some dirt or sand, or commercial incense. Have you noticed that I love using herbs? You can use whatever you have handy from the list on page 283. You'll burn these and carry them around the house, if you can, so put the dirt or sand in the bowl and then stick the charcoal in it. If not, sprinkle some around the house or make little sachets and stash them in hidden places, like at the back of a coat closet or in a kitchen cabinet.

Salt. Sprinkle some around the house to ground negative energy.

Water. Sprinkle water around to cleanse the house.

A white nine-day candle in glass. You can get these in many supermarkets. If you can't burn a candle, tape a piece of pure white paper on your wall.

A pot and a spoon. Oh, you'll see!

ALTAR LAYOUT

You'll be moving around the house, so your altar will be where you start and end the ritual. Put the candle (or piece of paper) on your altar, along with the other tools to charge them up.

Close all the doors and windows except one.

GO FOR IT

Move your dominant hand clockwise over all your tools, imagining white light pouring out and empowering them. I know, I said counterclockwise for banishing, but your actually *charging* this stuff with light to banish the funky energy.

Add a little salt to the water, bless, and charge it. Carry it around the

house, sprinkling a little bit everywhere. Leave the water and salt near the window or door that's open.

Light the candle. Carry it around the house and (carefully) poke it into every corner of every room. See the flame burning away the bad vibes. If you can't burn a candle, use your visualization to bring the color white firmly into your mind. Spread white light around the entire house by holding the image "white," breathing deeply, and moving that energy down into your dominant hand. Hold it out in front of you as you imagine white light flooding from your palm and saturating every inch of the house. Put the candle near the open window or door, still burning. (Make sure it's secure and in a safe spot.) Do the same thing with the incense.

Now, grab your pot and spoon. Start in the most remote corner of your house or on the top floor. Bang forcefully on it to start the magick. Then, walk slowly through your house, banging loudly on the pot, as you say in a loud but controlled voice: "*Out!* All negativity, *out!* Nothing angry, nothing cruel, nothing harmful can remain." (You could clap loudly if you feel nutty walking around with a pot and a spoon.)

Walk around every square foot of your house, ending up in front of the window or door you left open. Visualize the negative energy leaving through the opening. Chase it outside, if you can. Grab your water, salt, incense, and candle. Go outside. Leave the candle and incense burning on your stoop (safely). Take the other stuff around your yard, and sprinkle some of everything around the edges.

Take a cleansing bath after this, and wash any of the tools you used in hot running water. Dump the water onto the ground somewhere off your property (or flush it down the toilet), and bury any remains from the incense. Keep the candle on your altar and burn it for nine nights to continue the cleansing. If you can't burn candles, meditate on the white paper for nine nights.

COOL YOUR HEELS

Variations on this spell are pretty common, and you'll find it in a few different places. I hate to be redundant, but this is one of the first spells I was taught, and it's really effective! An excellent choice for obnoxious teachers or other people who seem to enjoy picking on you.

INTENTION

To freeze any negative energy that's aimed at you from a specific person.

TOOLS

A figure or other representation of the person you're thwarting, if you know who it is. If you dig poppets, this is a good time to use one. I don't like to use anything that resembles a person too closely for this; remember, it's the energy and effect you want to freeze. You could use a rock with the person's name on it, a piece of paper, or whatever's handy. If you don't know who's causing the trouble, just write "Troublemaker." On the other side, write "FROZEN," draw the rune for "winter" (see Chapter 11), or use other symbols that work for you.

A freezer. Put your image in here to stop that person cold!

ALTAR LAYOUT

You won't use a formal altar, but you may want to reinforce your goal (binding bad energy) by keeping a white candle on a table with runes or symbols for "stop," or something similar. You could also set up a spot like the one described in Banish a Bad Attitude.

※ GO FOR IT

Hold your antagonist's representation in your dominant hand, and say a brief incantation over the object; make sure you incorporate the idea of freezing the energy.

Put the image somewhere it won't be disturbed in the freezer. Joyce suggests putting the image in a plastic bag filled with water. Keep it in the freezer until the situation rights itself. Get rid of it when the energy isn't affecting you anymore.

BIND A TROUBLEMAKER

You can cast a Circle and set up an altar if you want to, but you don't have to. You will need:
· A photograph of the person (if you know who it is for sure), a poppet, or a rock
· Black cord
· A bowl of salt

Write the person's name on the back of the photo or other representation. Hold the image in your receptive hand and gather the psychic energy that you want to bind, like in Banish a Bad Attitude. Roll it into a sphere with your dominant hand and put it into the image. Repeat an incantation over it while you wrap the cord and knot it, being sure to reinforce the idea of binding or tying.

Repeat until you feel that the energy is safely tied up in knots. Put the image in a bowl of salt, and make sure it's completely covered. When the situation is resolved, bury the salt and the image away from your house, or simply "untie" the spell by undoing the knots.

THREEFOLD RETURN SPELL

Use this to return negative energy to its sender. You will need:
· A mirror
· A quartz point or your athame

Put up a simple white light Circle around you. Sit and meditate to clear your mind and ground yourself. Hold the mirror in your receptive hand and the quartz or athame in your dominant one. Think about the person who's bothering you, and imagine him or her starting trouble. Before you get upset, hold the mirror over your soft spot (wherever you feel troubling emotions in your body). Keep it there while you get your emotions under total control. Move the quartz point or athame to the side of the mirror, point facing out. Visualize the energy reflecting off the mirror, and guide it away from you with the quartz or athame, saying an incantation that includes returning the energy to its sender. Repeat until you feel the energy shift.

RITUALS TO HEAL A BROKEN HEART

It hurts. It really hurts. It totally sucks to have your heart broken, and I hate to tell you this, but chances are good that it'll happen more than once. They say that time heals all wounds, and it does, but it works even faster when you use a little Witchcraft! Ritual is great for cleansing your psyche, heart, and soul of all the aches and wounds that can accumulate through this lifetime. In fact, cleansing your aura and chakras is something you should do all the time—psychic hygiene! When the stresses or pangs of the day are too much, use these rituals to release, relax, and charge up to face another day.

PSYCHIC-WOUND SOOTHING

First of all, take a while to truly feel whatever you're feeling. Grieve over your lost lovey, or mourn someone who has passed away. The only way *out* of painful emotions is *through* them. If you don't let yourself feel the full force of your aching heart, you won't truly be able to mend it. So take a day or two, lay around in bed, cry until your face resembles a puffer fish, lounge in fuzzy slippers, and watch sappy movies. After you're done—two days, max!—get up and get ready to go on with life—with a little help from your witchy ways, of course.

ULTRA-MEGA DETOXIFYING SOAK

Once you've gotten out of your crummy sweats, do a major detox with this concoction.

2 cups Epsom or sea salts
5–15 drops frankincense, lavender, tea-tree, or sweet orange oil, or a combination

Add all the ingredients to a clean bathtub while you're running fairly hot water. Swirl the water to mix.

Or:

2 cups Epsom salts
2 tablespoons sage
2 tablespoons lavender
1 tablespoon rosemary

Infuse the herbs in a jar with boiled water. Add the infusion and salt to a warm bath.

As the tub fills, stir the water counterclockwise. Draw a banishing symbol in it, like the Adinkra symbol for changing yourself, or a pentagram. If you can, light a candle that you've inscribed with the same symbol. Leave it somewhere you can see it. Banishing incense, Peace Incense, or any other blend that pleases you would be a nice addition.

Slip into the tub. Splash the water over yourself and wash your grief away. Meditate on the flame as you breathe deeply and rhythmically. Visualize your body's inner workings as clearly

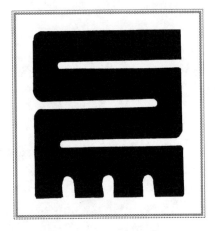

Adinkra Symbol for Changing Oneself

as you can, and breathe all that sorrow out of each cell. As you breathe in, enjoy the scent of the oils and let that pleasure replace your melancholy. After you've had a good, long soak, pull the plug and watch as the tub empties. Watch your unhappiness go down the drain. If you need something even more potent, do the . . .

HEALING-HEART RITUAL

If you can't use incense or light candles, get a quartz point to use instead. I'll explain in a moment.

INTENTION

To heal a broken heart

TOOLS

A bath. Take a ritual bath first to rinse your grief away and power up.

A white or red candle or quartz crystal. Use this to burn away your sadness.

Peace Incense or another soothing blend. Cleanse and rejuvenate your droopy aura with incense or an essential oil blend with which you can anoint yourself.

Paper and a pen. You'll see . . .

A Love amulet. The only way to get over it is to keep loving *yourself*. The Love amulet is to bring out your own loving energies and to remind you that love is everywhere.

A fireproof bowl and Essence-of-Love Oil (page 164) (optional). See below.

ALTAR LAYOUT

You can go two ways here. You can set up a formal altar (with all your working tools) and do a formal ritual (a good idea, since formalized rituals can help speed the healing process), or you can just do this in your room (or the bathroom) one night when you really feel lonely.

GO FOR IT

Cast a Circle however you like, and meditate to clear your mind. Keep an image of a circle firmly visualized for as long as you can. That image, the circle, will help you to get over emotional distress. It has no beginning and no end; it's a cycle, constant motion, and a perfect shape.

If you're working with candles and incense, light them now. If not, place the herbs in a bowl and give them a few pinches to release their scent, or use an essential oil blend to rub on your body. If you use a quartz point instead of a candle, hold it in your dominant hand and conjure your inner fire. See the crystal glowing with light.

Pass the candle or crystal around your body, imagining the light burning away any sadness. Do it again. Pass the candle or crystal around your body one more time, this time imagining the light suffusing every cell with its warmth and brightness, healing any tears or wounds in your aura. Do the same thing with the incense or oil blend. As you smooth the oil on or breathe in the incense, feel comforted and warm.

Concentrate on your breath and heartbeat to raise energy as you open your heart chakra by moving your dominant hand clockwise around it, physically touching the spot. Let your emotions well up. Cry, laugh, whatever. Release it. Visualize your emotions as a fine mist in front of you. Move your hands in a weaving motion, pulling the energy into a small sphere. Direct the sphere down onto the paper, and see it melting into the paper. Write your full name on the paper. Fold it in half once. Drip wax on it to seal it, if you're using a candle. Fold it in half again, and drip wax on it. Fold and repeat the process a third time.

If you can do this, it's a good one:

Hold the paper with your name over your heart, and say a prayer for healing and peace. Light the corner. Put the paper in the bowl and let it burn. Reserve the ashes and mix with a few drops of Essence-of-Love Oil.

(If you can't do that, tuck the paper away someplace private.)

Bless the Love amulet and anoint it with oil, if you're using any. If you did the burning part of the ritual, smear the ashes on the back of the amulet, the side you'll wear against your chest. Wear this until your heart heals.

CHAPTER TWENTY-ONE

POLITICS AND TEEN RIGHTS

SEX, DRUGS, AND PAGAN POLITICS?

If there's one question I hear over and over again, it's this one: "What's the official Pagan stance on premarital sex/abortion/euthanasia/same-sex marriage, or any other of a multitude controversial personal/political issues?" The difficulty with answering is that there *are* no pat answers. Remember, Wicca and Paganism aren't organized religions; we don't have a central leader who exercises absolute power over everyone's moral choices. In a coven setting, a Wiccan might go to the High Priest/ess to ask for advice on a specific problem, but, even then, a good Priest/ess doesn't dictate. He or she *listens,* advises according to the particular situation, and then encourages the person to think deeply for himself or herself. So the simple answer to the question is that Pagans don't have *any* official stances on political issues. We're Democrats, Republicans (believe it or not), Libertarians, and "other." Most of us *do* agree with "An it harm none, do as you will," and that's a complicated creed to apply to politics.

For one thing, how do you practice "harm none" when you're thinking about abortion or the death penalty? Does a Wiccan want to make abortion illegal and possibly curtail women's reproductive rights? On one hand, abortion ends a life, and that's harmful, right? On the other hand, a woman who's forced to be pregnant against her will is being harmed, isn't she? It's the same quandary with capital punishment. Should we pay for a confessed mass murderer to live and eat and let him continue to hurt society? But if we take a life, aren't we murderers, too? The debates are endless, unanswerable, and totally personal. In my opinion, the rule of thumb is slightly different when you start talking politics. I think keeping the greatest good of all involved is a key concept. While Witches don't have any authority figures to tell us how to live, we always answer to our own conscience and our personal deities. Witches take responsibility for their actions, and if that means we have to occasionally do something that goes against the accepted norm to live true to our selves, then we take that and own it.

Which brings me to the less understood implication of "An it harm none, do as you will": *If your actions harm none but simply aren't socially accepted, then you have the responsibility to live as you see fit and follow your heart.* If you feel that the way you live your life is good, wholesome, and happy, then it's your duty to live that way and be delighted. Sounds good, but sometimes it's really hard to buck the system constantly. Ask any gay person. For the same reason, it's important to give every other living creature the respect to let it live in its own best way.

I'd also like to point out that "harm none" includes *you!* Wicca doesn't have any "laws" about when, how, or with whom you have sex, for example. We're all about Nature, right? And sex is perfectly natural, right? So go ahead and have tons of sex without worrying, right? Not exactly. I used this example because the idea that Witches are promiscuous is a pretty common stereotype, especially for female Witches. Witches are generally sexually liberated, for sure, and the vast majority of us are open about and have a healthy attitude toward sex. However, being empowered and free doesn't necessarily translate into being a hoochie. Wiccans know that freedom means responsibility. We also know that sex is a sacred act. Read: Sex is natural, groovy, holy, and a huge responsibility. Therefore, Witches (I hope)

> "I think Pagans need to be more socially active. I grew up with food drives and clothing drives. I grew up knowing about politics, and I was encouraged to have strong opinions. I grew up with strong liberal Democratic ideals, and just because I changed religions doesn't mean I'm about to give them [my ideals] up. I hear Pagans talking about the good of the people, and how everyone is equal, and so on . . . so the logical conclusion is to live for the people."
>
> —MARJORIE, AGE 13

"I had been raised to think of the Earth as a nonentity. It wasn't alive really—it was just an inconsequential setting or backdrop to the all-important dramas of the human race. My mother would often throw bags of trash out the car window, even when we were only about a hundred yards away from our house. My brother continues this tradition, much to my dismay. I know it's wrong. It's a sin against Mother Nature. I've stood up against my mother and brother, refusing to litter or to let them do so without a considerable guilt trip. If we as individuals do what we can, however small, we might do a world of good for Nature."

—ATHENA, AGE 17

won't harm themselves by having meaningless sex or having sex with someone who doesn't respect us, *or* Witches won't harm someone else by disrespecting him or her or the relationship he or she may be involved in. See how the lines are blurry and everything gets complicated? That's the obligation of freedom. You have to think for yourself, follow your intuition, be willing to hear all sides of an argument, and act with your best effort by always consulting your intellect, heart, and soul.

Having said all that, I feel comfortable making one small generalization about Pagan ethics: We want freedom, justice, a healthy planet, and true humanity in the world. How you interpret those ideas is entirely up to you. What would you fix about the world? What is your definition of utopia? Figure it out and work for it every day! Politics is a game, but the game is serious. If you want to delve into the political world, here are a few suggestions for you—even if you're not old enough to vote.

PERSONAL ACTION IS POLITICAL ACTION

Remember Chapter 16? Some of the ideas in there are absolutely political. Every personal choice you make is political, from supporting those companies who make products that fit in with your Pagan lifestyle to calmly stating your views on the world. Politics isn't just voting or activism, although those things are important. Each time you make a decision about what you think is right and good and then act on it, you're making a political statement. So the first step to being a political Pagan is to know yourself. You are a part of society. Use your power!

- **Always speak your mind.** If you think something is unfair, unhealthy, or a restriction of your freedom, speak up! It's your right as a human being to put in your two cents. A word of advice: Follow the first rule of good debate and always keep your cool when you encounter opposition.

- **Money is power.** Spend your money wisely. If you find out that your favorite chocolate milk company destroys the environment with strange chemical by-products, give it up and find another favorite. You can also write to that company and express yourself, making sure to tell them that you won't buy their products anymore unless they clean up their act.

- **Money is power.** I know, I already said that, but it works another way, too. TeenPowerPolitics.com says that teens between the ages of ten and nineteen spent an estimated $153 BILLION in 1999! That's serious cash! Support those companies that are in tune with your ideals! Support your local farmers and your local Pagan shop, and you end up creating a world a little bit closer to your own utopia.

- **Learn the rules.** If you want to play the political game, you have to learn the rules. Stay informed about what's going on in your government and in other countries. Write to your representatives, even if you can't vote yet. If there's something that you and your friends are really steamed about, start a letter-writing campaign and don't relent until you get a response. You may not be able to vote right now, but you will someday, and you certainly have parents and teachers who vote. Remind your local political figures about that.

- **Start locally.** If you're unhappy about toxic waste, clean up a park. It's not saving the world from chemical sludge, but it *is* taking responsibility for your immediate environment. Work your influence in school, too. Petition your administrators when there's something ugly afoot, like censorship, or try to implement a recycling program.

· Always finish what you start.

STRENGTH IN NUMBERS

You have the right to freedom of speech, expression, and religion. If you find yourself in a situation that restricts those freedoms, shout, argue, kick, and fight for your rights. Not only is it imperative for you as an individual, you're also paving the way for the next person who's being bullied into silence and conformity. I hope you're close enough with your parents that you can go to them if you're being harassed and that they'll support you if you decide to take action.

There are lots of organizations out there that focus on political activism, and lots of those are especially for teenagers. Check out the Political Action section of the Appendices for contact information to get you started.

PROTECT YOUR RIGHTS

According to several constitutional scholars, a teenager is afforded exactly the same rights as adults under our Constitution. In reality, teens sometimes get squashed in school and out in the world. Why? Mostly because teens aren't aware of their rights, so they don't know how to defend themselves. Take a look at a copy of our Constitution, get really friendly with it, and don't let yourself be pushed around.

Read on:

In 1999, seventeen-year-old Crystal Seifferly was told that she couldn't wear a pentagram to school because it violated the school's dress code. The dress code banned several types of apparel, including Gothic makeup, black nail polish, and "gang/cult" symbols. In fact, the schools Gang/Cult Policy "specifically prohibits students from belonging to a Wiccan group."[1] Huh? Are you kidding me? Crystal contacted the ACLU (American Civil

Liberties Union), and they represented her in the proceeding court case against her school. The ACLU argued that the pentagram is a symbol of religious faith, and as such, students must be allowed to wear it openly. Interestingly enough, other religious symbols, like the Jewish Star of David and the Muslim crescent and moon, were also banned from the school as "gang" symbols, but crucifixes were allowed. Can anyone say "discrimination"? Needless to say, Crystal and the ACLU trampled that policy, won the case, and made a great stride for Pagan rights.

Another case that started in 1999 was fifteen-year-old Brandi Blackbear's lawsuit against her school for infringing on her freedoms. She's an aspiring horror-fiction writer who admires Stephen King, among others. Someone started a rumor that she had written a story that included a violent incident at school (this was shortly after the Columbine insanity). Her administrators freaked out, searched her book bag, and seized her belongings. They did, indeed, find a short story that had to do with a shooting at school . . . a *fictional* story. They confiscated her writings, and she was temporarily suspended for being a threat to the school. A few months later, Brandi found a book on Wicca in the library, where several students saw her reading it. Shortly after, a teacher was admitted to the local hospital for some kind of illness. You're not going to believe this, but the assistant principal at Brandi's school called her into his office and accused her of being a Witch and casting a spell on the sick teacher. Are we living in the thirteenth century? Again, the ACLU stepped in

> "About a year ago in my old hometown, an English teacher was suspended from her job because the Board of Education discovered that she was Wiccan. The teacher was devastated at her community's reaction. She was shunned by most of her former friends and colleagues, and feared for her and her husband's safety. It tore my heart out to watch her interview with the nightly news— she sat trembling on her couch, her eyes swollen and tearing as she recounted the treatment she had received after all the years she had spent in the community. She could have sued and gotten her job back, but she decided not to pursue it and resigned."
>
> —ATHENA, AGE 17

and the case was resolved in favor of sanity and freedom.

According to the ACLU, an organization that fights for our constitutional rights, where you go to school affects your freedoms while you're there. Public schools are given money by the federal government to help them operate successfully. Since they're under the federal government's rule, public schools *have* to follow constitutional guidelines. You cannot be forced to pray in school; you cannot be discriminated against because of your religion; and you do have the right to express yourself freely—as long as that expression isn't deemed "obscene" or "libelous." That's where the debate starts; what is obscene and libelous, and what is "disruptive" (another common excuse cited by school officials when they don't like your style)?

Private schools are different because they're privately funded. Since the federal government doesn't give them money, it doesn't have as much control over a private school's policies. It's still freedom, in a way. If your family is religious or wants to send you to a very specialized school, they have the freedom to choose it, and the school has the freedom to teach a specialized curriculum. Private schools can be a lot more strict in their rules regarding censorship, dress codes, and freedom of expression, so you're in a bit of a bind there. Still, you cannot be discriminated against, regardless of where your school gets its money.

How do you know if you're being discriminated against? Well, I can't answer that without hearing your story, but if a teacher or faculty member is picking on you for your beliefs, singling you out in class and making fun of you, or marking your papers badly for no reason other than the fact that your ideas are different from his or hers, then you may have a case. If you're not allowed to participate in clubs or organizations because your religion/gender/race/class is different from the other members, you're being discriminated against. If you aren't allowed the same rights as other people, like wearing a symbol of your religion to school, then you're being discriminated against. Your school officials don't have the right to take your stuff (unless it's illegal for you to have it, like drugs, guns, and all that), and they don't have the right to search your purse, book bag, or body without your consent.

DISCRIMINATION SUCKS . . . FIGHT THE POWER!

No American citizen has to stand for being discriminated against because of his or her race, color, creed, gender, or age. Our Constitution protects us from being harassed or otherwise penalized for our beliefs, and those same laws apply to teenagers. While Wiccans and Pagans aren't part of an organized religion, we are still afforded the same rights as anybody else. Unfortunately, Paganism is often misunderstood, and we have to fight a little harder to make ourselves and our beliefs accepted. If you encounter discrimination in school, at a job, or in some other public way, you have a right to stand up for yourself! Don't sit back and take it!

There are a few groups that offer resources for legal aid, information, and networking in cases of religious (or other) discrimination. Here are some for you to check out:

AMERICAN CIVIL LIBERTIES UNION (ACLU)

ACLU.org
National Headquarters
125 Broad Street
New York, NY 10004

This is a watch dog organization that works to protect American's civil liberties, namely those freedoms that are guaranteed by the Constitution. Check out their web site for all sorts of useful information about your rights and ways that you can help protect them. There's a section just for high school students and another one for colleges and universities. You can contact your local ACLU representative for legal aid if you feel that you're being discriminated against at school.

"I have been harassed at school by various people. What's worse is, the faculty didn't back me up. I've always held teachers (well, at least some of them) in high regard, but their reaction to my torment was incredibly disappointing. One instance that sticks out in my mind—and on my head—is when a jerk cut my hair in one of my classes about a month ago. I was devastated that he, being in high school, would do something so childish, and that the other girls at the table watched him do it without raising a hand. He giggled afterward, 'Now she really *does* look like a Witch!' The teacher claimed that, since he didn't see it, it might as well not have happened. *'Do you think I did this to myself!'* I demanded. He shrugged. I went to the guidance office and the disciplinary office with my mom. They assured us they would have a stern talk with the guy. Oh, wow. He had assaulted my person with a six-inch-long pair of scissors and had violated my physical appearance. What if he had slipped and the scissors had accidentally cut my neck? Yet they did nothing to punish this guy . . . whilst staring at my pentacle in an odd sort of way that made me want to wring their necks."

—ATHENA, AGE 17

RELIGIOUS LIBERTIES LAWYERS NETWORK (RLLN)

Phyllis Curott, Esq.
P.O. Box 311
Prince Street Station
New York, NY 10012
rllnhq@aol.com

Phyllis Curott, a Wiccan Priestess, NYU School of Law graduate, and fabulous author, has set this group up to provide attorneys for legal counseling and representation in religious discrimination cases.

ALTERNATIVE RELIGIONS EDUCATION NETWORK (AREN)

AREN.org

One of the groups that stepped in to work on Crystal Seifferly's case, this group offers legal assistance.

LADY LIBERTY LEAGUE

CircleSanctuary.org/liberty
Circle Sanctuary
P.O. Box 219
Mt. Horeb, WI 53572

Started in 1985 by Selena Fox, a prominent Witch and coproducer of *Circle Sanctuary* magazine, this group offers networking contacts for legal support.

EARTH RELIGIONS LEGAL ASSISTANCE NETWORK

Conjure.com/ERAL/eral.html

This site is a collection of contacts and also provides referrals for legal assistance.

WITCHES' LEAGUE FOR PUBLIC AWARENESS (WLPA)

Celticcrow.com
P.O. Box 909
Rehoboth, MA 02769
Or
P.O. Box 8736
Salem, MA 01971

Started by Laurie Cabot in 1986, this group works to fight stereotypes and educate the media. They can send you informational packets regarding your rights and how to protect them.

MERRY MEET, MERRY PART, AND MERRY MEET AGAIN!

So, now you've got a grip on what Wicca and Pagan Witchcraft are all about. I have a few parting words, and then I have to go.

RITUAL ETIQUETTE

All the Witches I interviewed requested one thing: that I include a few words about ritual etiquette so you know what's up when you finally come across a Pagan gathering. Although we're a relatively laid-back and tolerant bunch, there are a few simple rules to be aware of when you go to a Witch's Sabbat or Esbat, or one of the big festivals. Stick to these and you'll be sure to make a good impression.

· **Ask before you touch anything!** Some Witches are *very* particular about who touches their stuff, whether it's their Tarot cards, drum, ritual tools, or crystals. Always err on the side of politeness, and get permission before you put your paws on anything that isn't yours.

· **Be respectful of people's personal space.** What I mean is, don't assume that a ritual is an excuse to hit on someone. It's annoying when people get aggressive with their attention around a festival fire. If you think someone's cute, that's great, but be polite. While Witches are (mostly) sexually liberated, that doesn't mean we want someone bugging us when we're trying to work.

· **Don't show up drunk/stoned/with illegal drugs on you.** I can't tell you how totally annoying it is when someone comes to ritual totally ker-schnickered. Witches may have a reputation for being rebels, but that doesn't mean you should assume that we are. If you show up to an Open Circle with illegal substances on you, you put the entire group at risk for being arrested, and that really sets us back in the main-stream acceptance department.

Remember that magick comes from you, from the blood running through your veins, from your breath, and from your deep connection to the Universe around you. You are powerful. You are strong. If you work hard for something, it can be yours. Ignore the media, which tells you that you have to look a certain way or think the same thoughts as everyone else to be accepted. Your individuality is precious. Keep searching until you find other people who appreciate you for who you are. Always be willing to learn, grow, and fight for what you believe in. And have some other inter-ests and hobbies besides Witchcraft. Knit a sweater or go running or some-thing. Your mind needs a break every now and again!

One of my favorite parts of the Pagan community is the fabulous festi-vals. Starwood Festival, at the Brushwood Folklore Center in New York, is one of my favorites. It's a weeklong bash, and we all camp out on the beau-tiful grounds. Starwood usually attracts around fifteen hundred Pagans from different traditions. You'll find Wiccan Traditionalists, Eclectic Witches, Druids, Santeros, and people of all different races and nationali-ties, ranging from infants to elders. There's live music, workshops, incredi-ble vendors, and all sorts of Pagan mayhem to be had. My absolute favorite part is the drummers, who carry on all day and night.

One time, I fell asleep outside the drum circle, just lying on the ground on the outskirts of the Circle. My head was directly on the dirt, and I could hear and feel the soft pulse of the "third shift" (midnight to dawn) drum circle. I slept that way until sunrise, when I woke up totally refreshed and ready to go. I also love the merchant's lane, where the same people set up the same booths every year. There's one lady who makes the most incredi-ble pottery from clay she digs herself. It looks like milk chocolate, and it's so smooth and luscious, I just want to lick it! My friend, Johnathan, recently gave me a chalice that she made, and it stands proudly on my altar. At night, the campgrounds look like an enchanted Gypsy village, one tent more elaborate and lovely than the next. You can walk down the makeshift alleys and lanes, and everyone says hello, even if you've never met.

At the end of the festival, an absolutely enormous bonfire is built, and it takes the "woodbusters" (burly guys who chop the wood) an entire day to get it set up. Before the Sun goes down, everyone rushes around, taking a shower and putting on their best costume for the party. It's huge! Imagine a thousand Pagans in all their finery, laughing, dancing, and chasing one another around a bonfire that weighs hundreds of pounds! For a few days, I feel like the world is totally right and I understand what "community" means. When it's over, we all say "see you next time," pack our things, and know that our community will live on in our hearts until we get together again.

I hope this book has helped you on your journey. . . . Maybe I'll see you at one of the festivals! Stop by my website www.parkyourbroomstick.com to say hello.

Never say good-bye! Instead, say what the Witches say when the Circle is opened and everyone goes home: Merry Meet, Merry Part, and Merry Meet Again!

CORRESPONDENCES

These correspondences are to help you get your magickal connections started. Practice and experience will be your best teachers, so work with the information you find but always be open to learning directly from an herb, deity, color, or planet itself.

A WITCH'S PANTRY (COMMON INGREDIENTS)

Anise: divination, spirit work, invisibility
Apple: love, prosperity, healing
Basil: prosperity, love
Bay: luck, legal battles
Chamomile: sleep, prophetic dreams, eases pain
Cinnamon: stimulant, cleansing, banishing, healing, psychic awareness, prosperity
Clove: purification, healing, prosperity, power
Dill: prosperity, love
Fennel: peace, calming for nervous or upset stomachs
Garlic: healing, protection, banishing, willpower
Ginger: energy, healing, success, calming for upset stomachs
Lavender: peace, soothing nerves, meditation, clarity, concentration
Lemon: cleansing, healing, rejuvenating
Marjoram: peace, balance, soothing
Mint: stimulant or relaxing (depending on your need), concentration, cleansing, communication, prosperity
Nutmeg: psychic awareness, love, prophetic dreams
Orange: joy, love, peace, healing, cleansing, prosperity, attraction

Parsley: energy, healing
Pepper: banishing, stimulant, cleansing, healing, prosperity, sexual love
Oregano: invoke spirits, meditative trance
Rose: love, consecration, healing
Rosemary: love, enhance memory, concentration, power, consecration,
    cleansing, grounding
Sage: purification, banishing, healing, consecration, feminine energy,
    grounding
Vanilla (beans or extract): passion, self-love, joy

SOME SECRET INGREDIENTS FOR A WITCH'S PANTRY

Dragon's blood: power, psychic power, love, purification
Frankincense: consecration, banishing, meditation, spiritual growth, psychic
    awareness
Amber: wishes, love, riches
Bergamot: success, concentration, cleansing, prosperity
Patchouli: sexual energy, prosperity

TABLE OF COLORS

White: protection, repel negativity, purity of thought, peace, consecration,
    meditation
Black: protection, absorb energy, psychic ability, repel negativity, power
Gray: glamours, invisibility, creating confusion
Red: love, passion, healing, protection, power, Fire
Pink: love, gentleness, fun
Orange: inspiration, energy, cheer, friendship, Solar energy
Yellow: intellect, communication, Air
Green: prosperity, growth, healing, Earth
Blue: spirituality, soothing emotions, Water, Fire
Brown: grounding, healing, animals, Earth
Indigo: psychic ability, spirit work, invisibility, increasing spirituality
Violet: magick, psychic abilities, sooth anxiety
Silver: psychic abilities, Lunar energy, repel negative energy, glamours,
    invisibility
Gold: healing, Solar energy, energy booster, blessings

SPELL-CRAFT CORRESPONDENCES

LOVE SPELLS

MOON PHASE:

> To bring Love to you: waxing to full
> To heal a broken heart: full to new

SUN OR MOON IN:

> Taurus, Scorpio, Cancer, Pisces

STONES AND METALS:

> To radiate and draw Love: moonstone, rose quartz, amber, ruby, garnet,
>   rutilated quartz, copper, gold
> To balance emotions: amethyst, hematite, quartz
> To repel unwanted advances: moonstone, obsidian, onyx, jet, silver, iron

DEITIES:

> Goddesses: Aphrodite, Freya, Isis, Oshun, Shakti, Amaterasu
> Gods: Apollo, Chango, Shiva, Pan

HERBS AND OILS:

> vanilla, dragon's blood, cinnamon, orange, pepper, rosemary, basil, apple,
>   nutmeg, amber

COLORS:

> pink, blood red, gold, silver, white

TIMES:

> dawn, dusk, midnight, midsummer, Beltane, Lughnasadh, Venus in Pisces

HEALING SPELLS

MOON PHASE:

> To banish illness: full to dark
> To increase vitality: dark or new to full

SUN OR MOON IN:

> Virgo, Taurus, Libra

STONES AND METALS:

> citrine, hematite, malachite, amethyst, obsidian, garnet, moonstone, gold

DEITIES:

> Goddesses: Brigid, Gaia, Iduna, Ochun, Kuan Yin, Sekhmet
> Gods: Apollo, Inle

HERBS AND OILS:

> sage, parsley, orange, garlic, cinnamon, pepper, ginger, clove, frankincense

COLORS:

> green, gold, light blue, red

TIMES:

> Beltane, Mabon, Sun in Virgo

PROSPERITY AND SUCCESS SPELLS

MOON PHASE:

> To banish poverty or obstacles: dark and waning to dark
> To increase wealth and power: full and new to full

SUN OR MOON IN:

Taurus, Cancer

STONES AND METALS:

malachite, pyrite, quartz, silver, copper, gold

DEITIES:

Goddesses: Freya, Oshun, Amaterasu
Gods: Lugh, Nudons, Tyr

HERBS AND OILS:

bergamot, cinnamon, patchouli, amber, basil, mint, pepper, orange

COLORS:

green, gold, silver

TIMES:

noon, dawn, Beltane

PROTECTION SPELLS

MOON PHASE:

any time

SUN OR MOON IN:

Aries, Scorpio, Cancer

STONES AND METALS:

obsidian, jet, onyx, moonstone, labrodorite, hematite, quartz, silver, iron, lead

DEITIES:

Goddesses: Nyx, Morrigan, Cerridwen, Sekhmet, Hekate, Oya, Kali
Gods: Odin, Thor, Cernunnos, Helios, Ra, Obatala, Chango, Oggun, Brahma

HERBS AND OILS:

dragon's blood, frankincense, pepper, cinnamon, garlic, clove, rose, anise

COLORS:

black, white, gray, red, silver, dark blue

TIMES:

Sun in Aries, Mars in Capricorn

PSYCHIC-ABILITY SPELLS

MOON PHASE:

full or dark

SUN OR MOON IN:

Scorpio, Cancer, Pisces

STONES AND METALS:

moonstone, obsidian, herkimer diamonds, diamonds, silver

DEITIES:

Goddesses: Rhiannon, Brigid, Selene, Aradia, Hekate, Freya, Ochun, Nyx
Gods: Odin, Chaos, Apollo

HERBS AND OILS:

dragon's blood, nutmeg, cinnamon, chamomile, anise, rosemary,
frankincense

COLORS:

black, silver, dark purple, dark blue, white, gray

TIMES:

midnight, dusk, Moon in Scorpio

COMMUNICATION SPELLS

MOON PHASE:

any time

SUN OR MOON IN:

Gemini, Cancer, Scorpio

STONES AND METALS:

quartz, kyanite, tiger's eye

DEITIES:

Goddesses: Cerridwen, Rhiannon
Gods: Hermes, Ellegua, Ogma

HERBS AND OILS:

mint, cinnamon, bay, lavender, bergamot

COLORS:

light yellow, light blue, white

TIMES:

Monday, Wednesday, noon, Mercury in Gemini

BANISHING AND BINDING SPELLS

MOON PHASE:

waning or dark

SUN OR MOON IN:

Scorpio, Libra, Aries

STONES AND METALS:

obsidian, onyx, jet, moonstone, silver, lead, iron

DEITIES:

Goddesses: Kali, Morrigan, Cerridwen, Rhiannon, Aradia
Gods: Shiva, Chango, Chaos, Thor, Tyr

HERBS AND OILS:

dragon's blood, frankincense, sage, cinnamon, pepper, garlic, rose, clove, lavender

COLORS:

black, white, gray, red, silver

TIMES:

noon, midnight, Samhain, Mars in Scorpio

WEB DIRECTORY

THE TOP FIVE PAGAN SITES ON THE WEB

Witchvox.com (The Witches' Voice)
Neopagan.net
Wicca.com
BranwensCauldron.com
iit.edu/~phillips/personal/ (Mama Rose's Kitchen)

WEB SITES OF ESTABLISHED PAGAN ORGANIZATIONS

CoG.org (Covenant of the Goddess)
CircleSanctuary.org
CUUPS.org (Covenant of Univeralist Uniterian Pagans)
Reclaiming.org
EarthSpirit.org
ADF.org (Ár nDraíocht Féin)
AREN.org

"BOOT CAMP" WEB SITES

TeenWitch.com
WitchSchool.com
Reclaiming.org
CircleSanctuary.org

WEB SITES TO VISIT FOR GENERAL RESEARCH

PaganPath.com
TWPT.com (The Wiccan Pagan Times)

Bulfinch.org (Bulfinch's Mythology Online)
gofree.indigo.ie/~wicca/ (Wicca Na hErin: Janet Farrar and Gavin Bone)
WaningMoon.com
Sacred-Texts.com
About.com
ReligiousTolerance.org
AromaWeb.com
Yahoogroups.com (for mail lists)

GOOD WEB SITES FOR SHOPPING

All these sites have fairly extensive catalogs online, they all have going-rate prices, and they all accept money orders. If you see a star next to the name, I have ordered from them, so I can vouch for reliability and quality. Otherwise, you're on your own.

*FirstHerb.com
Starwest-Botanicals.com
CapricornsLair.com
Abaxion.com
PansPantry.co.uk/index.htm (Pan's Pantry)
*MagicParlor.com
*WLPSSP.com (Nu Aeon: White Light Pentacles/Sacred Spirit Products)
TheMagicalBlend.com
WhisperedPrayers.com

WEB SITES FOR THOSE INTERESTED IN POLITICAL ACTION

Alternet.com
TeenPowerPolitics.com
Greens.org
GenerationNet.org
FreeThePlanet.org
FreedomForum.org
PBS.org/merrow/trt/index.html (Listen Up)
FreeSpeech.org
YouthActivism.com
WhisperedMedia.org

APPENDIX C

ESSENTIAL READING

BOOKS

Bonewits, Isaac. *Real Magic*. 1989. York Beach, Maine: Red Wheel/Weiser.

———. *Witchcraft: A Concise History*. 2001. eBook. PocketPCpress.

Capro, Fritjof. *The Tao of Physics: An Exploration of the Parallels Between Modern Physics and Eastern Mysticism*. 2000. Boston, Mass.: Shambhala Publications.

Cunningham, Scott. *Cunningham's Encyclopedia of Crystal, Gem, and Metal Magic*. 1988. St. Paul, Minn.: Llewellyn Publications.

———. *Living Wicca: A Further Guide for the Solitary Practitioner.* 1993. St. Paul, Minn.: Llewellyn Publications.

———. *Magical Herbalism: The Secret of the Wise*. 1987. St. Paul, Minn.: Llewellyn Publications.

———. *Wicca: A Guide for the Solitary Practitioner.* 1990. St. Paul, Minn.: Llewellyn Publications.

Curott, Phyllis. *Witch Crafting*. 2001. New York: Broadway Books.

Farrar, Stewart. *What Witches Do*. 1983. Blaine, Wash.: Phoenix Publishing.

Farrar, Stewart, and Janet Farrar. *A Witches' Bible: The Complete Witches Handbook*. 1996. Blaine, Wash.: Phoenix Publishing.

Gardner, Gerald. *Witchcraft Today*. 1980. New York: Magickal Childe.

Hunter, Jennifer. *21st Century Wicca: A Young Witch's Guide to Living the Magickal Life*. 1997. New York: Citadel Press/Kensington Books.

Hutton, Ronald. *Triumph of the Moon: A History of Modern Pagan Witchcraft*. 2001. New York: Oxford University Press.

Starhawk. *The Spiral Dance: A Rebirth of the Ancient Religion of the Great Goddess*. 1999 (20th anniversary edition). San Francisco: Harper San Francisco.

Zimmermann, Denise, and Katherine A. Gleason. 2000. *The Complete Idiot's Guide to Wicca and Witchcraft*. New York: Alpha Books.

HIGHLY RECOMMENDED

BOOKS

Agrippa, Henry Cornelius. *Three Books of Occult Philosophy*. 1994. Ed. Donald Tyson. Trans. James Freake. St. Paul, Minn.: Llewellyn Publications.

Amber K. *True Magick: A Beginner's Guide*. 1991. St. Paul, Minn.: Llewellyn Publications.

Bradley, Marion Zimmerman. *The Mists of Avalon*. 2001 (reissue). New York: Del Rey Books.

Crow Dog, Mary. *Lakota Woman*. 1994 (reissue). New York: Harper Perennial.

Culpeper, Nicholas. *Culpeper's Complete Herbal: A Book of Natural Remedies of Ancient Ills*. 1998. Hertfordshire, England: Wordsworth Editions.

Fortune, Dion. *The Mystical Qabalah*. 2000 (reprint edition). York Beach, Maine: Red Wheel/Weiser.

———. *The Training & Work of an Initiate*. 2000 (revised edition). York Beach, Maine: Red Wheel/Weiser.

Huson, Paul. *Mastering Herbalism*. 2001. Lanham, Md.: Madison Books.

Javane, Faith, and Dusty Bunker. *Numerology and the Divine Triangle*. 1997. West Chester, Pa.: Schiffer Publishing. Covers numerology, Tarot, the Pythagorean theory, etc.

McGaa, Ed. *Mother Earth Spirituality: Native American Paths to Healing Ourselves and Our World*. 1990. San Francisco: Harper San Francisco.

Melody. *Love Is in the Earth: A Kaleidoscope of Crystals*. 1995. Wheat Ridge, Colo.: Earth-Love Publishing House.

Roberts, Richard. *From Eden to Eros: Origins of the Put Down of Women*. 1985. San Anselmo, Calif.: Vernal Equinox Press.

Sjöö, Monica, and Barbara Mor. *The Great Cosmic Mother: Rediscovering the Religion of the Earth*. 1991. San Francisco: Harper San Francisco.

Starhawk. *The Fifth Sacred Thing*. 1994 (reprint edition). New York: Bantam Books.

Teish, Luisah. *Jambalaya: The Natural Woman's Book of Personal Charms and Practical Rituals*. 1988. San Francisco: Harper San Francisco.

Telesco, Patricia. *How to Be a Wicked Witch: Good Spells, Charms, Potions and Notions for Bad Days*. 2001. New York: Fireside.

———. *Your Book of Shadows: How to Write Your Own Magickal Spells*. 1999. New York: Carol Publishing Group.

Wall, Carly. *Setting the Mood with Aromatherapy*. 1998. New York: Sterling Publishing.

Worwood, Valerie Ann. *The Complete Book of Essential Oils and Aromatherapy*. 1991. Novato, Calif.: New World Publishing.

PUBLICATIONS

Circle Magazine: Visit CircleSanctuary.org for further details.

Talisman: For the Magickal Teen.

The Witches' Almanac, Spring 2002 to Spring 2003: The Complete Guide to Lunar Harmony. Visit Amazon.com for ordering information.

Parabola. Visit Parabola.org for further details.

Sage Woman. Visit SageWoman.com for further information.

GLOSSARY

animism: seeing every object as alive.

anthropomorphic: the idea that deities look and act like humans.

asperger: a ritual tool used by some Wiccans, an asperger (or aspergilum) is used to shake small droplets of water on a person, around a Circle, etc., for purification.

athame: a ritual dagger, usually double-edged with a white handle.

besom: broom.

bibliomancy: divination by opening to random passages from books.

bolline: a ritual knife with a crescent-shaped blade, used to harvest herbs and carve objects.

Cabala: the Hebrew mystical tradition that views the relationship between God and man as expressed by the Tree of Life, the Three Pillars, and the 32 Paths of Wisdom.

cauldron: a Goddess symbol. Often made of cast iron, the cauldron is used to cook ritual foods or potions.

chalice: a ritual cup that symbolizes the Goddess. The chalice is used when blessing water or other liquid.

code: a religion's moral standard.

collective unconscious: distinguished from the personal consciousness, this is the deep underlying well of all humankind's experiences throughout time.

credo: a religion's philosophy on life.

cultus: a religion's particular set of rituals and mythology.

deosil: sunwise, clockwise (in the Northern Hemisphere), or movements, used to charge or create energy, that go in those directions.

duotheistic: the idea that the divine force is expressed by two deities, often a God and Goddess.

eclectic: drawing from many sources.

ecstasy: literally, "standing outside oneself." A state of consciousness that releases the boundaries between yourself and divinity; connection to the infinite.

ephemeris: a book of astronomical movement.

Esbat: a full Moon ritual.

evoke: to call forth emotional response.

grimoire: any one of several medieval instruction books for magick.

immanent: the idea that divine force(s) are within all things at all times, that divinity is present in the world.

infusion: drawing out an herb's properties by soaking it in boiling water or in oil.

invoke: to call forth a primal energy from the Universe.

libation bowl: a ritual tool; food and drink are poured into this as an offering to the Gods.

Neo-Pagan: a modern person practicing a modern version of Paganism.

occult: something that is hidden from view; usually refers to the study of magick.

Pagan: a general term for any religion that (a) is polytheistic, (b) worships Nature as a divine force, (c) isn't Judeo-Christian or Muslim.

pantheism: the idea that all Nature is alive and divine.

polarized: having two opposite forces that complete each other.

polytheistic: believing in many gods.

pyromancy: divination by scrying with fire.

Sabbat: the Witches' holidays: Samhain, Yule, Imbolc, Ostara, Midsummer, Beltane, Lughnasadh, and Mabon.

scry: divination by gazing at a reflective surface to receive visual impressions.

sephira/sephiroth: the ten levels of divine manifestation in the Cabala. Depicted as spheres on the Tree of Life.

shaman: a healer in tribal cultures that uses spiritual techniques to affect physical illness, like communicating with the spirit world.

smudge: Native American term for cleansing an area with incense smoke, especially sage.

stang: a staff with two points on the top, used by some Traditional Witches to represent the Horned God.

sympathetic magick: using the relationships between natural objects to harness their energy and affect other natural objects.

transcendent: the idea that divine forces are above or beyond human experience and understanding.

Tree of Life: a metaphor for the connection between God and man, used in Cabala.

Wicca: a modern Pagan religion that reveres Nature as alive with divine forces and Nature's cycles as holy; sees divine forces as male and female, transcendent, immanent, and anthropomorphic, depending.

widdershins: movement that goes against the Sun's pattern; antisunwise, counterclockwise (in the Northern Hemisphere).

Witch: a person, either male or female, who practices the art of changing consciousness to reconnect with the infinite universal energies and who affects changes in his or her life and self through that connection with Witchcraft.

Witchcraft: the art of understanding, combining, harnessing, and communicating with the energies of Nature to bring about change.

NOTES AND BIBLIOGRAPHY

NOTES

CHAPTER 1

1. Migene Gonzalez-Wippler. *The Complete Book of Spells, Ceremonies & Magic* (St. Paul, Minn.: Llewellyn Publications, 2000), p. 15.

2. Britannica.com (Encyclopaedia Britannica). See entry for "Prehistoric Religion."

3. Joseph Campbell. *The Masks of God: Primitive Mythology* (New York: Penguin Books, 1959), pp. 66–67.

4. Margaret Murray. *God of the Witches* (London: Sampson Low, Marston & Co., 1933; from online version, scanned by Sacred-Texts.com, 2000).

5. Joseph Campbell. *The Masks of God: Primitive Mythology* (New York: Penguin Books, 1959), pp. 9–10.

CHAPTER 2

1. Ronald Hutton. *Triumph of the Moon: A History of Modern Pagan Witchcraft* (New York: Oxford University Press, 1999), p. 241.

2. Isaac Bonewits. *Witchcraft: A Concise History,* 2nd ed. (PocketPCpress, 2001), p. 33.

CHAPTER 3

1. Alfred Métraux. *Voodoo in Haiti* (New York: Schocken Books, 1972), p. 27.

CHAPTER 4

Note: All planetary seals are from Henry Cornelius *Agrippa's Three Books of Occult Philosophy*. See the Bibliography for publication details.

CHAPTER 5

1. The meditation is based on one I tried from Ven. Balangoda Anandamaitreya's *Buddhism: Lectures and Essays* (Sri Lanka: Samayawardhana, 1997).

CHAPTER 6

1. If you're going to use canvas—a good choice for durability and widely available at art supply stores—you'll need some other stuff, too: gesso to prepare it (otherwise it won't take the paint—read the instructions on the back of the bottle), and acrylic paint (which won't crack as much).

CHAPTER 9

1. There are a lot of differing opinions on using metal during spell casting. Some Witches say that you shouldn't have any metal at all in a Circle—even the athame—because metal conducts energy, and they think it interferes with the Circle's psychic energy. Other Witches say the *only* metal you should have in a Circle is the athame, since it's used to conduct energy. They believe you *want* the metal athame to collect the psychic energy and direct it. Still other Witches say that it doesn't matter either way, and you can have anything you want in the Circle. I think it depends on your intentions.

2. Hot debate! Some traditions say the athame represents Air, and others say it's Fire. Same with the wand: Some say Fire, other say Air. I was taught that the athame is Air, and the wand is Fire. I've done some thinking on it, and I'm sticking with my original story. Here's why: Air is associated with East, and also with intellect. The athame (or sword) is used to control and direct energy—the same way your intellect controls and directs your energy. On the other hand, the wand is used to *invoke* energy, and it's usually made of wood—a natural energy amplifier. I'm not saying I'm right and anyone else is wrong. Try it both ways and see what works best for you.

CHAPTER 12

1. Based on Sir James George Frazer's classic text on magick, *The Illustrated Golden Bough* (London: George Rainbird Limited, 1978), pp. 33–44.

2. I realize that dragon's blood resin may be difficult to find, but it's one of the best ingredients for love and power spells there is. You can absolutely find it at any of the resources I list in the Appendices, but if you can't access them for some reason, try using frankincense and rose petals instead. Add a drop or two of red food coloring to get the same visual effect, and make this ingredient a top priority on your Witch's Wish List!

CHAPTER 21

1. Quote from ACLU of Michigan brief.

BIBLIOGRAPHY

Adler, Margot. *Drawing Down the Moon,* 2nd edition. 1986. New York: Penguin.

Agrippa, Henry Cornelius. *Three Books of Occult Philosophy.* 1994. Ed. Donald Tyson. Trans. James Freake. St. Paul, Minn.: Llewellyn Publications.

Anandamaitreya, Balangoda. *Buddhism: Lectures and Essays.* 1997. Sri Lanka: Samayawardhana.

Bell, Jessie Wicker. *The Book of Shadows by Lady Sheba.* 2000. St. Paul, Minn.: Llewellyn Publications.

Buckland, Raymond. *Buckland's Complete Book of Witchcraft.* 1990. St. Paul, Minn.: Llewellyn Publications.

Cunningham, Scott. *Wicca: A Guide for the Solitary Practitioner.* 2000. St. Paul, Minn.: Llewellyn Publications.

Frazer, Sir James George. *The Illustrated Golden Bough.* 1978. London: George Rainbird Ltd.

Gardner, Gerald. *Witchcraft Today.* 1954. Thame, England: IHO Books.

Gonzalez-Wippler, Migene. *The Complete Book of Spells, Ceremonies, and Magic.* 1988. St. Paul, Minn.: Llewellyn Publications.

———. *Santeria: The Religion: Faith, Rites, and Magic,* 2nd edition. 1994. St. Paul, Minn.: Llewellyn Publications.

Harner, Michael. *The Way of the Shaman: A Guide to Power and Healing.* 1980. New York: Bantam Books.

Harrow, Judy. *Wicca Covens: How to Start and Organize Your Own.* 1999. New York: Carol Publishing Group.

Hutton, Ronald. *Triumph of the Moon: A History of Modern Pagan Witchcraft.* 2001. New York: Oxford University Press.

Jordan, Michael. *Encyclopedia of Gods.* 1993. New York: Facts on File.

———. *Witches: An Encyclopedia of Paganism and Magic.* 1996. London: Kyle Cathie Ltd.

Leland, Charles, *Aradia, or the Gospel of the Witches.* Sacred-Texts.com.

Mathews, John. *The Druid Sourcebook.* 1996. London: Blandford Press.

Métraux, Alfred. *Voodoo in Haiti.* 1972. New York: Schocken Books.

Mircea, Eliade. *A History of Religious Ideas: From the Stone Age to the Elusinian Mysteries.* 1981. Trans. Willard R. Trask. Chicago: University of Chicago Press.

Monaghan, Patricia. *The New Book of Goddesses and Heroines.* 1997. St. Paul, Minn.: Llewellyn Publications.

Murray, Margaret. *God of the Witches.* 1933. London: Sampson Low, Marston, and Co. Sacred-Texts.com.

Nicholson, Shirley. *Shamanism.* 1988. Wheaton, Ill.: Theosophical Publishing House.

Orion, Loretta. *Never Again the Burning Times: Paganism Revived.* 1995. Prospect Heights, Ill.: Waveland Press.

Telesco, Patricia. *365 Goddesses: A Daily Guide to the Magic and Inspiration of the Goddess.* 1998. New York: HarperCollins.

JERRY SANDER, A.C.S.W, is a psychotherapist in private practice in Warwick, New York.

WYLD WYTCH, age nineteen, lives in Plymouth, Connecticut. You can visit Wyld Wytch at www.wyldwytch.com or email: Wyldwytch@wyldwytch.com

MARJORIE C., age fourteen, lives in Randolph, New Jersey. You can email her at: lefteyeisanangel@aol.com

ATHENA SKYEFOREST, age seventeen, lives in Laurinburg, North Carolina. You can email her at athenaskyeforest@hotmail.com

GWINEVERE RAIN, age seventeen, lives in Florida has has been a Wiccan practitioner for over three years. She is the author of *Spellcraft for Teens: A Magical Guide to Writing and Casting Spells,* due out September 2002. To find out more about Gwinevere and her writing endeavors, and find hip, fun, and unique Wiccan products, please visit her website: www.get-me.to/TeenWitch.

JONATHAN ARCHIE, HELAINE LUBAR, and JOYCE VALENZANO all live in Broome County, New York.

INDEX